...e militarized racism of the last cen-
...hicago, guns have promised Ameri-
...again and again. *Beating Guns* dives
deep and uncovers the pathologies of violence in our society. Claiborne and Martin
shine light on a path out of the madness. It's time to never again say 'never again.'"

—**Lisa Sharon Harper**, founder and president of FreedomRoad.us

"*Beating Guns* fills a spiritual void in our national conversation on guns. This
powerful book employs pragmatic wisdom and challenging biblical insight to
offer a fresh, humane, and sacred view of our guns, our violence, and the nation's collective response to human suffering."

—**Otis Moss III**, writer, activist, sacred troublemaker,
and pastor of Trinity UCC, Chicago, Illinois

"This is the quintessential pro-life book if there ever was one! The tireless,
intrepid Shane Claiborne is joined by Michael Martin in a summons to face up
to the claims of faith in response to gun pathology. This book is both a bold
summons to imagine a gun-regulated society and a mandate to act in the public
domain. A must for those who care but who have not yet cared enough to weigh
in actively for the sake of an abundant life that overrides the lethal power of fear."

—**Walter Brueggemann**, Columbia Theological Seminary

"Outrage about gun violence in this so-called Christian nation is the easiest
path of resistance. In fact, outrage is too easy. It is much harder to grieve over
those suffering from gun violence and over how Christians have embraced a
legal right—called the Second Amendment—as their Christian right. But the
most difficult path is hope carried by love, and it is this love that empowers
Beating Guns. It is time for Christians to turn from the insane violence of guns
and their defense by rights to a cross-shaped vision of how we ought to live."

—**Scot McKnight**, professor of

"This book could change America and awaken
such a combination of documented history, co
als, and practical, readable theology in one bo
decide whether you need to weep or rejoice.

—**Richard Rohr, OFM**, Center for Action and Contemplation

"This is a book worth reading and then doing something about."

—**Bob Goff**, *New York Times* bestselling author of *Love Does*

"Anyone who is worn out by our country's day-to-day infatuation with violence needs the hope that is contained in this skillfully written tour de force. The authors ask the question, Can one carry a cross in one hand and a killing machine in the other? Some *may* answer yes. But, if one reads this book, no simplistic answers are possible."

—**James E. Atwood**, retired Presbyterian pastor and author of
America and Its Guns: A Theological Exposé and
Gundamentalism and Where It Is Taking America

"A story behind every statistic. *Beating Guns* is a book of stories that will crack our hearts wide open—stories that will convince us that if we value life, if we are pro-life, we have to find a way to beat guns. Mike Martin beat a gun at Middle Collegiate Church, beat it into a farming tool. Shane Claiborne's honest prose will convert you. Together these visionaries show us the way to beat guns."

—**Jacqui Lewis**, senior minister, Middle Collegiate Church,
New York; executive director, The Middle Project

"*Beating Guns* helps gun lovers and gun haters to suspend their assumptions and look afresh at lethal firepower and find surprising solutions to the deadly problems associated with them. A very timely book that can be enormously helpful to individuals, churches, and whole communities who know that something must be done."

—**Rob Schenck**, subject of *The Armor of Light*, an Emmy Award–winning
documentary on evangelicals and guns; president of
The Dietrich Bonhoeffer Institute

"The violence epidemic in America that has made guns a part of America's wardrobe is making our children 'road kill.' It comes from a love affair with guns and the deception that they somehow make us safer. In *Beating Guns*, we are reminded of what Dr. King taught us, that if we can change our hearts we can change our world."

—**Michael L. Pfleger**, pastor of The Faith Community of Saint Sabina

"For any who feel helpless in a society that seems to accept gun violence as inevitable, this book will change you. Being faithful to Jesus requires taking seriously the message of this book."

—**Tony Campolo**, professor emeritus, Eastern University

BEATING GUNS

BEATING GUNS

HOPE for PEOPLE
WHO ARE WEARY of VIOLENCE

SHANE CLAIBORNE
AND MICHAEL MARTIN

Brazos Press

a division of Baker Publishing Group
Grand Rapids, Michigan

Published by Brazos Press
a division of Baker Publishing Group
PO Box 6287, Grand Rapids, MI 49516-6287
www.brazospress.com

Printed in the United States of America

Library of Congress Cataloging-in-Publication Data
Names: Claiborne, Shane, 1975– author. | Martin, Michael (Founder of RAWtools Inc.), author.
Title: Beating guns : hope for people who are weary of violence / Shane Claiborne and Michael Martin.
Description: Grand Rapids : Brazos Press, 2019. | Includes bibliographical references.
Identifiers: LCCN 2018036421 | ISBN 9781587434136 (pbk. : alk. paper)
Subjects: LCSH: United States—Church history—21st century. | United States—Social conditions. | Violence—Religious aspects—Christianity. | Firearms—Religious aspects—Christianity. | Firearms—United States.
Classification: LCC BR526 .C5668 2019 | DDC 261.8/3—dc23
LC record available at https://lccn.loc.gov/2018036421

Unless otherwise indicated, Scripture quotations are from the Holy Bible, New International Version®. NIV®. Copyright © 1973, 1978, 1984, 2011 by Biblica, Inc.™ Used by permission of Zondervan. All rights reserved worldwide. www.zondervan.com

Scripture quotations labeled CEB are from the Common English Bible © 2011 Common English Bible. Used by permission.

Scripture quotations labeled ESV are from The Holy Bible, English Standard Version® (ESV®), copyright © 2001 by Crossway, a publishing ministry of Good News Publishers. Used by permission. All rights reserved. ESV Text Edition: 2011

Scripture quotations labeled NRSV are from the New Revised Standard Version of the Bible, copyright © 1989, by the Division of Christian Education of the National Council of the Churches of Christ in the United States of America. Used by permission. All rights reserved.

Photo credits for collage on page 263: Shovels: Pedro Reyes, Palas Por Pistolas; Gun guitar: © Sergio Moraes / Reuters Pictures; Steel flower and gun/plow: made by Fred Martin; Saxophone: photo by Jana Meyer, Mennonite Central Committee in Mozambique; Menorah: "Loaded Menorah" by Boris Bally, https://BorisBally.com

Interior design by Brian Brunsting

19 20 21 22 23 24 25   7 6 5 4 3 2 1

To all the lives lost to guns

To all the families affected by gun violence

To those who are committed
to building the world
foretold by the prophets

Where people beat swords into plows
and turn from death to life

CONTENTS

NOTE TO THE READER

IF YOU OWN GUNS and want to see fewer people killed, this book is for you.

If you've never even touched a gun and want to see fewer people killed, this book is for you.

If you are a victim of violence or have lost a loved one to murder, this book is for you.

If you have hurt or killed someone, this book is for you.

Basically, this is a book for everyone who is tired of violence.

This is a book for people who believe—or who want to believe—that things can be different than they are right now.

Even if you're a doubter or skeptic, if you have to fight back despair and cynicism, this book is for you.

A man once came up to Jesus and said, "I do believe; help me overcome my unbelief" (Mark 9:24). We all have days like that. That might be a good prayer for us to begin with—"I do believe; help me overcome my unbelief."

Our hope is that this book will give you courage and imagination, and stir in you a defiant hope that guns and violence are not the most powerful forces in the world.

Love is.

INTRODUCTION

WHISPERS OF ANOTHER WORLD

> You see things; and you say, "Why?" But I dream things that never were; and I say, "Why not?"
>
> —George Bernard Shaw

SOME PEOPLE ARE MOTIVATED BY THEIR HEADS, and others are moved by their hearts. We hope to engage both the head and the heart in this book.

Not many people get argued into thinking differently, but experiences and stories move us, especially when we have the humility to listen and to view the world from a different lens, from someone else's eyes. We are going to share many stories in this book—many of them from people who have been directly affected by guns. But first, let's start with a personal story.

I (Shane) grew up with guns in the good ole state of Tennessee. I went hunting and frog gigging (spearing bullfrogs) with my grandpa. He used to throw smoke bombs into groundhog holes and have me shoot the groundhogs when they ran out. I was lethal to squirrels. I remember shooting two squirrels with one shot of my .410 shotgun, making Papaw really proud that day. To be fully transparent, one of the squirrels wasn't entirely dead, just wounded, and my grandpa had to grab him by the tail and crack his head on the tree. Looking back now, that may be one of the first hiccups in my love of guns. I had a hard time killing squirrels after that one.

My wife, Katie Jo, was a hunter too. I remember knowing she was the right woman for me when I heard a story about her skinning a deer. She was on her way to youth group at church, driving with her dad, and they hit a deer. Instinctively, they both had the same thought: dinner. They ran out and cut that thing up and put it in the trunk. When she got to youth group, she had blood all over her clothes. But it was North Carolina. No big deal. It probably just added new meaning to the hymn "Nothing but the Blood" that night.

Down South, God and guns go together like Oreos and milk. We have country-music songs that say things like "Our houses are protected by the good Lord and a gun / And you might meet 'em both if you show up here not welcome, son." It never even occurred to me to question whether it was a good idea to have guns in our house growing up.

Then I had a friend in elementary school who was playing one of those childhood games of cops and robbers with his best friend. They had grabbed a real gun but were convinced it wasn't loaded. I'm sure you know what happened next, because it happens all the time. My friend pulled the trigger and killed his best friend. That little boy died immediately. Last I heard, the other little boy is still in a therapeutic hospital and may never leave.

Butch Brotherton

Katie Jo hunting with our family in North Carolina

I had an uncle who went into his front yard, laid out a tarp, and shot himself. He had two kids.

Obviously, I grieved these tragedies, deeply. But they didn't make me question guns, not immediately anyway. Accidents and suicides happen in other ways too, after all. My uncle could have hung himself just as easily. My concerns regarding gun violence didn't come all of a sudden. They emerged over time. Maybe it's the same for you.

Many of us are growing weary; we have gun-violence fatigue. We don't want to grow numb, but it's hard to stay heartbroken and outraged when so many lives are lost each day. My weariness grew one mass shooting at a time, one tragedy in our neighborhood at a time. We've held so many vigils on corners with candles and painted RIP murals. I began to see how avoidable so many of these catastrophes are. Not all of them, but many. I've gotten to know so many people who have been directly affected by gun violence, and their stories have wrecked me—people who have survived mass shootings, parents who have lost their kids, even people who have committed violent crimes and carry the weight of that for the rest of their lives. And as I've traveled to war zones like those in Iraq and Afghanistan, I've seen the devastation of violence on a larger scale. I've held kids in hospitals in Baghdad who were victims of our wars, and I've held veterans who wept over the damage war did to them. Like many of you, I grew weary—not hopeless, but weary—of violence.

Most of us have been touched by gun violence in some way, so let's honor the massive pain that exists in our world—in our schools, on our streets, in our hearts. The right place to begin seems to be a deep lament. All is not well in the world, and we need to allow the blood that God hears crying out from the ground to affect us. We need to listen to that pain.

Before we explore some ways that we might better protect life, let's begin by mourning the lives that have been lost—by homicide, by suicide, by accident, and on purpose. Every person is created in the image of God. And every one of those lives, from Abel to my pal Jason, who was killed in elementary school, is a child of God. Every time a life is lost, we lose a glimpse of God in the world, for each one of us is an image-bearer of our God.

We also want to say from the get-go that we are really grateful for all of you reading this who are gun owners, even gun enthusiasts. Our friend James Atwood says, "Gun violence is nonpartisan."[1] It's also color-blind. Guns kill Republicans, Democrats, and people who hate politics altogether. The victims of violence are white, black, and brown. They are boys and girls, gay and straight, young and old. They are Christians, Jews, Muslims, Sikhs, Buddhists, and atheists. They are rich and poor, urban, suburban, and rural. No one escapes the reach of guns.

Joe Roebuck

Cutting up the first gun donated to RAWtools

Nothing is going to change as long as the country is polarized, with people talking *at* each other rather than *to* each other. I (Mike) started facilitating this conversation when I formed RAWtools (RAW is "war" flipped around). One of my friends was a gun owner who began to question why we have assault rifles on our streets. He owned a number of guns, and one of them was an AK-47. After the 2012 shooting at Sandy Hook Elementary, which claimed the lives of twenty kids and six adults, he donated the AK-47 so that it could be destroyed and repurposed. My dad and I met with a blacksmith and learned how to create garden tools from that AK-47—and RAWtools was born. Five years later my friend donated his handgun.

Meanwhile, on the other side of the country, here in Philadelphia, I (Shane) had just teamed up with my pal Ben Cohen (from Ben & Jerry's ice cream) to do a memorial event on the tenth anniversary of the September

11 attacks in New York, Pennsylvania, and Washington, DC—we called it "Jesus, Bombs, and Ice Cream." In addition to dropping ice cream from the sky with helium balloons, we decided it could be powerful to have a welder friend of mine perform a live weapon transformation during our event. So we put out a call for weapons (it's amazing what you can do with social media), and someone donated an AK-47, which we turned into a shovel and a rake. My friendship with Mike felt like it was divinely appointed. And it all started with a couple of AK-47s.

An assault rifle beat into a shovel and a rake

The Simple Way, by metalcrafter Josh Seltzer

While pounding an AK-47 into a garden tool makes an incredible statement and has been healing for many, this isn't a new idea. Many artists have been making farm tools from guns and implements of war for decades, especially after World War II. These artists have created the space for RAWtools to exist.

This is the age-old story of turning all kinds of weapons into all kinds of farm tools in the midst of a world that is telling us it won't work, that we are idealists or dreamers. The dominant culture often tells us that we can't escape the violence, so we should therefore join the violence. Instead, this counter-story of turning swords into plows insists that violence is the problem, not the solution. It is about the transformation that happens when, before she ever met the shooter, a mother forgives the teen who killed her three-year-old son. It's about the mass shooting survivors who refuse to be labeled

The Simple Way

A peacemaker's uniform

as only victims, but are instead wounded healers. It's about those who have been affected by unimaginable trauma but who then choose to lean into their communities and tell us that those ripples of trauma affect us all, so listen up.

As we've converted weapons into tools, we've had veterans, police chiefs, grandmothers, and little kids take part in the action. And in the movement to reduce gun violence, some of the best allies have been hunters against gun violence, folks who have a gun to hunt with or to keep coyotes off the farm but who don't believe AK-47s should be on the streets of our cities. We all need to work together.

In fact, an overwhelming majority of gun owners are concerned about gun violence. They aren't necessarily the loudest voices in the NRA, but they are by far the majority. That's good news, and it is also critical to remember. This book is not about demonizing gun owners. It is about saving lives and working with everyone who is committed to that.

For those of you who are pastoring churches, issues like this one require a special sort of grace and patience—and courage and wisdom and prayer. We want to encourage you to see this as a moral, spiritual, pro-life issue. Pro-life does not mean just antiabortion. It means standing against death in all its ugly forms and becoming a champion of life consistently, across the board. Stopping gun violence is a pro-life issue.

There are those who say, "We do not have a gun problem; we have a heart problem." We would make a slight change: we have a gun problem *and* a heart problem.

So let's gather around a table. But it's not an ordinary table; it's the top of an anvil. And that oven over there isn't baking bread; it's baking gunmetal. Gather round, all you who are weary, you who are wounded, you who are cynical and angry, you who have much faith and you who would like to have more, you who have tried to follow Jesus and you who have failed. Gather round the forge, and let's dream of a world where weapons become garden tools and where cold hearts are brought back to life again.

One

TURNING WEAPONS INTO FARM TOOLS (AND OTHER LOVELY THINGS)

> God will judge between the nations,
>   and settle disputes of mighty nations.
> Then they will beat their swords into iron plows
>   and their spears into pruning tools.
> Nation will not take up sword against nation;
>   they will no longer learn how to make war.
>
> —Isaiah 2:4 (CEB)

THERE'S THIS THING about turning guns into garden tools. You have to add some heat—a little more than two thousand degrees of controlled flame. If it's too hot, the steel melts or burns off. If it's too cold, the steel cracks under the hammer. There is a happy medium range of heat where the magic happens—where transformation takes place—and it's a beautiful glowing orange. The steel feels like thick clay when the hammer makes contact, and it cools as you work on the anvil. As the orange glow fades, the steel hardens into its new form. But you can't make a tool in just one "heat." You have to repeat the process. You put the gun barrel back into the forge and bring it out to shape it some more. Then again. And again. You repeat that cycle over and over using various tools designed to make the gun barrel into a garden tool. The heat brings transformation. Steel is literally shaping steel.

Coe Burchfield

Forging peace

How much did the prophets Micah (4:3) and Isaiah know about blacksmithing when they both called their audiences to transform the metal tools of death into the tools of life, to beat swords into plows and spears into pruning hooks? We don't know if they had spent much time at the forge, but they surely knew heat is required. Fire refines; it burns away impurities. Our deepest growth often comes as we rise from crisis or trauma or a heated moment in our lives. The prophets knew that with a little holy fire metal can be reshaped—and so can people. They knew weapons that kill can be transformed—and so can people who kill. The prophets of old were not so much fortune-tellers as they were provocateurs of the imagination. They weren't trying to predict the future. They were trying to change the present. They invite us to dream of the world as it could be and not just accept the world as it is. That takes faith.

Both Micah and Isaiah tell of this holy movement where God's people turn from death to life and transform their weapons into garden tools. And the prophets go on to say that, in the end, nation will not rise up against nation; the world will no longer learn to make war (Isa. 2:4). We are offered a vision of a world free from violence and bombs and guns and drones and all the ugly stuff of death.

According to the prophets, though, peace does not begin with kings or presidents or heads of state. They're the ones who keep creating the wars. Peace begins with "the people." It is not politicians who lead the way to peace; it is the people of God who lead the politicians to peace. Peace begins with the people of God, who refuse to kill and who insist on beating their weapons into farm tools. The prophecy ends with the vision of a world free of violence, but *it begins with us*.

It is people with prophetic imagination who will become the conscience of our world and lead the politicians and presidents and kings to turn from war and stand on the side of life. We will make violence extinct by refusing to kill.

Might it be that we are the people that we have been waiting for?

Some will say we are idealists if we talk of peace in a world of war. But faith is about believing in what we hope for and about being certain of what we do not yet see (Heb. 11:1). Faith is all about not letting the current reality hijack the future. Faith refuses to accept the world as it is and insists on moving the world toward what it should be.

We can't wait on politicians to change the world.

We have the audacity to believe that it is not the will of God for approximately 105 people to die from guns each day in the United States.[1] The world doesn't have to be this way. And we can begin by telling the truth about the world as it is now and reimagining how this world could be a better, safer, and more beautiful place. We can begin reimagining our world by telling the stories of deep lament, of lives lost. Then, through the prophetic hope that we have, we can transform metal—and the world. Hope makes us live differently, unsatisfied with the way things are, and it gives us the audacity to believe they can be different.

Photos and stories are scattered throughout this book. Let them stir a different part of your brain and your heart. **We will not change the world with facts alone.** Or words alone.

Eventually we've got to pick up the hammer and put words into action.

Forging Life

It's been said that you can count the number of seeds in an apple but you can't count the number of apples in a seed. We live in a world of abundant life, where one apple can produce hundreds of offspring. But the same may be true of bullets—they do not kill just one person. A bullet can destroy an entire family, community, or neighborhood. A bullet can produce many more bullets as the spiral of violence escalates, as conflict begets conflict, as wars beget wars, as hatred produces more hatred. And any time a person is killed, the person who did the killing can feel something in them die as well. We were not made to kill, and when we do, something in us dies. We were made to love and be loved, to cultivate life, not death. So we need to discover how to live on the side of life again. Death, as we will see, is one of the first things that came after the fall of Adam and Eve way back in the garden of Eden.

The call to turn swords into plows is as much about transforming our way of life as it is about transforming a gun into a garden tool.

On the front door at The Simple Way, the faith community Shane and friends have been building on the north side of Philadelphia for over twenty years, there is a prayer that God would heal all that is broken—in our hearts, in our streets, and in our world. We have a God who is healing individuals. But God is also healing the world and wants us to be a part of the action.

We want to live in a way that moves the world toward love and away from fear. We want to live in patterns that generate life rather than exploit it, that see people and creatures as precious instead of disposable.

The hard thing about transforming a life, like transforming metal, is that it requires work, sweat, heat, and constant attention. There's a beautiful Scripture that says, "Continue to work out your salvation with fear and trembling" (Phil. 2:12). Salvation is a movement, not just a moment. Trans-

The front door at The Simple Way

formation is a process. This is the paradox of waiting for the steel to reheat. You know that transformation is coming, even though it may feel like you are taking a pounding, but you are also thankful for the rest that you are given while you reheat in the fire. And then as you are being healed, you become a healing presence in this broken world.

In that same passage about beating swords into plows, the prophet Micah offers another image, this time of a vine and a fig tree. He says, "Everyone will sit under their own vine and under their own fig tree, and no one will make them afraid" (Mic. 4:4).

Can you imagine that? A world where people have enough food and live without fear? What does it look like to move from a world of scarcity and violence into this vine-and-fig-tree world the prophets speak of?

A fig tree can take two to six years from when it was planted

Fig tree

to produce fruit. What's fascinating is that trees mature at their own pace. Some trees bud younger and some older, just like people. This long juvenile period often tempts humans to speed up the pro-

GOD'S DREAM FOR THE WORLD

Everyone will sit under their own vine
and under their own fig tree,
and no one will make them afraid,
for the LORD Almighty has spoken. (Mic. 4:4)

cess by overfertilizing or overwatering. In a world where we can buy Fig Newtons at the local grocery store, we would need a whole new level of patience to wait for a fresh fig off a branch. Turning swords into plows takes patience. You can't stick a sword in a microwave for two minutes (or until golden brown) and pull out a plow. We need patience with each other as our cold hearts are being transformed into hearts that beat with life and love and hope again.

And communities take time to transform. One of our mentors is Dr. John Perkins, who's almost ninety years old. At one point, I (Shane) was explaining to him that I was growing impatient because our neighborhood was not changing as quickly as I wished it would. We had been working tirelessly for almost five years, and folks were still getting shot on our corners and overdosing on our sidewalks. Dr. Perkins said, "Be patient, my brother. You will see things begin to change and transform, but it may take another ten years."

Sometimes we are tempted to turn up the heat on the forge to make things move a little faster. But that only means we run the risk of burning off the metal from too much heat. God's grace moves slow and steady. We live in a world that wants everything to happen in an instant: fast food, quick money from the ATM, movies on demand, news at our fingertips. But the stuff that really gives life takes time. A baby takes nine months. A good meal doesn't come in three minutes. It takes time to learn a new skill or language. And lives that are beautiful take time to produce, just like any work of art. You begin to wonder if guns are our default because they seem like a quick and

Memorial to the Lost

On February 14, 2018, seventeen students and staff at Marjory Stoneman Douglas High School in Parkland, Florida, were fatally shot, and seventeen others were wounded. Witnesses identified the assailant as a nineteen-year-old former student. The weapon used was an AR-15-style semiautomatic rifle. Here are the names of those who died.

Alyssa Alhadeff, 14

Scott Beigel, 35

Martin Duque, 14

Nicholas Dworet, 17

Aaron Feis, 37

Jaime Guttenberg, 14

Chris Hixon, 49

Luke Hoyer, 15

Cara Loughran, 14

Gina Montalto, 14

Joaquin Oliver, 17

Alaina Petty, 14

Meadow Pollack, 18

Helena Ramsay, 17

Alex Schachter, 14

Carmen Schentrup, 16

Peter Wong, 15

easy answer in the short term. They give us access to immediate power and force. But violence is often the instrument of those who are impatient, those who lack imagination, those who cannot wait on justice or freedom or redemption.

Turning swords into plows reorients how we do life. We move from instant gratification to seasonal patience.

The fact that something can be made new is a miracle. Caterpillars to butterflies, weapons to tools, sinners to saints. The old is gone, the new has come. Nothing is beyond redemption. In Philadelphia, we've turned old tires, televisions, and computer monitors into garden planters. We've made sunflowers out of hubcaps and turned one ugly wall after another into a piece of art. Transformation is magical. When we turn guns into garden tools, we turn fear into feasts. When we no longer train to annihilate fear, we train to face it. When we don't train for war, we train for transformation. When we begin to turn our swords into plows, we experience a paradox of vulnerability and opportunity. Each dip into the fiery heat of the forge brings us closer to the vine and fig tree.

One of the profound things about making a garden tool is that it is hard to do alone. Many of the important steps require two sets of hands. When you punch a hole for the handle, you need at least three or four hands— one for the hammer, one for the punch, and one or two to hold the tongs with the heated metal. This process can't happen alone. Another lesson from the forge: we are not meant to do life alone. Jesus sent the disciples out in pairs and elsewhere promised that "where two or three gather," he would be with us (Matt. 18:20). We are created in the image of God, who reflects community to us—Father, Son, Spirit. We are made to do life together. If you want to be a help in your community, you need to allow your community to speak into your life, and you need to be vulnerable to those around you. **As iron sharpens iron, so we sharpen one another (Prov. 27:17).**

In our heated, raw vulnerability, it's not uncommon to be formed by a hammer held by an enemy, a punch held by a friend, and tongs held by our community. When we invite people who don't think, act, or look like us into the process, we allow transformation to take root. We start that seasonal process toward a vine and fig tree.

Gathered around the forge in Toledo

Dan Brearley / The Simple Way

Transformation requires tools—whether we are talking about changing swords to plows or about ourselves being made into new persons. When we repurpose metal, we trade some of our old tools in for new ones. In America, this means trading the Second Amendment for the Sermon on the Mount. Romans 12:2 says we are not to conform to this world but to be transformed by the renewing of our minds—new hearts, new minds, new eyes to see the world. That's what God is up to in the great project of transforming the world. Transformation begins inside each of us.

It takes faith to believe that something (or someone) can be different from what it is now or that the world can be different than it is right now. Faith is all about believing despite the evidence we currently see—and watching the evidence change. Before every major social movement that has changed the world, people said, "That is impossible." And after every social movement that has changed the world, people say, "That was inevitable."

So it is with the movement to turn a world from weapons to garden tools. It is about believing in a God who is transforming death into life and inviting us to participate, daring us to stand on the side of life.

Transformation requires hope—and hope changes the one who hopes. Think about a pregnant mother. She doesn't just passively wait for the baby. She waits actively. She prepares. She gets the crib ready, prepares the room, eats healthy, sleeps well. And so it is with those of us who want to be mid-wives of a new and better world.

If we believe swords are going to be converted to plows, it makes less and less sense to keep making swords. If we really believe the prophets were right and that this is what is coming, then we can't help but begin enacting it now. We adjust our lives now to get ready for the future that we know is coming.

Other Lovely Things

Let's not limit what we make out of a gun to garden tools alone. As you will soon see, when we at RAWtools started transforming guns into plows, we began getting images from folks all over the world who were likewise inspired by the idea of turning swords into plows. There were guitars made out of handguns, and saxophones out of semiautomatics. We've had folks send images from Iraq of guns being crushed in the streets. We've seen enormous pieces of public art made from melted guns, and we've seen folks make Christmas ornaments out of tear-gas canisters.

On Halloween in 2015, a Colorado Springs man used an assault rifle to kill three people and then later died in a shootout with police. One year later, a silent walk was organized by local residents that followed the path of the shooter to reclaim the neighborhood as their space and not the space of a shooting.[2] The walk ended at a church, where a feather was passed around a circle of about one hundred people. Native Americans have a practice of using a feather as a talking piece in mediation circles. Whoever is holding the feather has the right to speak their truth. Whoever held that feather was invited to share how gun violence affects them. It didn't matter what side of the gun-violence

Peace feather made from various gun components

issue someone fell on, they were welcome to share how their life has been changed since that shooting.

The feather being passed didn't come from a bird. RAWtools made a spine from the spring in an AK-47 magazine; the rubber grip of a revolver was sliced and formed the shape of the feather; a spent bullet casing was used to seat the spine of the feather. This feather and others like it continue to be used by restorative-justice facilitators in Colorado.

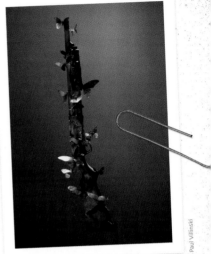

Epitaph (2014), shotgun, aluminum (found cans), soot, steel

Many lovely things can be formed from a gun. Even gun enthusiasts make artistic and functional pieces from gun parts (though probably not from perfectly functioning guns). Changing swords to plows requires us to open our imagination to what we can make of our guns. Instead of dreaming of bigger, faster, more technologically advanced weapons, we can imagine a world of plowshares that points both toward a vine and fig tree and toward the past we came from. This is why art is so important. Imagine what we could make from a tank.

We love seeing artists share their work that speaks to gun violence and peacemaking—from dozens of shovels being formed out of bulldozed guns in South America to a giant plowshare in Virginia made from weapons confiscated in Washington, DC, to bombshells in the Middle East with "Made in USA" stamped on the side being turned into planters. America is infected with violence,

Mourn (2014), handgun, aluminum (found can), soot, steel

THE NARROW WAY THAT LEADS TO LIFE

But I tell you, do not resist an evil person. If anyone slaps you on the right cheek, turn to them the other cheek also. (Matt. 5:39)

Calvary (2018), bullet shells

Celtic (2018), decommissioned firearms

and art points the way to the cure. It's work like this that allows changing swords to plows to even exist. It dreams of neighborhood block parties with balloons instead of bullets. The art is prophetic because it has escaped to the wilderness and is begging us to create communities that value life over ego. Artistic expressions of changing swords to plows have been happening for a long time. Micah and Isaiah have an idea of what that healing process might look like.

It's a process—a Jesus process—this art of loving your enemy and turning the other cheek. These are the prerequisites for sitting under a vine and fig tree without fear. It's not so much that we are never afraid or anxious but that *love is stronger than our fear*. Fear does not have to control us and change the nature of who we are.

Poet and pastor Dale Fredrickson says, "My heart is a fragile trigger."[3] There is a trigger in all of our hearts. When we are under our own vine and fig tree and able to say that we are in fear of nothing, it's because fear is no longer allowed to pull the trigger of our hearts. This is not some magical state we attain and then keep forever. It's a never-ending process and discipline of resilience that is impossible without the support of a community. In fact, without the support of a community, any one of us is capable of pulling a trigger on a gun. Gun triggers are just as easy to pull as the triggers in our hearts.

Changing swords to plows is about the holy, sacramental work of transforming hearts as much as it is about transforming metal. The questions we'll raise in this book go to the very heart of what it means to be free. Is true freedom having a right to own a gun, or is true freedom the ability to live unarmed and fearless, refusing to fight violence on its own terms? Perhaps it is the powerful realization that our faith does not rest in "chariots and horses," or in handguns or assault rifles. Beating guns is about creating a community—a world—where gun violence is a thing of the past, where we study violence no more.

Nobody likes gun violence. And lots of people have their own ideas on how to stop gun violence (including owning more guns). There must be a comprehensive effort that transforms a country plagued by violence, a country that uses a gun as its primary tool for carrying out that violence. Communities of faith have an opportunity to step up right now, to lean into the wisdom of those prophets of old and allow them to lead us toward a world of plows instead of a world of swords and guns. The prophets of old can inspire us to raise up new visions of how we can build a world where everyone is under the vine and fig tree without fear.

As with all fruit, the seeds only exist in tandem with the fruit. As the fig tree needs time to mature and produce fruit, so we need time to shift our imagination and create practical alternatives to guns and gun violence.

Once a fig tree is mature and produces fruit, it must be cared for. If neglected, it retreats to a state where it cannot produce fruit. It can take many years to be fruitful again. The same is true for the survivors of gun violence. The trauma is everlasting. Recent studies show that grandchildren of holocaust survivors have inherited trauma.[4] Trauma can literally affect our genetic makeup. We owe it to the generations that follow us and to survivors of gun violence to help them with their trauma and to make continual efforts to end gun violence in our country. Let's start in our neighborhoods by turning guns into garden tools, feathers, and other lovely things that will change what our children inherit. Who knows? Maybe changing swords to plows will be part of the genetic moral makeup of our grandchildren.

Two

THE MESS WE FIND OURSELVES IN

> While they were in the field, Cain attacked his brother Abel and killed him. . . . The LORD said, "What have you done? Listen! Your brother's blood cries out to me from the ground."
>
> —Genesis 4:8, 10

VIOLENCE IS AS OLD AS HUMANITY. It goes all the way back to the garden of Eden. One of the first stories in the Bible, the inaugural sin outside the garden of Eden, is a brother killing a brother—the ancient story of Cain and Abel.

The Bible says that Abel's blood cried out to God from the ground (Gen. 4:10). The blood cried out.

And the blood has been crying out to God ever since.

Tubal-Cain was Cain's descendant. According to Genesis, Tubal-Cain "forged all kind of tools out of bronze and iron" (Gen. 4:22). The ancient historian Josephus regarded him as one of the strongest men in the world, an expert in martial performance, and one of the pioneers of working brass. Not only did Tubal-Cain create and design weapons; he demonstrated better than anyone else how to use them.

Tubal-Cain is the natural conclusion to a path that started with his ancestor killing his brother. The continual need to have a larger rock than your brother turns into a catapult with a giant boulder, which turns into a cannonball—and eventually the explosive that propels the cannonball is put in the cannonball and called a bomb. And don't forget that we miniaturized the cannonball into a bullet, to be placed into a weapon that can be held in the palm of our hand.

There is no room to imagine a garden when your mind is consumed with the next best way to destroy. If all we imagine is the martial performance necessary to harm our adversary, exact our revenge, or engage an intruder, there is little room to imagine a performance of another Spirit.

Today we recognize the dangers of guns when they get in the wrong hands. Everyone admits this. The advent of "smart" guns tells us that the industry is aware of a problem. We now have the expertise, but not the incentive, to make guns that work only with a fingerprint reading as you grip it or a ring worn on your trigger finger that tells the gun you are a "safe" shooter, similar to how some phones have fingerprint technology that recognizes their owners. We have smartphones, but why not smarter guns that require fingerprint technology for activation? Some banks even use facial recognition, instead of a password, a pin, or a fingerprint, to access a customer's account. Imagine what we could do if we used our best minds and best technology to make the world safer. Some within the gun industry resist the idea that this technology is needed, as it can be skewed as one more limitation on an industry that has enjoyed unprecedented exception from any regulation. We need more imagination.

We are desperate to be able to keep using our guns, to be able to kill our neighbor if we have even a remote sense of fear. Perhaps you remember the fourteen-year-old boy in Michigan who missed his school bus and went to a nearby home to ask directions, only to find himself running for his life as the homeowner shot at him with a shotgun.[1] This is the world we've created. It's not hard to imagine a remix of Matthew 25 where Jesus says, "When I was a stranger, I came to you in need . . . and you pulled a gun on me."

We have trained ourselves to defend, so much so that a knock on our door means we grab our gun. Recently, in Colorado Springs a man shot his stepdaughter as she was sneaking back in the house after curfew because he thought she was an intruder.[2] Americans are encouraged to impulsively grab a gun because, in an active robbery, a victim only has seconds to respond and yet the police are minutes away. But we must search our imagination for alternatives to this fear-based response.

Then there is another Colorado Springs man, Mel Bernstein, often called "the most armed man in America," who is a gun-shop owner and who has acquired more than four thousand weapons—from machine guns, to bazookas and flamethrowers, to tanks and attack jeeps (jeeps armed with loaded machine guns). And it's all legal.

We Have a Problem

The United States is the most dangerous industrialized country in the world. When all the murders of civilians in all the developed countries of the world are tabulated, 86 percent occur in the United States.[3] Of all the children killed in the world's twenty-three developed countries, 87 percent are American children.[4]

We may not all agree on how to solve the problem. Some say more guns will help: "The answer to a bad guy with a gun is a good guy with a gun." Others will say more regulations or tighter restrictions.

We may not all even agree on what the problem is. Some folks say it is a gun problem. Others say it's a heart problem: "Guns don't kill; people kill."

MEL BERNSTEIN

Mel Bernstein rents and sells weapons. He has 260 acres of combat zone, often called Dragonland or Dragon Man's (the nickname comes from his custom motorcycle that resembles a dragon). On the compound are six shooting ranges, a military museum, a paintball park, and a gun shop, in addition to his home.

One person with more than four thousand guns. That's America in 2018. In Mr. Bernstein's own words, "You get addicted to them. . . . You know, it gets in your blood."

He talks about how gun sales skyrocketed after the mass shooting in Las Vegas. "Whatever the killer used, that's what they want." He talks like mass shooters are the best salesmen. He even holds up some of the weapons used in the shooting at the church in Sutherland Springs, Texas, and in the Vegas massacre, making sure folks know they are for sale in his shop. "We've been selling more guns in the last three weeks than we have in the last eight months."

He shows off the 12-gauge pistol-grip shotgun used in Columbine, and he boasts of another gun that can shoot five hundred bullets in a minute. "We sell real men's guns," he says, smiling. And according to Mr. Bernstein, you can walk out of his shop with a gun in fifteen minutes.

Mr. Bernstein is not just an eccentric gun enthusiast; he also talks about being bullied as he grew up in Brooklyn, having to pay twenty-five cents per day to keep the bullies away. "They bullied me, then I got older and I bullied the other kids. It's a whole cycle. . . . I was bullied and I became a bully."

We don't doubt he's had a hard life. He lost his wife a few years back in a tragic malfunction of artillery, as a smoke canister exploded and went through her body. He also experienced a robbery at his shop when four people used Bernstein's truck to smash into the store and steal nearly one hundred guns. It turns out that two of the suspects are members of Bernstein's own family. So now he lives alone.

Accompanying his arsenal of guns are four life-size mannequins, which he calls "the girls." He dresses them up and gives them names—Betty, Jill, and so on. "I need someone to talk to, to tell them my problems." They don't talk back. They don't want to go shopping or out to eat, he explains, laughing. They are easy to live with—in his words, "very polite." He comes home from work, turns on the jukebox, talks with the girls about machine guns and hot rods, builds them a fire, and drinks some coffee. "When it gets cold in the winter, I even put underwear on them. . . . I'm a good boyfriend."

Honestly, we know plenty of people who have eccentric personalities and live in their own fantasy worlds and alternate realities, but the difference is that they don't have four thousand guns. And Bernstein sells them with such enthusiasm.

When I (Mike) was in high school, I took a trip with my youth group to play a few rounds of paintball at Dragon Man's. There is a fairly long driveway with wrecked cars and mannequins sticking out of them, simulating a war scene, not a car crash. They are warnings to what would happen if you crossed a line, be it political or personal. When you check in to get your equipment, you can also see into the gun store where Mr. Bernstein has his collection of weapons.

Anyone who has played paintball knows the connection between paintball and real guns. It's not a giant leap when you are playing capture the flag on one of the paintball courses to imagine this in real life. The whole experience is a glimpse into the next level. While you're playing, you can also hear the gunshots from the firing range nearby. People who don't play paintball or haven't grown up with real guns may not know the difference between the two types of guns without the paintball hopper attached. If I spent most of my life in the bubble of Dragonland, I imagine I would be a different person.

Paintball guns designed to look like real guns

Though an extreme case, Mel Bernstein isn't alone with his collection and story. In fact, only 8 percent of gun owners own about 40 percent of the guns in the United States. Beyond that, there are stories of folks accidentally shooting their own family and friends when they were seen as intruders in various cities across America. It's getting messy.

A gun barrel in the coals, with "USA" engraved on it

We say it's both. We have a gun problem, and we have a heart problem. That's one of the false binaries that thankfully we don't have to take sides on. As we peel away the layers of this issue, we will be careful to address both the gun problem and the heart problem. People kill people. And people with guns kill a lot of people. Hopefully, we can all agree that we want to save lives if we can. And we are convinced that we can.

But let's start with this: we have a problem.

We've learned from friends in recovery from drug and alcohol addiction that the first step to recovery is recognizing that we have a problem.

Considering that some say we are addicted to guns, the first step in our recovery is staring the problem in the face and acknowledging the damage done. In 2016, thirty-eight thousand people died from guns. That's about 105 per day, up from 90 per day in 2013.[5] And it's been this way for far too long. Since 1979, the nation's gun deaths have not dropped below thirty-two thousand per year. That means for nearly forty years we've allowed more than 1.2 million lives to be lost to guns—by homicide, suicide, and accidental shootings.

Our country started keeping records of gun deaths in 1933. Since then, hundreds of thousands of lives have been lost. We've had more Americans killed domestically by guns in two decades—right here in our own country—than we have seen killed in all our foreign wars in the past 250 years.[6] Students routinely practice active shooter drills, and school entrances are being redesigned to mitigate school shootings. We now have companies selling bulletproof blankets and backpacks. Some folks think we need to arm teachers. And some of our own politicians have argued that we need to arm schoolchildren as young as *four* years old![7] It might not be an exaggeration to say that our country feels like a war zone. Kids are scared to go to school. Teenagers have enough to worry about—taking final exams, dealing with acne, finding a date to prom. They shouldn't be afraid of mass shootings, and yet over and over they are happening in our

Memorial to the Lost

On June 12, 2016, forty-nine people were killed in an act of hatred at a gay night-club on "Latin Night." Many of the victims were Latinos, and it was the deadliest attack against LGBTQ people in US history. It was the worst act of domestic terrorism since September 11—and at the time it was the deadliest mass shooting by a single shooter, though that record sadly was soon surpassed by the Las Vegas massacre. The weapons used included a SIG Sauer MCS semiautomatic assault rifle and a semiautomatic Glock 17 pistol. In addition to the forty-nine people killed, fifty-three others were injured, many in life-altering ways. Here are the names of those who died.

Stanley Almodovar III, 23

Amanda Alvear, 25

Oscar A. Aracena-Montero, 26

Rodolfo Ayala-Ayala, 33

Alejandro Barrios Martinez, 21

Martin Benitez Torres, 33

Antonio D. Brown, 30

Darryl R. Burt II, 29

Jonathan A. Camuy Vega, 24

Angel L. Candelario-Padro, 28

Simon A. Carrillo Fernandez, 31

Juan Chevez-Martinez, 25

Luis D. Conde, 39

Cory J. Connell, 21

Tevin E. Crosby, 25

Franky J. Dejesus Velazquez, 50

Deonka D. Drayton, 32

Mercedez M. Flores, 26

Peter O. Gonzalez-Cruz, 22

Juan R. Guerrero, 22

Paul T. Henry, 41

Frank Hernandez, 27

Miguel A. Honorato, 30

Javier Jorge-Reyes, 40

Jason B. Josaphat, 19

Eddie J. Justice, 30

Anthony L. Laureano Disla, 25

Christopher A. Leinonen, 32

Brenda L. Marquez McCool, 49

Jean C. Mendez Perez, 35

Akyra Monet Murray, 18

Kimberly Morris, 37

Jean C. Nieves Rodriguez, 27

Luis O. Ocasio-Capo, 20

Geraldo A. Ortiz-Jimenez, 25

Eric Ivan Ortiz-Rivera, 36

Joel Rayon Paniagua, 32

Enrique L. Rios Jr., 25

Juan P. Rivera Velazquez, 37

Yilmary Rodriguez Solivan, 24

Christopher J. Sanfeliz, 24

Xavier Emmanuel Serrano Rosado, 35

Gilberto Ramon Silva Menendez, 25

Edward Sotomayor Jr., 34

Shane E. Tomlinson, 33

Leroy Valentin Fernandez, 25

Luis S. Vielma, 22

Luis Daniel Wilson-Leon, 37

Jerald A. Wright, 31

schools. What a strange world we live in, in which the number of kids killed by guns since Sandy Hook surpasses that of US soldiers killed in overseas combat since 9/11.[8]

Even our own military service members are more likely to die at home than they are in combat overseas. Soldiers are being killed by their own guns more often than by the guns of any foreign enemy. Suicide by gun has surpassed war as the military's leading cause of death; over twenty veteran and active service members die each day from suicide—nearly one per hour.[9] Two-thirds of them use guns to take their lives.[10] It is a national health crisis, an epidemic of violence.

In the United States, we have the most guns in the world, by far. And we have the most gun deaths in the world, also by far. When it comes to gun homicides, the United States leads the world. We have more gun homicides than all the other industrial countries combined. There are 29.7 gun homicides per million people in the US.[11] The next most violent country when it comes to guns is Switzerland, with seven per million. So we have four times more gun violence than the next country. We have six times more gun homicides than Canada, and sixteen times more than Germany.[12]

Those are the lives lost. Sometimes we only count the casualties, but there are tens of thousands each year who are victims of gun violence and yet survive. An estimated seventy-three thousand people per year are injured by guns, many of them in life-altering ways.[13] There are over four hundred thousand crimes involving guns each year.[14] Young people from ages eighteen to twenty commit a disproportionate amount of gun violence, accounting for only 5 percent of the population but nearly 20 percent of homicide and manslaughter arrests.[15] Young people—not old enough to buy beer or rent a car—are able to buy and carry guns.

We have a problem.

The United States has about 5 percent of the world's population, but we have almost half of the world's privately held guns (42 percent).[16] There are nearly five times more licensed gun dealers in America than there are McDonald's restaurants.[17] And those are just the licensed dealers.

OVERSUPPLY AND OVERDEMAND

We manufactured an average of 9,458,172 guns annually in the US from 2012 to 2015.
That's 25,912 per day.
That's 1,079 per hour.
That's 17.9 per minute.
That's 1 gun every three seconds.

We have as many guns as people—maybe more. Recent data shows that we have around three hundred million guns in the United States, which is about one per person.[18] Each year millions of new guns are added to the arsenal—in 2016, a record 27 million guns were sold.[19]

We have a problem. We are addicted to guns. We are addicted to violence.

But here's an interesting caveat: even though we have as many guns as people, only 32 percent of US households have guns.[20] So a small portion of people have a lot of guns. Three percent of our population owns half of those three hundred million guns, with an average of seventeen guns each.[21] Nearly two-thirds of our guns are owned by 20 percent of gun owners.[22]

It is largely a man's obsession. Further, 61 percent of gun owners are white men, even though white males make up only 32 percent of the overall population.[23]

And where there are more guns, there are more gun deaths. This is the mess we find ourselves in.

Read over the gun facts on the opposite page. That's a lot of bad news. But let's put a face on it, as injustice is always personal, always has a name. After all, that's what puts a fire in our bones and moves us to action.

That Problem Has a Name

I (Shane) will never forget the night we heard the gunshots outside. Sadly, it's not uncommon to hear gunshots in Kensington, on the north side of Philly

- The United States has about 5 percent of the world's population, but we have almost half of the world's privately held guns (42 percent).
- One Black Friday, two hundred thousand guns were sold in the US. That means two per second.
- There are 170,000 guns for sale online.
- There are nearly five times more *licensed* gun dealers in America than there are McDonald's restaurants.
- We hold the world record for the most civilian-owned guns—one hundred guns for every one hundred people, or about one per person.
- Guns kill about thirty-eight thousand people per year, and over half of those are suicides.
- Over one hundred people die from guns every day in America.
- There are seventy-three thousand gun-related injuries each year.
- There are over four hundred thousand crimes involving guns per year. That's forty-five crimes involving guns every hour. Young people from ages eighteen to twenty commit a disproportionate amount of gun violence, accounting for only 5 percent of the population but nearly 20 percent of homicide and manslaughter arrests.
- The US leads the world in gun homicides. We have twenty-nine gun homicides per million people. The next most violent country when it comes to guns is Switzerland, with seven per million. So we have four times more gun violence than the next country. We have six times more gun homicides than Canada, and sixteen times more than Germany.
- Another source shows that we have thirty-six gun homicides for every one million people—the highest in the world. That's twenty-five times higher than other high-income countries.
- When all the firearm deaths in all the developed countries of the world are tabulated, 80 percent occur in the United States. Of all the children killed by guns in the world's twenty-three developed countries, 87 percent are US children.

But here are some interesting caveats:
- Even though we have almost one gun per person in the US, only 32 percent of households have guns. That means some folks have a *lot* of guns. Three percent of the US population owns half the guns. The folks in that 3 percent own an average of seventeen guns each, a total of 133 million guns.
- Thirty-two percent of Americans are white men, but 61 percent of gun owners are white men.
- Sixty-five percent of guns are owned by 20 percent of gun owners. Fifty percent are owned by 3 percent of the total population.
- We have eleven gun deaths per one hundred thousand people. Japan has 0.07 per one hundred thousand.

and where I've lived for twenty years. But these were close, so I ran to the door and found a young man falling to the ground in front of my house. I grabbed his hand, prayed over him, and held him until the ambulance came. The next morning we found out that he did not make it.

His name was Papito. He was nineteen years old.

We had a candlelight vigil, as we always do after someone is killed. But that didn't feel like enough. We can tell kids not to shoot each other, but eventually we also start to ask deeper questions like, Where are they getting the guns?

Martin Luther King Jr. was right when he said that we are all called to be the good Samaritan and lift our neighbor out of the ditch, but after you lift so many people out of the ditch you start to realize that we need to transform the whole road to Jericho. We've got to figure out why people keep ending up in the ditch.[24]

When our community asked where the guns are coming from, we didn't have to look far. About two blocks away was a gun shop called the Shooter

The Shooter Shop

Shop. It wasn't just any gun shop. It was one of the worst gun shops in the country. What we know is that there are a few gun shops that are notoriously irresponsible. Over half the guns found at crime scenes are traced to 1 percent of gun dealers.[25] Five percent of gun shops are responsible for 90 percent of guns used in crimes.[26] The worst of the worst. The Shooter Shop was one of those gun shops.

My friends and I on the block knew we needed to do something. We had held vigils and protests plenty of times before, at the Shooter Shop and at other similar gun shops. But this time we did something different.

The Simple Way

When Papito was killed, it was Lent—the season that begins forty days before Easter and when Christians around the world spend a lot of time contemplating the life, death, and resurrection of Jesus. So on that Friday before Easter, what we Christians often call Good Friday, rather than having a church service in a sanctuary, we took things into the streets. We had our Good Friday service outside the Shooter Shop.

Good Friday service at the Shooter Shop

Jamie Moffett

The young men in our neighborhood, many of whom have seen their friends wounded or killed on these streets, carried a large wooden cross to the front of the gun shop. We listened to the familiar passage from the Gospels recounting Jesus's violent murder on the cross on that first Good Friday. We heard the Gospel writers speak of how the women wept at the foot of the cross. And then, after the Gospel reading, we invited the victims of gun violence to share their stories. We listened to mothers, with tears rolling down their faces, share about losing their kids.

Something profound happened that Good Friday. The tears of those women two thousand years ago met the tears of these women standing among us. Calvary met Kensington. The suffering of Jesus met the suffering of our streets.

After the service, a woman came up to me, deeply stirred. "I get it. I get it!" she said. "I understand something today." I held her as she went on, tears streaming. "God understands my pain, because God knows what it feels like to lose your son."

I realized in that moment that this woman was Papito's mom. And she had encountered the gospel. The good news is that we have a God who understands our pain, who knows what it feels like to lose a son.

This gun crisis is not just an "issue." Its casualties have names, faces, and tears. And this is also a deeply spiritual matter. *It is about a God who suffers with those who suffer*, who grieves with those who grieve, and who promises that the tomb is empty and death will lose its sting. This is a redemption story. It is about a God who redeems Cain, Tubal-Cain, the young man who killed Papito, the person who sold him the gun, Mel "the Dragon Man" Bernstein, and even you and me.

Three

GUN HISTORY 101

> We certainly are in a hell of a business. . . . A fellow has to wish for trouble so as to make a living, the only consolation being, however, if we don't get the business, someone else will. . . . It would be a terrible state of affairs if my conscience started to bother me now.
>
> —Frank Jonas, Remington dealer

ONE OF THE FIRST GAMES I (Shane) can remember playing as a kid was cowboys and Indians. The cowboys had cap guns that popped and smoked and smelled like gunpowder. The "Indians" had tomahawks and feather headdresses. Looking back, I'm embarrassed.

One of my favorite places to go as a kid growing up in Tennessee was Silver Dollar City, before Dolly Parton bought it out and renamed it Dolly-wood. It took the Wild West theme over the top. Granted, there weren't tons of entertainment options in East Tennessee at the time; nonetheless, Silver Dollar City was a blast. It was built to resemble an old Western town, with live metalcrafting workshops, candle-making shops, and folks riding around on horseback. And my favorite—the saloon. We used to go in the saloon and watch the ladies dance, which undoubtedly was toned down for the underage audience (I was eight). At the end of the show, the women, with their puffy dresses and big hair, would come into the audience and plant big kisses on the kids, leaving giant red lips on us. There were gunfights and people playing banjos and bluegrass in the street. I was convinced this was exactly how life used to be in the old days.

But the best part was the train. There was an old-timey coal-powered train that you could ride through the mountains. It would huff and puff, and the steam engine would scream out with blast after blast. Midway through the ride, there was an announcement that we were experiencing a problem. You'd see some alarmed faces, especially among the kids. Then out of nowhere we heard guns popping, and masked bandits on horseback would take over the train. It used to scare me to death. Then, just in the nick of time, the good guys would come—also on horseback and also with guns, of course—and they would save the day. Was I glad for those good guys with guns!

The Wild West also took over my living room growing up, as *Bonanza*, my grandpa's favorite show, blared from the television.

Heck, I'm even named after a cowboy. Legend has it, my parents were having a hard time landing on a name and eventually found inspiration from the old Western *Shane*. Almost providential.

The Wild West seemed to follow me even after I left East Tennessee. When I lived in India as a college student, all the kids asked me if I was a cowboy. That's how pervasive the Wild West imagery is. They thought everyone from the US was a cowboy, especially if they had a Southern accent. I told the kids in India that, while I wasn't a cowboy, I was named after one. That's the best I could do.

The Wild West has shaped our imaginations—and our facts.

The Myth of the Wild West

History tells a different story than the popular folklore of the Wild West. Pamela Haag and other historians have gone to great lengths to separate truth from fiction in the tales of the great American heroes and villains, the outlaws and gunslingers of old.[1]

In the late 1800s, dime novels became a massively profitable business, and the Wild West was where they hit gold. They were sensational, mass-produced fantasy books, and most of them were about the Wild West. One of the authors told an interviewer in 1902 that you needed three things to write a bestseller: "a riotous imagination, a dramatic instinct, and a right hand that never tires."[2] The novels all had a similar plotline, which later shaped radio Westerns and the television Westerns that my grandpa watched. The good guys win. The bad guys get caught or die. One author of the novels said you had to "kill someone in almost every paragraph." In the words of Pamela Haag, figures like Buffalo Bill, Billy the Kid, Belle Starr, and Calamity Jane became American legends and went "from lowbrow fiction to highbrow historical fact."[3] **Truth was the first casualty of our romanticism with guns.**

The dime novels eventually turned into TV shows and movies (and more books). At least 1,400 Western films came out from 1935 to 1960. They were pretty much all you could watch. Eight of the top ten television shows in 1959 were Westerns. It's clear that far more folks died in the movies than on the real frontier.[4]

Publishers sold thirty-five million paperback Westerns per year in the 1950s. There were magazines too—*Gunslingers of the West*, *True Frontier*,

Wild West legends moved "from lowbrow fiction to highbrow historical fact"

Outlaws of the Old West, *Badmen of the Old West*, and *Best of the West*. By 1969 the word *cowboy* was everywhere. One scholar compiled a bibliography of Western gunman works and came up with a grand total of 2,491—by 1969![5] As Haag says, "The myth flourishes in the space between what happened and what we wish had happened."[6] She says the gun was "retroactively fetishized."[7] It may not be the history that was, but it is the history that we wish it were. Even now, many older folks are nostalgic about a past that never actually existed.

Spoiler alert: the cowboys of old are not like they were in *Bonanza* or *The Magnificent Seven*. Both the lethality and the moral righteousness of the cowboys are exaggerated. Historians say cowboys were lower-class bachelors who were laborers and usually lived a disreputable life ravaged by alcoholism and vagrancy. Historian Wallace Stegner shows the cowboy not as an iconic hero but as an "overworked, underpaid hireling, almost as homeless and dispossessed as a modern crop worker."[8] David Cartwright, another historian of the West, says we have had to do "moral surgery"[9] to transform the historical cowboy into the mythical icon of rugged individualism and superhero-like qualities. Most often cowboys were not saving the day but sleeping off a night of drinking and womanizing.

The violence that we have glorified in the cowboy legends may not have existed as we wish it had, but today that almost doesn't matter. It has become common understanding despite the facts. Even in the 1800s, most murders were also, just as they are now, among people intimately involved—domestic violence—and guns were not always the means of choice.[10] Historians point out that poisoning (with things like arsenic), stabbing, and simply beating someone to death were more common.[11] It wasn't cowboy renegades killing outlaws but abusive husbands killing their wives. I know we love our Wild West stories, and I hate to burst the bubble, but we exaggerated the violence and the moral righteousness of the heroes. In the words of one historian, "The body count of gun casualties on the frontier at Saturday matinees far exceeded the number of casualties on the actual frontier."[12] Sorry, John Wayne.

Many of us learned in history class that the gun saved the Wild West from Natives and outlaws. The truth is, **our mythology about the West may have helped save the gun.**

So Where Did We Get All These Guns?

In 2018 the NRA showcased a gun that is disguised as a cell phone. (What could go wrong?) We've got big guns and little guns. Guns that are disguised as lipstick. Six-bullet revolvers that can be worn as rings. There are Hello Kitty guns designed for kids and pink guns made for women. There are guns that can shoot one hundred rounds per minute. There are even 3-D printed guns. We have a hard time wrapping our minds around 3-D printing in general, but even more with the implications of being able to print your own gun made from the same material as a LEGO piece. But where did all these guns come from?

Guns are older than America. Humans have been making guns, cannons, and weapons that use gunpowder since around AD 1000. The word *gun* is first recorded in referring to a personal, handheld firearm around the end of the 1300s. But what is new, and uniquely American, is the gun market. We are the ones who mastered the art of mass-producing and selling guns, both domestically and around the world.

The gun business started as the war business. Unsurprisingly, Uncle Sam was the sugar daddy of the gun industry. But, as we shall see, the government turned out to be a tricky business partner, and the war economy proved to be economically unsustainable during peacetime. Peace was bad for business.

The inventor Eli Whitney played a big role in the history of guns in America, especially when it came to the transition from gun as craft to gun as commodity. Whitney invented the cotton gin, but perhaps his more lasting contribution to the world (for better or worse) is the idea of interchangeable parts for mass manufacturing. This is where he became a major player in the history of guns in America.

Whitney's cotton gin transformed the economy of the antebellum South, massively boosting the economy of slavery. But despite the booming slave economy, Whitney went broke. Turns out he was a better inventor than he was a businessman.

For Whitney, guns were sort of his Hail Mary to survive financially. With bankruptcy looming, the opportunity to make guns for the government surfaced, and he jumped on it.

In 1798 the US government issued twenty-seven contracts for a total of 30,200 guns.[13] Eli Whitney signed up to make ten thousand of those all by himself! And get this: he had never made a gun before. But he turned out to be good at making the machines that made the guns. The problem was cost and the time it would take. It took him years and thousands of dollars to make the first gun. Because he was pioneering mass production, he knew that making the first gun would be harder than making the next ten thousand guns—it would be easier once he had the process and technology in place. There were many skeptics and doubters, but he delivered on those ten thousand guns. It wasn't long before businessmen capitalized on his ideas.

The Gun Capitalists

Businessmen invented the gun market. They made the gun as commonplace as a sewing machine. And it was not an easy task. Most of the gun capitalists would have preferred to stick to selling typewriters or hammers, but guns promised to make more money. Businessmen stumbled into guns because they were looking for the most lucrative thing they could sell.

This is one of the most striking things that surfaces as you dig into the history of guns in America. The gun capitalists weren't actually big fans of guns. Guns were a means to an end. It's just how they made money.

Love of money was what sparked the unlikely romance of what has been called the gun empire's incestuous family tree—Remington, Colt, Smith, Wesson, Winchester, and a few other lesser-known cousins. It was "incestuous" because they were constantly buying, selling, and merging as they struggled to survive amid competing friends, allies, buyers, and an undeveloped market for guns. The lines of where one company ended and another began were often blurry.

The gun capitalists didn't love guns. They loved money.

Eliphalet Remington was actually a pacifist, a poet, and a deeply religious man.

Before Samuel Colt got into guns, he had been traveling the country on a bizarre, circus-like "laughing-gas tour," showcasing the effects of nitrous oxide and undoubtedly having some fun as he did it. He made submarine batteries before he patented the multi-shot revolver that made him his fortune.

Daniel Wesson had apprenticed as a shoemaker, the trade of his father. Horace Smith was a carpenter like his father.

These are the icons of the gun dynasties, and several of them didn't even like guns that much.

Though Christopher Spencer (inventor of the Spencer repeating rifle) sold record numbers of guns, he spoke of rejoicing when wars had ended and guns were rendered useless, when "the return to a peaceful industry of silk would be hailed with delight."[14]

Even later in life, Oliver Winchester—the King of Guns—is known to have had only two guns, which he may not have even fired. They were family heirlooms—a pair of engraved, ivory-gripped pistols.[15] He didn't drink the Kool-Aid he was selling. The man who made a fortune off guns didn't seem to care much about guns at all. He was a businessman. He might well have sold other things if that would have made more money.

Early gun businessmen were hardworking folks who knew how to make something out of nothing. And that's exactly what they did with the civilian gun market—or lack thereof. They made something out of nothing.

The War Business

The gun business did not start as a private business enterprise but was instead funded and kept financially viable almost entirely by defense contracts from the only guaranteed bulk purchaser, the US government. The gun business began as a war business. But it didn't stay that way.

In its early days, hands down the United States was the biggest buyer, the mother of all clients. From Eli Whitney on, the government was supplying the venture capital to get the gun business going and, later, to keep it afloat.

War was certainly the most convenient market. The government relied on the private gun companies to provide guns for war. But that meant that the private arms makers found themselves utterly dependent on the government contracts. Any business person knows you want to diversify your market.

It created one of the greatest conflicts of interest in American history. The private gun capitalists ended up telling the government, their biggest client, essentially this: "If you don't allow us to freely sell guns everywhere we can in the off-seasons of war, then we will all go bankrupt and you won't have any guns for the next war."

Building a business around war is terribly difficult—and we're not even talking about the bloodshed. War is not a sustainable business. It creates massive surges followed by catastrophic lulls.

In times of war, the gun manufacturers couldn't create enough guns. And after the wars, they couldn't get rid of them.

The spasms of war were manic—a desperate buildup of capacity to fulfill huge, time-sensitive orders of weapons in wartime, followed by a period where there were more guns than anyone needed and a surplus production line that could never sell the guns it was producing—which meant layoffs, debt, and massive amounts of excess space.

The gun industry would not survive off war alone. The gun business had to become something other than the war business.

Samuel Colt is said to have been as "poor as a churchmouse" at one point and was done with government work entirely.[16] He looked for new clients. He bypassed the government and tried to sell directly to soldiers. His major production plant in Paterson, New Jersey, went bankrupt in 1842.[17]

Remington may have done the same if he hadn't diversified beyond the gun, selling other items like washers, sewing machines, and typewriters.

In 1861 Winchester said, "From the commencement of our organization, there has not been a month in which our expenditures have not exceeded our receipts." At one point he was in debt $77,437—equivalent to $23.7 million today.[18] They all struggled to stay alive financially.

They had not yet invented the gun market.

The crisis became: What will we do when all the Natives are killed or subdued? And what if there is not war on the horizon?

In sadistic irony, the gun was too effective. It killed so quickly, it brought about its own demise. Colt's lawyer said, "The thing was so good that it ruined itself. . . . It killed all the Indians. . . . If it had been a slower process, the . . . Company would have prolonged business; but the moment the Indians were extirpated, there was no market for their guns."[19] Chilling. Sickening.

Colt looked for a new market. He tried to sell to state militias. He tried selling to Mormon leader Brigham Young. He gave away guns all over the world as gifts, hoping to lure in an international market. And that was quite effective—for a while.

Winchester went after folks fighting Natives in unofficial wars. We can see this turned out to be very profitable—and catastrophic for Natives. One man fighting Seminole warriors (and who was known to shoot them and hang them from trees as a warning) said this: "I honestly believe that but for these arms, the Indians would now be luxuriating in the everglades of Florida."[20] Thus we see the horror of American history and the unique role the gun played in that history.

It turned out to be very difficult to sell guns to ordinary Americans.

So the gun capitalists went overseas. Profits were to be made selling guns to countries involved in wars, conquest, and fragile situations.

Arming the World

One American living in Vienna, Austria, said to gun inventor Hiram Maxim: "If you want to make a pile of money, invent something that will enable these Europeans to cut each other's throats with great facility."[21]

As the domestic gun market was still being invented, the international market kept the gun industry afloat. The irony is that many of the countries that are baffled by the gun epidemic in the United States helped create it. They were the folks who kept the gun market alive in the mid-1800s.

The gun icons like Colt and Winchester were nursed into being, or nursed back to life, by the international market. Without that revenue during the mid-1800s, the private industrial gun business would likely have gone belly up after the Civil War.

All the major gun capitalists—Winchester, Colt, Remington, Smith & Wesson—relied on international markets for their survival. Winchester armed the Ottoman Empire and Benito Juárez in Mexico in 1866. Remington armed Egypt and Cuba, among others. Russia kept Smith & Wesson going in the 1870s.

Memorial to the Lost

When we think of mass shootings, we often think of recent tragedies such as Columbine, Sandy Hook, and Pulse nightclub. But guns have been used in mass shootings for hundreds of years.

One of the largest mass shootings on US soil happened on the morning of November 29, 1864, when a US volunteer soldier troop of roughly seven hundred men descended upon peaceful Cheyenne and Arapaho camps. Carbine rifles and howitzer cannons were used to murder roughly 230 people, most of whom were women and children. Their names have been lost over time, but we memorialize them here as a reminder that guns have been instrumental in the murder of native people and in the subjugation of Africans. We honor the lives lost, and lament the inability to name them.

Lord, have mercy on us.

On December 3, 2014, Colorado Governor John Hickenlooper formally apologized to the descendants of the Sand Creek massacre victims, gathered in Denver to commemorate the 150th anniversary of the event. Hickenlooper stated, "We should not be afraid to criticize and condemn that which is inexcusable. . . . On behalf of the state of Colorado, I want to apologize. We will not run from this history."

In recent years, Arapaho youth have taken to running the length of the Sand Creek massacre trail as an endurance test to bring healing to their nation.

The first batch of 3,211 Winchester Model 1866 guns, named after the year it was born, went to Paris, the first of over eight million guns that would be sold by 1930.[22] That was enough to keep the factories going. Gun industrialists traveled the world showing off guns and gifting guns to tsars, revolutionaries, and tyrants alike. Russia basically saved Smith & Wesson from its financial crisis, as Grand Duke Alexei Alexandrovich went hunting with Buffalo Bill in 1869. (Buffalo Bill Cody is credited with fighting in sixteen battles with Natives and killing buffalo to supply railroad workers, including as many as sixty-nine buffalo in one day.) After the hunting trip, Russia bought 250,000 Model 3 guns—five years' worth of business.[23]

The worlds collided. Former enemies found a common friendship in their love of guns. Japan, Australia, Cuba, Spain, England, Denmark, Sweden, Norway, Luxembourg, Greece, Peru, Argentina, the Dominican Republic, Mexico, Curaçao, Guatemala, Costa Rica, Haiti, El Salvador, Honduras, the Bahamas, Brazil, Ecuador, Chile, Liberia, Hong Kong—even the Vatican. All were buying guns. Yes, Remington sold five thousand guns to the pope.

Remington alone recorded sales of 10,000 to Puerto Rico, 89,000 to Cuba, 130,000 to Spain, 55,000 to Egypt, 50,000 to Mexico, 12,000 to Chile, and an "unknown quantity" to China.[24] Winchester began to translate catalogs into other languages to scatter the guns around the world. They were indiscriminate in whom they sold guns to.

The gun business stood to make money off both sides of conflict (a precursor to the Iran-Contra affair). There was a vested interest in international conflict. Winchester in 1866 went to Mexico willing to sell "to either warring party"—whoever was the highest bidder, no doubt.[25]

One article in London pointed out that Russia and Turkey were outbidding each other in the race to arms as they prepared to slaughter each other, stating that "it is in the US alone that they find the means of gratifying their wishes promptly available."[26] As early as the 1800s, American companies were already arming the world and making a killing off of killing.

There were laws and standards about one government selling guns to another government, violating neutrality. But just like today, there were many ways around those technicalities. For instance, Remington purchased $9 million worth of guns from the US federal government and sold them to France during the Franco-Prussian conflict.[27]

There was a moral agnosticism to it all. Ignorance is bliss. Money is worth the same amount from revolutionaries and democracies, tyrants and criminals.

One of the brokers of the deal with France was interrogated by Congress and asked, "Was it not your business to inquire where the guns were going?" He answered, "I think not. We sell arms to arms-dealers. . . . They dispose of them to their own advantage."[28] It was not his duty or responsibility to know where the guns were going. His job was to maximize profits.

This small group of business folks in New England would arm almost the whole world in just over twenty years.[29] Before the 1860s the US had imported most of its guns. By 1881 all that had changed, and the world was looking to America for its guns. We now had the corner on the market. All of this momentum continued to build until the first embargo on arms exports, in 1898.

Back in the 1850s Winchester was still a shirt man. He was more interested in the sewing machine than the gun machines. But there was a very important intersection. Winchester had discovered the wonder of mass production—and how lucrative it could be. He had found the superiority of machine over man. In 1853 he replaced workers with sewing machines. He decreased his workforce by 4,500 people, converting as much as possible to an entirely machine-run production line.[30] And it proved to be very profitable. His shirt business was worth over $200,000 (over $4 million today).[31] As business success often does, profits led to a desire for more profits. The gun business was booming, and to it Winchester now turned.

As did many others.

Inventing the Domestic Market

As we moved to the second half of the nineteenth century, with a dwindling international market (due largely to embargos, increased competition, and new laws), the gun capitalists looked to the domestic market. There was much doubt about whether Americans would buy guns. Most farmers who needed them already had them. Most urban folks did not have them or need them. The gun was still seen mostly as a rural instrument for hunting or farming. How many shovels do you really need, and do you really need one in the city?

Unlike some countries after wars, we did not melt down our guns after the Civil War. We did not tell our citizens, as Mandela did after apartheid fell, "Take your guns . . . and throw them into the sea."[32] Nope. We let people take them home with them after the war. It was the informal "inheritance of the Civil War."[33] And men on opposing sides of the war came home with their guns, in the same country, sometimes the same town, now being reconstructed after the war.

Half a million men went home from the Civil War with guns. And the federal government sold its excess guns uninterruptedly from 1865 to 1871, making $17 million net proceeds.[34] This all made the civilian gun market tricky from the start. In 1871 we were already one of the most heavily armed countries in the world when it comes to our own citizens. Our Constitution backed that up with the right to bear arms, which moved from a collective right to an individual right (see chap. 10).

The challenge for the gun manufacturers became: How do we get people to love guns like people love horses? How do we get them to see that just one is not enough? And how do we get people who really don't *need* one to *want* one?

In the beginning, guns were very expensive. Only the wealthy could afford them, and most wealthy people didn't think they needed them. Guns were often frowned on as the poor man's—the farmer's—tool. And the folks

GUN TIMELINE

1364	First recorded use of a firearm.
1380	Hand guns are known across Europe.
1400s	The matchlock gun appears.
1498	Rifling principle is discovered.
1509	Invention of wheel lock (rose lock).
1540	Rifling appears in firearms.
1607	Settlers arrive in Jamestown, Virginia.
1630	The first true flintlock.
1637	First use of firearms proof-marks.
1750–1850	Dueling pistols come into fashion.
1776	American Revolution.
1807	Percussion-detonating principle patented.
ca. 1825	Percussion-cap guns are in general use.
1830	The back-action lock appears.
1835	The first Colt revolver.
1840	Guns begin to use pin-fire cartridges.
1847	The telegraph is invented.
1850	True shotguns in common use.
1854–1856	The Crimean War. The last war to use only muzzle-loaded guns.
1859	The first full rim-fire cartridge.
1860	Spencer repeating carbine patented.
1861	Breech loaded guns in common use.
1861–1865	American Civil War. Both breech and muzzle loaded guns used.
1862	The Gatling gun is invented.
1869	Center-fire cartridge introduced.
1870–1871	The Franco-German War. Breach-loaded guns are dominant.
1871	First cartridge revolver.
1873	Winchester rifle introduced.
1876	Custer defeated at Little Big Horn.
1877	First effective double-action revolver.
1879	Lee box magazine patented.
1892	Advent of automatic handguns.
1900	Historical firearms period concludes. Contemporary period begins.

DEVELOPING A DOMESTIC GUN MARKET AFTER THE CIVIL WAR

It proved very difficult to invent a domestic market for guns. In the early days of the 1850s, Winchester had fifty men and four women on deck to help manufacture guns. Orders were so exceptional that when there was an order, Winchester would blow a whistle to call in help. And then everyone would go back to their farms when the order was completed. As hard as manufacturers tried, the gun did not sell well. Many investors withdrew. Winchester took his own money, largely coming from the shirt business, to keep the hemorrhaging young gun business alive. In 1857 his cash was down to less than $100. Even though the Winchester guns were advertised in the *New York Times* as "A Triumph of American Ingenuity" in 1859, it was more of a dream than a reality.

In the 1850s, even a mere two hundred rifles per month were hard to sell. Smith & Wesson was making only fifteen guns per month in 1867. Colt leased out his surplus factory space, which was not needed in peacetime. Employment declined in the Winchester company from seventy-two during the war to twenty-five after. Remington called the postwar reality the "great struggle to survive," and the company had more than $1 million worth of merchandise with nowhere to send it.

Gun manufacturers were all but dead in the 1870s. Gun companies diversified and began making sewing machines, horse cars, bridges, plows, mowers, reapers, or "anything else that strikes their fancy." They were, after all, committed more to the dollar than the gun.

But these were businessmen, and they kept their minds going on how to convince people to buy stuff they did not really need. They came up with plans for bulk orders to try to move product and shift the burden of responsibility to sellers. There was a 20 percent discount for orders of $100 or more, 25 percent for $1,000, 30 percent for over $5,000—pretty innovative strategies for the 1800s. But as profits were cut by bulk orders, there was an ongoing desire to maximize profits through smaller gun buyers or, as Winchester said, "scattering our guns as much as possible." The more guns scattered, the more gun makers profited.

The preference became small, steady orders that could counteract the spasms of the war revenue. As Pamela Haag puts it, "The gun industry was on the leading edge of the first wave of economic globalization." The venture capital needed to create the market in the United States was largely provided by the international market in the late 1800s.

who needed guns for their farms and in rural areas often could not afford them. The task became how to sell guns to rich folks who didn't need them and to poor folks who couldn't afford them. That's why marketers have to be savvy, even conniving.

Men were the most obvious market, and that's exactly where much of the early marketing turned. Marketers targeted civilians in the South who might need protection from Confederate rebels after the war. They went after farmers who might need to defend themselves from "Indians or other varmint."[35] Civilians had to be convinced that they needed guns. There was a new image of the citizen-defender who would step in when the government did not. "It behooves every loyal citizen to prepare himself . . . with the best weapon of defense."[36] There were rumors of secret rebels who could reignite violence after the Civil War. "Rebels" and "outlaws" and "guerrillas" and "Indians" were all buzzwords in the gun market.

Gun marketers pounced on the gold rush out West, an opportunist attempt to sell guns to protect all the gold one found. One ad said, "You may sleep soundly and safely, with your hard-earned nuggets by your side." Even though many of the fears were perceived rather than actual, marketers took advantage of fear, saying things like: "My friend, if you have regard for your life or your scalp, do not fail to get one or more of these invaluable weapons."[37]

Soon there were ambitious attempts to sell to women. There was the "lady's pistol" of 1859, a gun the size of a pocket comb that could fit in a purse or

Antique gun advertisements

Shane Claiborne

bag or even be tucked away in a corset. Guns were developed for other niche markets as well. A cane gun came out in 1858, perhaps alluring because of its covert nature but also because of its utility to the elderly or the disabled. Some of these attempts, like in any business, flopped. (Remember "new Coca-Cola"? #BadIdeas.)

Gun advertisements featuring women

Shane Claiborne

There was a transition from focusing on consumers who needed guns but did not want them to creating the consumer who wanted guns but didn't need them. In the former, the marketing focused on the functions of the gun as a tool (precision, ease, firepower, comfort, etc.); in the latter, none of that mattered as much as the magic of the gun. It became common to see ads that didn't even have a gun in them or that had guns not drawn to scale. It was more about the romance of having a gun in the wilderness or having a gun ready to protect your family.

When the market had exhausted all the buyers who needed a gun for its practical value, it began to create buyers who attached an emotional value—or even a spiritual value—to guns. It's what Pamela Haag calls the gun "mystique." No longer would the gun be seen as a hammer or a drill or a sewing machine. In Haag's words, "What was once needed now had to be loved."[38]

In the early 1900s, a very ambitious strategy called the "boy plan" had a goal of specifically reaching over three million boys ages ten to sixteen (their exact target number was 3,363,537, though it's unclear why they chose such a precise number).[39] They were the target market in one of the biggest gun-marketing campaigns in history. Owning a gun was pitched as synonymous with becoming a man. Fathers and mothers who had concerns about their kids owning guns were laughed off, even shamed. To address safety concerns, shooting centers began to proliferate in the country. Even groups like the Junior Rifle Corps helped prepare young boys for gun ownership. Each young man was given a chance to be in the NRA.

Gun advertisement targeting boys

The gun executives were brilliant marketers. Colt is said to have coined the phrase "new and improved."[40] He made one of the first attempts at utilizing prison labor—to make guns and munitions (what could go wrong?).

While the gun industry did have some critics, one of the most stunning things is how little resistance there was to the proliferation of the tools of death—earning many of these businessmen the title "Merchants of Death." And as guns grew more and more powerful and precise, they began to change society.

Army of One

One of the most interesting social developments is the rise of the heroic individual, the lone ranger, and vigilante justice, which arguably has evolved into some of the armed militias we have today. We moved from an army of many to an army of one. What used to need a brigade of soldiers with a clear division of labor was now able to be carried out by one person. Me versus the world. You can still see the tension, which continues to this day, of the individual "army of one" versus the real defense provided by the federal military and police. You can even see some of this in the Wild West movies of John Wayne and in old films like *Rambo* and *James Bond*. More recently, we find the lone hero with a gun in the Jason Bourne series, in the *Taken* films, and in *American Sniper*, which is about the life of Chris Kyle, who was said to have killed 255 people as a sniper in the US military and who was later killed by a fellow veteran.

The vigilante savior with a gun began to emerge as an American icon. But it wasn't without its critics. Some gun enthusiasts warned of the danger of firepower replacing bravery, even mocking some of the modern guns, by use of which an "infamous coward" could kill someone with a "random ball" from whence no one knew where it was shot. Just as some might say of drone warfare today, the new firepower made bravery less necessary and gave cowardice much more power. Some said it "cheapened war and corroded bravery."[41] A stealth sniper shooting from one hundred yards was much different than the face-to-face combat of musket loaders and cavalry. Without a doubt the "army of one" phenomenon, accompanied by increasingly powerful and accurate technology, has contributed to lone-wolf killers and domestic terrorists. Even now we see individuals armed with hundreds of guns and a few conspiracy theories who call themselves "patriots" but are prepared to fight the US military and kill soldiers should they deem the government too corrupt.

War moved from being a communal ritual to being an individual one. As guns and the right to own them evolved from being commonly shared to individually owned, there were voices of concern about guns that had such massive and precise firepower readily available to all. Some worried about "egotistical impulses" in a shooter. What would happen if every person in America began to think of themselves as a one-man militia? Rapid-fire guns invited and emboldened individuals. A contemporary example is the lone gunman responsible for the 2017 massacre in Las Vegas. With military-style weapons (and bump stocks to make them more lethal), he fired more than 1,100 rounds into the crowd at a music festival from a hotel window—killing 58 people and injuring 851 others—in a total of ten minutes.

Everyone, good and bad, had the opportunity to purchase invincibility and confidence and power by buying a gun.

Before the rapid-fire guns of the nineteenth century, a skilled shooter could shoot only twice in a minute. In the nineteenth century, that number grew to twenty-five shots per minute. As early as 1864, one man boasted that he could shoot ninety rounds so fast that the gun became too hot to touch. "I spit on it, and it would sizzle," he said.[42] Now, an unskilled shooter can shoot over one hundred rounds in a minute with a legally owned semiautomatic handgun or rifle. If a gun is customized with bump stocks, a person can even shoot multiple bullets *per second*. Gun barrels are made thicker in part to handle the heat of rapid fire.

Guns weren't the only gun product businesses could make money from. In the early twentieth century, folks like Marcellus Hartley saw that the real money was to be made in bullets. After all, most people would probably own only one or two guns in a lifetime, but they would shoot a whole lot of bullets. Hartley founded the United Metallic Cartridge Company and made his fortune off bullets.

There was a new empowerment, and not everybody was happy. But certainly the gun capitalists were. The "steady stream of lead" that one of the Winchester family members spoke of meant a steady stream of profits.[43] The more bullets fired, the more money rolled in. The more that dangerous people bought guns, the more that unarmed good people would think they needed them. For every "outlaw" there would need to be a "hero."

There were no obstacles when it came to legislation, no federal regulations to worry about. Gun makers were free to sell and didn't even need a gun lobby for quite some time. The biggest battle for the first generation of the gun empire was more of a court battle than a legislative one—they were fighting over patents: who owned the guns and the money made from selling them. Things like patent extensions ensured profits, which meant that the gun executives did some major hobnobbing and bribing of those who helped secure patents. Colt's brother said he must have spent over $60,000 in banquets and presents to secure a much-needed patent—a small investment in the financial security of his product's future.[44]

Eventually cowboys, militiamen, pioneers, renegades, revolutionaries, criminals, and wannabe heroes all bought in. They may not have had the same politics or religion or ethnicity, they may have had nothing else in common, but they learned to love the gun. And if they did not need it before, they could not imagine life without it now.

From Craft to Commodity

What was once a craft was becoming a mass-marketed commodity. Blacksmiths who made guns often made all sorts of other stuff too. They made cookware, forks, keys, shovels, razors, ladles, dishes, locks, hinges, horseshoes, wagon wheels, knives, and scissors. Their skills were invaluable to the community, and they were celebrated for their specialized contribution to society.

Undoubtedly, blacksmiths of old thought of the gun as one more tool they made to help out on the farm. No two guns were alike. It was a craft, an art. During times of war, some of them were conflicted about making guns, as they did not want to contribute to bloodshed. They were making guns for hunting and keeping away coyotes, not for taking human life.

Earlier, when the Revolutionary War came, a group of blacksmiths in Lancaster, Pennsylvania, refused to make arms for war. (To this day, Lancaster is known for having a high concentration of pacifists, with roots in the historic peace churches like the Quakers, Amish, and Mennonites. William Penn was a Quaker.) When the Lancaster blacksmiths refused to make guns for war, the government threatened to confiscate their tools, calling the war-resisters "enemies of their country."[45]

Whereas each gun had previously been handcrafted, with the gunsmith taking great pride in the merits and uniqueness of each product, the war economy created another need: interchangeable parts. Guns needed to be exchangeable, and ammo needed to be universal to adapt to the battlefield.

The gun companies moved from crafting guns to mass-producing guns, making them a commodity. Gun production went from a specialized skill to a corporate enterprise, creating tensions that still exist. Many of the folks who profited didn't know how to make a gun. And the folks actually making the guns weren't profiting. The person who knew the least about the craft was making all the money selling the product. Capital had triumphed over, and cheapened, craft.

Blacksmiths felt the collision. It was man versus machine. People became enraptured by mass production—the profits, the ingenuity, the precision of mechanized manufacturing. Praise for the machines grew, with people celebrating how they never tired, cost little, didn't complain, and didn't need homes or health care.[46] But it came at a cost. The collision of man versus machine was so intense that one gunsmith named Ebenezer Cox marched into the corporate office and killed his boss, Thomas Dunn—with a gun, of course.[47]

Cox became a bit of a legend, a folk hero who shot the corporate elite boss who didn't even know the art of metal. In 1842 gunsmiths walked off the job in Harpers Ferry, West Virginia, chartered a boat to Washington, DC, and made a direct appeal to President John Tyler, saying they were reduced to slaves or, in their words, treated like "machines," not people. But alas, gunsmiths were fighting a losing battle. The gunsmiths no longer made guns—they only made gun parts. Gunmaking was now about mass production.

One of the remarkable things about the gun capitalists is their moral agnosticism. Rarely did you hear them speak about the dark side of their industry. Even Eli Whitney said little if anything at all about the injustice associated with his line of work—both the cotton gin that became the backbone for slavery in the South and the mass production of guns.

It's important to recognize that the gun business is, first and foremost, a business. It always has been, from the very beginning. The gun industrialists did not want people to die; they wanted to sell guns.

You certainly wonder what those early gun capitalists, if they were alive today, would think of the industry they gave birth to and the tremendous loss of life we see on a daily basis.

I (Shane) went on a pilgrimage to the gun capital of the world—Hartford, Connecticut. I was speaking at Yale Divinity School, which is built on the site of the Winchester estate. There was something powerful about seeing all this land that had been the heart of the gun economy now a center for theological reflection. It was a swords-to-plowshares story in its own right. Down the street I walked through the old Winchester factory, now turned into condominiums.

I drove a few miles down the road and found the Eli Whitney Museum and his old house and estate. I went into the building, which was filled with kids doing artwork. An older man with an eye patch stopped me to ask what I wanted. I told him I came to visit the Eli Whitney Museum, and he laughed. "This is it. It's mostly used for educational activities these days." I explained to him my interest in Whitney's gunmaking business, and he assured me I had found the right guy. Chuckling a bit, he told me that he was a Quaker (known for their commitment to nonviolence), and we laughed at the irony.

Eli Whitney Museum

"Come with me," he said, taking me into a back room. "This is the gun room. We don't use it much." He moved some clothing racks and chairs so that I could stumble around the room and see some of the cases of guns—undoubtedly some of the oldest guns in the world. I love that they were buried in clutter and art supplies for kids. When I asked where the original armory was, he told me it was "over there where the kids are playing." Something felt very special about this old space that has much bloodshed tied to it—now transformed into a playground. I don't know if Eli Whitney is happy about what's become of his estate, but I sure was.

The gun room at the Eli Whitney Museum, now a nondescript storage space

Four

THE GUN EMPIRE

> Tell me who profits from violence, and I will tell you how to stop it.
>
> —Henry Ford

In LOUISVILLE, KENTUCKY, there is an event called the Festival of Faiths. The focus one year was "Pathways to Nonviolence." That year the National Rifle Association had also planned its annual convention in Louisville at the same time. The NRA convention was held at a space near the airport, while the Festival of Faiths was held downtown. The two groups crossed paths only at the airport and at tourist sites. One of the most interesting parts of that weekend was seeing the advertising juxtaposed throughout the city. The Festival of Faiths had reserved advertising space on both sides of Main Street long before the NRA but then had to give up one side at the request of city officials. On one side were banners imagining paths to nonviolence, while the other side was covered in NRA ads for guns and concerts.

I (Mike) was there with RAWtools to turn guns into garden tools. We had our forge and anvil set up every day, which drew people to check out what our fire and banging was all about. While most of the folks in town for the NRA convention who came up to see what we were doing were very civil and open to conversation, those who weren't walked off without a word. There were

only a few who walked off enraged, shouting things like, "They're killing our guns!" (The narrative "guns don't kill people" breaks down when you personify them.)

Are we better at protecting guns than at protecting people?

Founded in 1871, the NRA has some five million members. To put that in perspective, there are roughly 325 million people in the United States, and about a third own guns. So the NRA represents less than 5 percent of gun owners. That means at least 90 percent of gun owners—nine out of ten—are *not* represented by the NRA.

Without a doubt it is one of the most influential lobbying groups in the country—it has tons of money and tons of power. The NRA is officially a nonprofit and has half a dozen subsidiaries, including the Political Victory Fund, which funds politicians with its $434 million annual budget.

The NRA was established to advance marksmanship and teach firearm competence, and it was run mostly by former military folks. In the early days, the focus was setting up rifle clubs and recruiting for the military.

For nearly seventy years the NRA had very little to do with lobbying or legislation. Then, in 1934, they were confronted with one of the first federal gun control laws—the National Firearms Act. It regulated machine guns, sawed-off shotguns, and silencers. NRA president Karl Frederick had this to say during the hearings: "I have never believed in the general practice of carrying weapons. I seldom carry one. . . . I do not believe in the general promiscuous toting of guns. I think it should be sharply restricted and only under licenses."[1] It's true, the NRA once believed in commonsense gun laws.

In a similar move in the 1960s, the NRA supported another historic gun control bill—the Gun Control Act of 1968. This law required dealers to have a license; created a way to regulate firearms, transfers, and sales among gun dealers around the country; and regulated what guns they could sell. It got the NRA's stamp of approval.

Until the mid-1970s, the NRA mainly focused on sportsmen, hunters, and target shooters and didn't have much to do with gun control issues. It was also around that time that the Political Victory Fund was established, just in time for the 1976 elections.

The 1977 NRA annual convention is often called "The Cincinnati Revolution." At that convention was one of the NRA's charismatic leaders, Harlon Carter, who had been president for a couple of years during the late 1960s, during the civil rights movement. He wasn't just a sportsman; he was a vigilante and had killed a fifteen-year-old kid when he was seventeen. At the convention, he declared a new day before a cheering crowd: "Beginning in this place and at this hour, this period of NRA history is finished." It's safe to say he was taking the organization in a new direction. What he meant by his convention statements was clear to everybody. No longer would the NRA be focused on hunting courses and safety lessons, or target shooting

"I do not believe in the general promiscuous toting of guns. I think it should be sharply restricted and only under licenses."

NRA President
Karl Frederick, 1934

and marksmanship. It was going to become a political force to be reckoned with. The NRA was going to fight to make sure that nothing stood in the way of Americans and guns. The Second Amendment moved front and center—and one of the goals became squashing gun control laws just like the ones they had supported a decade earlier.[2]

The 1970s were the golden age for the NRA, as membership leaped from nine hundred thousand to three million. Under the leadership of Harlon Carter, Neal Knox, and Charlton Heston, the NRA won some major political battles that

THE TEEN KILLER WHO RADICALIZED THE NRA

Harlon Carter was arrested and convicted of murdering a fifteen-year-old Hispanic youth named Ramon Casiano. He was sentenced to three years in jail but was released after two years when a higher court ruled that the judge in the case had issued incorrect instructions regarding self-defense. He would later become the US Border Patrol chief in 1950. He championed an operation to remove undocumented immigrants—it was called Operation Wetback. Eventually he would become the head of the NRA's legislative action arm, one of the most powerful lobbying forces in the country.

have led us to the crisis we are in right now. For instance, in the 1980s the association led the way to reduce the powers and cut the finances of the federal Bureau of Alcohol, Tobacco, Firearms and Explosives (ATF). They basically overpowered the largest federal agency that stood in their way. It would be like the mafia getting rid of the local police. Years later NRA vice president Wayne LaPierre referred to ATF agents as "jack-booted government thugs." George H. W. Bush resigned his lifetime membership in the NRA over that comment.[3]

Things continued to ramp up over the next two decades, even though the NRA lost one of its major political battles in 1994 when the Federal Assault Weapons Ban passed. But the pendulum swung back in their direction as they successfully lobbied for the bill to expire in 2004. A year later they had another major victory that has set the tone for where we are now. In

Memorial to the Lost

The morning of April 16, 2007, a senior at Virginia Polytechnic Institute and State University opened fire on two individuals in a dorm. A couple hours later the gunman proceeded to an academic building with a Glock 9mm semiautomatic pistol, a Walther P22 semiautomatic pistol, and hundreds of rounds of ammunition. After nine minutes of shooting, thirty-two people were killed. As of this writing it is the deadliest mass shooting on a college campus in the US. These are the names of the victims who died from the shooting that day:

Ross Alameddine, 20

Jamie Bishop, 35

Brian Bluhm, 25

Ryan Clark, 22

Austin Cloyd, 18

Jocelyne Couture-
  Nowak, 49

Daniel Perez Cueva, 21

Kevin Granata, 45

Matthew Gwaltney, 24

Caitlin Hammaren, 19

Jeremy Herbstritt, 27

Rachael Hill, 18

Emily Hilscher, 19

Matthew La Porte, 20

Jarrett Lane, 22

Henry Lee, 20

Liviu Librescu, 76

G. V. Loganathan, 53

Partahi Lumban-
  toruan, 34

Lauren McCain, 20

Daniel O'Neil, 22

Juan Ortiz, 26

Minal Panchal, 26

Erin Peterson, 18

Michael Pohle Jr., 23

Julia Pryde, 23

Mary Karen Read, 19

Reema Samaha, 18

Waleed Shaalan, 32

Leslie Sherman, 20

Maxine Turner, 22

Nicole White, 20

Source: Mike Spies and Ashley Balcerzak, "The NRA Placed Big Bets on the 2016 Election, and Won Almost All of Them," The Trace, November 9, 2016, https://www.thetrace.org/2016/11/nra-big-bets-election-2016-results.

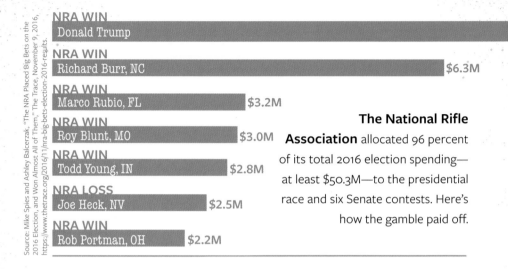

NRA WIN
Donald Trump

NRA WIN
Richard Burr, NC — $6.3M

NRA WIN
Marco Rubio, FL — $3.2M

NRA WIN
Roy Blunt, MO — $3.0M

NRA WIN
Todd Young, IN — $2.8M

NRA LOSS
Joe Heck, NV — $2.5M

NRA WIN
Rob Portman, OH — $2.2M

The National Rifle Association allocated 96 percent of its total 2016 election spending—at least $50.3M—to the presidential race and six Senate contests. Here's how the gamble paid off.

2005 they backed the Protection of Lawful Commerce in Arms Act, which George W. Bush signed into law, preventing firearms manufacturers and dealers from being held liable for any negligence when crimes have been committed with their products. No other industry enjoys the protection that the gun industry does.

The NRA backed their first presidential candidate in 1980—Ronald Reagan. To show how wildly things have devolved, even from the 1980s, keep in mind that Reagan once said, "I do not believe in taking away the right of the citizen for sporting, for hunting, and so forth, or for home defense. But I do believe that an AK-47, a machine gun, is not a sporting weapon or needed for defense of a home."[4] Reagan also said, "There's no reason why on the street today a citizen should be carrying loaded weapons. . . . [Guns are] a ridiculous way to solve problems that have to be solved among people of good will."[5]

In 1998 the NRA became the biggest contributor in congressional elections.[6] Only a decade later, the NRA spent $40 million on US elections, including $10 million in opposition to Barack Obama. And of course, in

2016 they endorsed Donald Trump and broke another record, donating over $30 million to help him get elected.

In recent years, the NRA has gone on the offensive. The NRA lobbied for a bill that granted them and other gun advocacy groups the right to sue municipalities in order to overturn local firearm regulations. The (still-embattled) bill stated that if a city passes laws in attempts to curb gun violence—such as banning high-capacity cartridges or semiautomatics—the NRA can sue them. The NRA sued Philadelphia, Pittsburgh, and Lancaster, contending that new regulations passed by those municipalities violated the Constitution. The regulations included things like reporting stolen guns within twenty-four hours. Similar lawsuits were also filed in California. The city of Sunnyvale passed an ordinance banning certain weapons, limiting guns to only ten bullets. It also required that guns in homes be locked up, that gun dealers keep logs of ammunition sales, and that stolen guns be reported within two days. And the NRA took them to court! Thank goodness those offensive moves have proved unsuccessful so far.[7]

In 2018, of the seventy-six members of the NRA board of directors, sixty-three were males. All but seven of the board members were white. The NRA has a major identity crisis when it comes to race. In 2017, NRA spokeswoman Dana Loesch released a video ad attacking an unspecified group of people referred to as "they." The ad shows images of

protests and marches and slams "the resistance," with accusations that they "smash windows, burn cars, . . . bully and terrorize the law abiding"—all of this on the heels of the movement for black lives. Here's her full statement:

> They use their media to assassinate real news. They use their schools to teach children that their president is another Hitler. They use their movie stars, and singers, and comedy shows, and award shows to repeat their narrative over and over again. And then they use their ex-president to endorse the resistance. All to make them march. Make them protest. Make them scream racism and sexism and xenophobia and homophobia. To smash windows, burn cars, shut down interstates and airports, bully and terrorize the law abiding. Until the only option left is for the police to do their jobs and stop the madness. And when that happens, they'll use it as an excuse for their outrage. The only way we stop this, the only way we save our country and our freedom, is to fight this violence of lies with the clenched fist of truth.[8]

As this ad reveals, some within the NRA are militantly opposed to the movement surrounding Black Lives Matter. And the NRA hasn't been consistent with their support for African American gun rights, as we see in the outrageous case of Philando Castile. In 2017 (the same year that the video ad quoted above came out), Castile was pulled over for a traffic stop. He had a valid firearm permit and informed the officer. Without any provocation or warning, the officer shot him seven times, in front of his girlfriend and four-year-old daughter, as Castile was retrieving his wallet. As much of the country raged over the injustice, the NRA was awkwardly silent. Over a year later, an NRA spokesperson called it "a terrible tragedy that could have been avoided."[9] The NRA has supported some new initiatives, though, such as Black Guns Matter, that it hopes will connect with a "new constituency." We shall see.

One thing we can say to their credit is that the NRA doesn't sit around and wait on politicians. They make stuff happen. In a recent study, nearly half of NRA members say they have contacted a public official to express their opinions on guns, and about a quarter of them say they've done that this year. When the same question was asked of folks not in the NRA, only 15 percent said they had, and only 5 percent this year.[10] It reminds me of a quote from Martin Luther King Jr.: "Those of us who love peace must learn to organize as effectively as the war hawks."[11]

There have been moments of truth-telling within the ranks of the NRA, but those have come at a great cost. One classic example is of Jim Zumbo. He is arguably one of the most influential and skilled gun enthusiasts in the country. But Zumbo began to raise some basic, commonsense questions like, Why do hunters need assault rifles? He said this in one of his last articles, which pretty much ended his professional career: "As hunters, we don't need the image of walking around the woods carrying one of these weapons. To most of the public, an assault rifle is a terrifying thing. Let's divorce ourselves from them. I say game departments should ban them from the prairies and the woods."[12]

The gun empire turned on Zumbo and launched a "Dump Zumbo" website. Their wrath was vicious and unrelenting. Despite his public apology, sponsors dropped him, many of them major players such as Remington. It was the end of his top-rated weekly TV show and the end of his long-time career at *Outdoor Life*, one of the nation's leading outdoor magazines. Even those who defended Zumbo became targets of the NRA and felt the backlash.[13] The NRA made its message strikingly clear—if you question the goodness of any gun, including assault rifles, the NRA will do its best to destroy you, whether you are a politician or a lifetime member of the NRA like Jim Zumbo. The kids in Florida after the Parkland shooting felt the wrath of the NRA and endured countless death threats. Ten years after the Zumbo incident, the NRA still has the Zumbo statement on its website, applauding the "wave of grassroots response" that led to Zumbo's downfall. It includes a warning to the "new Congress" to take heed lest anyone else fall prey "to the tragic demonization of gun owners."[14]

But times do seem to be changing.

In a recent survey, 74 percent of NRA members supported universal background checks on all gun sales, compared to 84 percent of gun owners in general (and 90 percent of all Americans).[15] When asked about prohibiting gun ownership for ten years after a person is convicted of violating a domestic-violence restraining order, 62 percent of NRA members, 76 percent of gun owners, and 83 percent of non–gun owners supported the notion. When asked if someone convicted of selling an illegal gun should have a mandatory minimum of two years in prison, 70 percent of NRA members said yes (along with 71 percent of gun owners generally and 78 percent of non–gun owners).[16] Hopefully, the NRA will follow the lead of its members, return to its roots, and advocate for some sensible changes.

The tide may be turning: the NRA recently reported that it might go broke due to legal fees from ongoing lawsuits and that it has lost its insurance coverage, claiming that its carrier wouldn't renew for "any price."[17]

Five

DO BLACK GUNS MATTER?

> The Winchester rifle deserves a place of honor in every Black home.
>
> —Ida B. Wells

MAYBE IT'S NOT SURPRISING that the NRA is supporting a new movement called Black Guns Matter. A disproportionate 84 percent of gun owners are white (whites make up 61 percent of the US population).[1] Expanding its constituency beyond white folks will be a challenge for the NRA given its history—and, well, US history in general. As of 2018, of the seventy-six members of the board of directors, all but seven are white. Sixty-three are males. It is about 90 percent white and 83 percent men.[2]

Guns and the NRA have a complex history with regard to racial subjugation and slavery in America. Any book on guns would be incomplete if it didn't look at these dynamics of race.

Some of the first arguments in support of armed militias and the Second Amendment were primarily concerned with keeping enslaved people subjugated, squashing any armed rebellion, and capturing fugitive slaves. In the words of Reverend William Barber, "The law [i.e., the Second Amendment] that was used to put on the books to kill slaves is now killing our children, white and black."[3] For many decades, that is what "policing" looked like in America—armed slave patrols. We still have a long way to go to heal those wounds of history.

It's hard to imagine America existing today without the existence of guns. Guns were used to take land from Natives and to keep enslaved Africans subjugated as the new experiment called the United States of America was being conceived and born. There are countless stories, and many more that we don't even know about, of conquest and the horrors of slavery. In Blackfoot territory, white miners riddled Native bodies with bullets with the help of the then-new invention of repeat-firing rifles (repeat-firing referred to guns capable of shooting multiple bullets without reloading) and arranged the bodies in an evil, seditious manner "so that survivors might . . . contemplate the fatal results of their terrible encounter with weapons that obviously appeared never to be reloaded at all." After the massacre, the Blackfeet were so horrified that they believed such a vindictive instrument could only come from a malevolent deity and so they called the rifles "spirit guns."[4]

George Schofield, after whom one of the most legendary guns in history—the Schofield revolver—is named, said that he wanted "no other occupation in life than to ward off the savage and kill off his food until there should no longer be an Indian frontier in our beautiful country."[5] Guns have an ugly and evil past in the birthing of this country. It's hard to confront the truth, but the truth sets us free. Telling the truth about the past is the first step toward building a healthy future.

A part of that history is the complex relationship of African Americans with the gun. Guns got mixed reviews to say the least. The abolition movement and civil rights movement are known for their revolutionary patience, steadfast hope, and nonviolent resistance. We think of Rosa Parks and Martin Luther King Jr. as champions of nonviolent direct action, but both of them owned guns at one point in their lives. Despite the many critics of the gun, it did have some champions among African Americans. Some came to see the gun as an equalizer. What the failed government, so infected with white supremacy, could not do, the gun promised to do. Where juries and courts failed black folks, the gun promised to level the playing field and help achieve what racist, broken police and judicial systems could not achieve. While "Equal Justice Under Law" is inscribed on the front of the Supreme Court, it was only an aspiration. The gun promised power and protection where the government had failed. "War is diplomacy by other means, and Winchester was equality by other means," says Pamela Haag. And as one proverb went: "God made man, and Colt made them equal."[6]

Nicholas Johnson, in his incredible book *Negroes and the Gun*, points out some stunning postbellum sentiments from African Americans on guns. Among gun champions in the African American community, journalist Ida B. Wells is often called the "celebrity endorsement." She bought a pistol after a lynching, saying, "The Winchester rifle deserves a place of honor in every Black home."[7] With lynchings happening nearly every week, and mobs of angry white men sometimes being thwarted by African Americans with guns, others echoed her call to arms. Even African American church leaders such as African Methodist Episcopal bishop Henry McNeal Turner turned to the gun for defense, saying, "Get guns Negroes, keep them loaded, and may God give you good aim when you shoot."[8] W. E. B. DuBois once wrote that he bought "a Winchester double-barreled shotgun and two dozen shells filled with buckshot," and said, "If a white mob had stepped on the campus where I lived I would without hesitation have sprayed their guts over the grass."[9]

Black folks had been traumatized by lynchings and racial terror, and at least some of them embraced the gun—sometimes passionately, sometimes with reservation, sometimes temporarily. There were plenty of voices of dissent against guns: Booker T. Washington voiced his concern about how the "custom of going armed" would undoubtedly contribute to "the high record of violent actions, most of the time directed toward other negroes."[10] Even still, the Black Panthers and other black nationalist organizations openly displayed guns and advocated for the right to carry them in public. Originally called the Black Panthers for Self-Defense, the Black Panthers organized "police patrols" to shadow police officers and share legal advice with African Americans who were stopped. The Panthers held a nuanced view on self-defense—advocating for people not just to have a gun in the privacy of their home but to openly carry a gun in public to protect from the corrupt government and racist police officers. In 1967 thirty members of the Black Panthers protested by openly carrying guns on the steps of the California statehouse (which was legal at the time) and announcing, "The time has come for black people to arm themselves."[11] This open display of weapons led to some of the strictest gun laws in US history, beginning with the Mulford Act, which prohibited the open carry of loaded firearms in California, ironically championed by Republican California governor Ronald Reagan. Reagan saw "no reason why on the street today a citizen should be carrying loaded weapons." This is the very ideology that militant white nationalist groups use a half century later as they perform similar displays of weaponry in public and even occupy government property with weapons in hand.

Certainly the brazen display of weapons in the streets and on government property by the Black Panthers raised the question: Was the Second Amendment intended just for white folks?

The Only Thing That Stops a White Man with a Gun . . . ?

There are black gun legends just like there were legends of the Wild West. Most of them similarly have some "truthiness" in them but over time became

Memorial to the Lost

On June 17, 2015, a twenty-one-year-old white supremacist murdered nine African Americans and injured five others during a prayer service at the historic Emanuel African Methodist Episcopal Church in downtown Charleston, South Carolina. The 202-year-old church, known as Mother Emanuel, has been an icon in the movement for civil rights and racial equality. And it continues to be. Here are the names of those who lost their lives, often referred to as the Emanuel Nine.

Cynthia Marie Graham
  Hurd, 54
Susie Jackson, 87
Ethel Lee Lance, 70
Depayne Middleton-
  Doctor, 49
Clementa C. Pinckney, 41

Tywanza Sanders, 26
Daniel Simmons, 74
Sharonda Coleman-
  Singleton, 45
Myra Thompson, 59

folk stories, similar to how stories morph a little when you whisper them around a circle. These stories include ones like the story of Robert Charles, who, in 1892, was sitting on his stoop in New Orleans when police officers approached him. The officers were aggressive and violent and injured Charles, who ran inside, grabbed his gun, and shot the police captain. Charles was also killed and became sort of a lone-gunman folk hero of a different sort. Ida B. Wells spoke of Charles as a man who "fought off a mob of 20,000 single-handed and alone."[12]

Though gun legends often fade under the light of scrutiny, the gun itself prevails. By the mid-1920s the African American homicide rate in US cities was seven or eight times that of whites.[13] From 2001 to 2016, the city of Chicago had more murders than the number of Americans killed in the wars in Afghanistan or Iraq, and a majority of those victims were young African American men.[14] One recent study has shown that Americans as a whole are 128 times more likely to be killed in everyday gun violence than by any act of international terrorism. But, for specifically African Americans in urban areas, that number shoots up to 500 times more likely.[15] Firearms are the first leading cause of death for African American children and teens in the US, and they are ten times more likely than white kids to die by gun homicide.[16]

The lives of especially black and brown people are endangered on so many fronts, one of which is gun violence—and sometimes it seems as if the most dangerous place to be is your own neighborhood or school.

It's Complicated

It's clear that guns and African Americans in the US share a complicated history. At one point the NRA chartered a chapter so that blacks could arm themselves against the KKK. Even though Rosa Parks and Martin Luther King Jr. were gun owners at one point, King later said this: "I was much more afraid in Montgomery when I had a gun in my house. When I decided that

I couldn't keep a gun, I came face-to-face with the question of death and I dealt with it. From that point on, I no longer needed a gun nor have I been afraid. Had we become distracted by the question of my safety we would have lost the moral offensive and sunk to the level of our oppressors."[17]

Gun advocates who might claim King as one of their own would quickly backpedal if they were to see how committed King became to nonviolence, especially after the time he spent with Gandhi. "I cannot make myself believe that God wanted me to hate. I'm tired of violence, I've seen too much of it. I've seen such hate on the faces of too many sheriffs in the South. And I'm not going to let my oppressor dictate to me what method I must use. Our oppressors have used violence. Our oppressors have used hatred. Our oppressors have used rifles and guns. I'm not going to stoop down to their level. I want to rise to a higher level. We have a power that can't be found in Molotov cocktails."[18]

And of course we can't miss the obvious—King was killed with a gun.

Stephen Colbert, in his characteristic brilliance, said, "Dr. King is progun just as surely as Jesus would be pro-nails." We're pretty sure King would be quick to join us at the forge to beat a gun into a plow.

The gun never brought about equality. White privilege and power has always meant that the people who suffer most from the gun are the most vulnerable and subjugated members of society. Guns might promise temporary safety or justice, perhaps even fulfill those promises on occasion, but they could never right the wrongs of history or fix a criminal justice system or constitution written by, and for, white folks. Equal justice under the law will not come from the barrel of a gun.

Flash forward to 2016. The election of Donald Trump. The new rise of white supremacy—in Charlottesville and beyond. After the election of Trump, gun store owners reported that the number of black and minority customers quadrupled. An increase in violent incidents and hate crimes directed at people of color and other minorities since the presidential election is thought to have spurred the increase in gun purchases, especially among African Americans. Philip Smith, founder of the National African American Gun Association, says, "Most folks are pretty nervous about what kind of America we're going to see over the next 5–10 years."[19] This same logic drove progun demographics to file for a record number of background checks (2.3 million) before the election, in preparation for the possibility that the new president (if it had been Hillary Clinton) might take away the right to own guns.[20] At the end of the day, the gun empire made a lot of money over the past few years. And a lot more guns have ended up on our streets without any of us feeling much safer. In fact, our country feels as fragile as it ever has, and the festering wounds of our violent, racist history remain to be treated with the care they deserve so that healing is possible.

To this day the NRA is one of the most overtly racist organizations in the country. You can see a list of hundreds of quotes from NRA board members on the NRA on the Record website (www.nraontherecord.org). There are the obvious ones from folks like Ted Nugent, who called Obama a subhuman mongrel and said that if Obama got reelected, Nugent would either be in jail or dead, implying in not-so-subtle terms that he would try to kill him.[21] In 2016 he posted on social media a racist meme with a fake moving company called "2 n——ers and a stolen truck."[22] He has said several hundred more terribly offensive things. But what is most offensive is that, after all of that, he got reelected to the board of the NRA and still serves.

Another NRA board member, Jeff Cooper, commenting on the massive numbers of people killed in Los Angeles, said we are doing society a service by keeping them armed so they can kill each other. Here's the quote: "The consensus is that no more than 5–10 people per 100 who die by guns in LA are any loss to society. . . . It would seem a valid social service to keep them well-supplied with ammunition."[23]

So that is what we are up against.

But keep in mind, 90 percent of gun owners are not members of the NRA.

Outside the NRA, polls show that people of color are only half as likely as white folks to support gun rights.[24] And more and more companies continue to put pressure on the NRA to be more reasonable or else they will cut ties to the organization.[25]

At gun shows, there are plenty of Confederate flags, and wherever you find white supremacists and Nazis, like the folks who marched in Charlottesville and left Heather Heyer dead, you can be sure to find some NRA stickers.

Some of the racism is overt, and some is subtle.

Gun enthusiast Troy Newman, a panelist on the "Faith and Guns" special on PBS, said this: "White, middle-class evangelicals use guns for protection, and unfortunately the people on the lower social economic rung of the ladder are victims of gun violence."[26] The image of my (Shane's) mortified face after that comment went viral. I am rarely speechless. All I could say during the live recording was, "We need a commercial break." I actually did respond after the break. But only later did I realize how hurtful and offensive his comments must have felt to the other people of color in the audience. There were people there from Mother Emanuel AME in Charleston, where black folks were massacred during worship. And Mr. Newman was sitting directly in front of Lucy McBath, the mother of Jordan Davis, who was killed at a gas station by a white man who complained that Jordan was playing his music too loud.

The residue of slavery and racism continues to surface all over our country, in almost every facet of society. We have not healed the historical wounds of racialized terror and violence. And we cannot get our future right until we get our history right. The consequences of America's original sins can be seen plainly by looking at the victims of gun violence and police violence in America today.

CONSIDER
This

GALLERY OF THE ABSURD

THIS GALLERY OF THE ABSURD is not meant to treat lightly the madness of gun violence. Quite the opposite; our goal is to expose how tragic, obscene, and totally avoidable many gun deaths are.

Exhibit 1

In my (Shane's) home state of Tennessee, state representative Curry Todd pushed for legislation that would allow guns in bars. What could go wrong? He said, "Drinking with your gun is something that no responsible handgun owner would ever do." Two years later he was jailed and charged with drunk driving and the possession of a loaded handgun while under the influence.[1] A similar law in Virginia passed that allows people to take guns into bars, provided they do not consume alcohol while there. Isn't that why folks go to bars?

Exhibit 2

After the tragic shooting in Sutherland Springs, where twenty-six people were killed at a rural church in Texas, there was a push to bring guns to church. One congregation even posted a warning at the front of the church: "Welcome to Church. This is not a gun-free zone. We are heavily armed. Yes, we are a church, and we will protect our people." In Tennessee, a man brought a gun to church and was showing it to other members of the congregation, making the case for how guns protect us, when the gun went off, shooting him in the hand and his wife in the stomach. Another church member thought it was an attack and called police. They locked down every school within fifteen miles, thinking there was an active shooter. Thank God the man and woman both lived. We're guessing the proposal to bring guns to church didn't fly when the deacons took it to a vote.[2]

Exhibit 3

There are numerous shootings at weddings. I'm sure some are from romantic feuds, but many are unintentional. Apparently it's a thing to pose with a gun on your wedding day. One couple accidentally shot their photographer.[3] Another bride gave her husband a handgun, and he accidentally shot both of them.[4]

Exhibit 4

After the Columbine massacre, former vice president Dan Quayle said, "I hope they don't blame this on guns." Donna Dees-Thomases of the Million Mom March countered, "Well, then, Dan, what should we blame it on, the trench coats?"[5] Touché.

Now we have companies that stand to make a ton of money off products that are meant to protect kids in school—like bulletproof backpacks, blankets, walls, and the like. It wouldn't be surprising if the same companies producing assault rifles were also producing bulletproof backpacks for protection. There is even an insurance policy (that has faced lawsuits over its legality) that would cover someone who is sued for shooting a person in self-defense. One life insurance policy even offers a special provision for teachers who are killed in their schools. Needless to say, all this seems like we have missed something.

Exhibit 5

The Barrett 82A1 Centerfire Rifle, a .50-caliber rifle that can shoot five miles, is advertised with these words: "A round of ammunition purchased for less than $10 can destroy or disable a modern jet aircraft."[6] One has to ask: Why do we have guns that can shoot down an aircraft? What's more is that the fellow it's named after, Ronnie Barrett, was named man of the year by the National Industrial Defense Association. He has contracts for sales of his gun with the US government and fifty other governments. He praised God for the gun: "It really is a gift from God."[7] A gun that can shoot a plane from the sky. It reminds me of when President Truman thanked God for the atomic bomb used on Hiroshima and Nagasaki: "We are now prepared to obliterate more rapidly and completely," he explained, adding a few days later, "We thank God that it has come to us, instead of to our enemies; and we pray that He may guide us to use it in His ways and for His purposes."[8] We don't know that God.

Exhibit 6

There is a gun that is made to look exactly like a cell phone. It's the same size, shape, and overall look, but beneath the face is a .22-caliber pistol. It's a phone that is capable of firing four rounds in succession with the touch of the keypad. It also looks pretty easy to take into places where cell phones are allowed but guns are not.

Exhibit 7

Did you know that some cities require every person to own a gun? If you don't like guns, it's best not to live in Kennesaw, Georgia; Nelson, Georgia; Nucla, Colorado; Virgin, Utah; or Gun Barrel City, Texas (fitting name).

Exhibit 8

One of the laws that is often considered wise is limiting the number of handguns one person can purchase to twelve per year, or one per month. This is only for handguns, and it's just limiting how many a single individual can buy. It's an attempt to cut down illegal sales, theft, and accidents and to keep someone from loading up a truck with guns and selling them on the streets. The bill has been blocked because some gun advocates think it starts the "slippery slope" to taking all guns away. One more strange law: a gun dealer who sells two or more handguns to the same person within five days must report the sales to the ATF, except if they are AK-47s, which don't have to be reported.

Exhibit 9

Florida created a statewide database of pawnshop transactions to aid police officers in tracking stolen property. The database includes pawned jewelry, televisions, tools, computers—everything except guns. The law stipulates that details of gun transactions are to be purged after forty-eight hours.

Exhibit 10

There's a thing called a "fire sale loophole." It allows a gun dealer who loses his license for misconduct to dispose of his inventory privately without being charged for illegal sales. Can you imagine shutting down a bad liquor store and saying, "You are responsible for disposing of all your inventory"?

Exhibit 11

The Bureau of Alcohol, Tobacco, Firearms and Explosives (ATF) keeps records of all gun sales through licensed dealers but must destroy them after ninety days. The law was enacted in 2001 through the efforts of Attorney General John Ashcroft, a former NRA board member. The ATF can check gun dealers for illegal sales, but only *once* per year. The ATF also collects data on gun dealers who regularly sell large quantities of guns that end up used in crimes (only 5 percent of gun shops are responsible for 90 percent of guns used in crimes[9]), but the ATF cannot release that information publicly. So no one knows which gun shops are good and which are bad. The ATF is not even allowed to have computers because doing so would be considered a "national database," so they have thousands of boxes of records. Obviously it is the epitome of inefficiency, which is exactly the goal of the NRA.

Exhibit 12

In 2003 Congress passed a law that bars federal law enforcement from releasing any information that links guns used in crimes back to the original purchaser or seller. It is impossible to build consumer pressure, facilitate boycotts, or put a gun shop out of business if we don't know which ones are the bad gun shops.

Exhibit 13

In 2010 fifty-six police officers were killed in the line of duty. All but one were killed by a gun. Seven were killed by their own guns—and these are professionals trained to use their guns. Still on the market are armor-piercing bullets, often called "cop killers." They are designed to go through anything, including body armor. And, of course, we also know that in a country saturated with guns, police are often on edge. In 2017 police killed nearly one thousand people, many of them unarmed, and disproportionately people of color.[10]

Exhibit 14

Every minute a gun is stolen in the US.[11] What's more, stolen guns aren't required to be reported in many states. In places that have required gun dealers to report stolen guns, say within a day or two, gun advocates have sued. Fifteen guns disappear each day from gun shops—over five thousand per year. Every year three hundred thousand guns are stolen from other places like homes, cars, and even directly from the military or gun factories. Up to a third of these stolen guns are used in crimes.[12]

Exhibit 15

In the United States, we register births, marriages, divorces, and deaths. We register houses, land, trucks, boats, animals—everything but guns.

Exhibit 16

There are more safety regulations on toy guns than real ones. The Consumer Protection Act of 1972 prohibits the Consumer Protection Commission from examining the quality or safety of any gun or any piece of ammunition. In late 2005, the US Congress and President George W. Bush passed the Protection of Lawful Commerce Act, which denies victims of gun violence the right to sue the manufacturers, distributors, or dealers for negligent, reckless, or irresponsible conduct. No other industry in America enjoys such blanket immunity and protection.

You can hardly miss the irony. If you shoot your friend's eye out with a Nerf gun, you can sue Nerf. But you can't if it's a Winchester rifle or an AR-15. You can sue a toy gun manufacturer but not the company that makes assault rifles or a gun shop that sells a gun to a drunk man who walks out and kills someone. Unprecedented immunity. It's one more reason that guns that don't even have safety controls are legal in our homes and on our streets. Teddy bears, dolls, and toy guns must pass four sets of strict regulations before they can be sold. Not so with guns.

Exhibit 17

In an attempt to make guns more attractive to women, and especially young women, gun dealers have started making Hello Kitty assault rifles and bubble-gum-pink pistols. Two kids in North Carolina, ages three and seven, found one of them, and the three-year-old was killed as they played with it. And of course the manufacturers are immune from any liability, even though they intentionally created weapons that would attract children.

Exhibit 18

In some states, concealed carry permits are issued to people who are legally blind.

In many states, an eighteen-year-old can own a handgun. You can have a gun, and even join the military, before you are old enough to drink a beer. Young people between the ages of eighteen and twenty have the highest rates of killing. Still, in the states where the legal age to own a gun is twenty-one, the gun lobby has filed lawsuits to force them to lower the age to eighteen. For the record, we're not advocating for dropping the drinking age. It's just interesting what we trust our teenagers with—guns but not alcohol.

Exhibit 19

In most states, a person can buy and own a gun without knowing how to use it, and there are no requirements that gun owners be trained in the safe operation of guns. Imagine letting someone drive a car off the lot without ever having driven one.

Exhibit 20

Folks on the no-fly list can still buy weapons. In a study from 2004 to 2010, individuals on the terrorist watch list were involved in firearm and explosives background checks 1,228 times. Of those attempts, 1,119 were approved, and 109 were denied. That means roughly 91 percent of attempts made by people we know are potentially dangerous were permitted. Over a thousand people on the no-fly list have bought weapons and explosives. You can't fly on an airplane because you might be dangerous, but you can still buy weapons.[13]

Exhibit 21

Hundreds of couples toting AR-15 rifles packed a
church in Pennsylvania one Wednesday to have their
marriages blessed and their weapons celebrated as
"rods of iron" that could have saved lives in a recent
Florida school shooting. Women dressed in white and
men in dark suits gripped the guns, which they had
been urged to bring unloaded to the Sanctuary
Church in the rural Pocono Mountains, about one hundred miles north of Philadelphia. Many celebrants wore
crowns—some made of bullets—while church officials
dressed in flowing pink and white garments to go with
their armaments.[14]

© Eduard Munoz / Reuters Pic...

Exhibit 22

It's hard to explain a gun show, especially to those of you who don't live in the
United States. Imagine a giant open-air market with guns everywhere. And you
don't even need a permit to buy one. It's like a rummage sale or, as one friend
said, "a Tupperware party with weapons." One of the gun shows advertised: "1000
tables . . . the size of 2 football fields . . . 1.5 miles of guns, knives and accessories."

I (Shane) just went to one of these gun shows that boasted of one thousand
tables. Before you even entered the convention center, you passed by folks selling guns outside. One of them told me all I needed was $400 cash—no ID, no
paperwork—and the gun was mine. You can buy a gun as easy as you can a cup of
coffee. My wife wanted to find a .410 rifle like the one she had as a kid but didn't
have any luck. The irony was that while table after table was filled with assault

weapons, it was almost impossible to find a .410. We found a handgun that shot one hundred rounds per minute, and then came upon a grenade launcher. I couldn't stop myself and had to ask a few questions. Sure enough, I could buy it on the spot—even the grenades to go with it. The lady behind the counter told me all I needed was two things—an ID and $6,000 in cash. She even added, "The most important thing is the cash."

The ATF regards gun shows as the second-leading source of crime guns in the country, second only to corrupt gun dealers. There are more than five thousand gun shows each year. It is the easiest way for felons, criminals, terrorists, abusive husbands, youth, and mentally ill folks to get weapons, cheap and quick, with no questions asked.

Exhibit 23

Many gun purchases are what is often called a "straw purchase": one person buys guns for someone else who is prohibited from purchasing. A lot of the time the "straw purchaser" is a woman buying guns for a man who can't. Video footage of such a purchase looks a lot like an adult buying a minor alcohol. Often both people go into the gun shop. One person will point out the guns he wants, or hand the buyer a list, and then leave the store as the guns are purchased. Sometimes you can even see them get in the car together or exchange money and guns outside the shop. It's nearly impossible to miss, and gun-shop owners can spot a straw purchase a mile away. Some gun shops have made a killing—literally—off of these sales, which is why they are so hesitant to stop them.

We're reluctant to try to "legislate morality" and would prefer that gun-shop owners voluntarily refuse to sell to straw purchasers, which they can surely do just as a liquor store owner can refuse to sell to someone buying alcohol for a minor. We should always prefer for folks to do right because they want to, not because they have to by law. Nevertheless, some simple procedures can nearly end straw purchases of guns, similar to how we have ended sales of alcohol to minors. A lot of the responsibility lies on the gun-shop owners, just as it does with liquor stores or bars. And we always know there are some irresponsible businesses that are going to make illegal sales because they can—and because they make money from those sales.

A few bad gun shops are responsible for a vast majority of the guns used in crimes. Ninety percent of crime guns can be traced to 5 percent of the gun shops in this country.[15] A handful of the worst gun shops in the country are responsible for a majority of the guns used in crimes. That's important to remember. And absurd.

Exhibit 24

Not only can you find plans and parts online to build your own unregistered firearm, but now you can find the blueprints to print a gun on a 3-D printer. These 3-D guns are made out of ABS plastic, the same material as LEGO pieces. Guns like "The Liberator" are known as "downloadable guns" because you can literally find everything you need to print your own gun on the internet. Because they are made almost entirely from plastic, they can easily pass through metal detectors and make their way into schools, courthouses, or airplanes. Law enforcement officials refer to them as "ghost guns" since they have no serial number and are untraceable. ATF agents decided to test out the blueprint and found that the gun fired with the accuracy of a commercial handgun. There have already been one million downloads. This definitely belongs on the absurd list.[16]

How did we get to this point?

---

six

MYTHBUSTING

Fifty percent of all statistics are wrong.

—Fake fact

WHEN IT COMES TO distilling the information about guns, it's important to note that there are limited resources available for researching and studying gun violence. One of the most seditious strategies of the militant gun lobby is to cut all funding for research. Much of the research we draw on has been privately funded, sometimes even by the researchers themselves, who passionately want to reduce gun violence and are convinced that the more people know, the more we can reduce gun violence. The NRA often accuses research findings of being "political opinion masquerading as medical science" and has pushed to cut millions of dollars in research money. Even the funds that are available for research purposes have a direct order from Congress, prompted by the NRA: none of the funds made available for research into injury prevention and control can be used "to advocate or promote gun control." It's kind of like saying we want to research the causes of cancer but want to make sure no one discourages folks from smoking or makes the tobacco companies look bad.[1]

This has all but stopped any funding and projects, and remains one of the top priorities of the NRA. They do not want any research that could cast doubt on the claim that guns save lives. This is nothing new—other self-interested corporations and lobby groups have done the same thing. Remember how hard tobacco companies worked to block research or information that showed that tobacco use leads to cancer? They worked viciously around the clock to keep us all in the dark. But the truth shall set us free! Aren't we glad that so much research has been done to make cars safer? Don't we want to find out how we can keep fewer people from dying of opioids? Gun violence is also a public health crisis. And we need to study it to understand it.

One of the major changes many of us could push for is more resources toward research and data collection. Research and information, studies and data, help us solve a public health crisis—whether that crisis is guns or opioids or cancer. We can't solve what we don't understand.

Having said that, here are some things we do know, and they are vitally important to remember as we look for common ground and try to save lives in the years to come.

Myth No. 1: The Slippery Slope

The slippery slope myth is one hundred years old. It gained popularity after the NRA and others led the way in restricting tommy guns and other "gangster weapons" in 1924. While the NRA and nearly all major players in the gun-rights community were much in favor of limiting these dangerous weapons, gun advocates began talking about all guns as a bundle of sticks, the bundle being strong only when held together but weak when the pieces are separated out. It's the idea that if we allow "them" to take any guns, they will take all the guns. The idea that "any gun means all guns" was not without controversy, even in the gun community, where many sport shooters, hunters, and other reasonable gun owners did not want to see machine guns and war weapons on our streets. But paranoia and fear won that battle, at least in the gun-rights world at the time. It has dominated much of the gun debate as a cliché talking point, primarily among extremists, who even have T-shirts and bumper stickers with an assault rifle that says, "Come and take it." The idea that "they" are coming for our guns is still prevalent, but it is losing steam, as most gun owners don't buy into it, which is why so many would like to see restrictions on assault rifles and high-capacity cartridges. The implied "them" is "the government," but hopefully in a semi-functional democracy like ours, "we" are "them." We can set the limits on our own government. It's done all the time with tobacco, alcohol, and now marijuana and other drugs. We can do the same with guns. Banning semiautomatic weapons or high-capacity magazines that allow guns to shoot one hundred rounds per minute does not lead to taking away hunting rifles or even a handgun purchased for self-defense.

Myth No. 2: Stranger Danger

Random acts of violence, assault, and burglary do happen, but they are by far the exception rather than the norm. When it comes to gun violence, the odds of getting killed by someone you know are massively higher than being killed by a stranger.[2] One fact that is proved true over and over is that the person who is most likely to kill you already has a key to your house.

Most of America's murders and assaults are not committed by strangers or criminals; they are committed by family members, friends, and acquaintances who, in acts of passion, take up a gun.

But we can change the way the game is played. You are more likely than not to know your intruder, which only strengthens the argument to use nonviolence in these situations—and perhaps the familiarity you have with the person could open the way for nonviolence as you try to de-escalate or distract them from their violent intentions. (We will work on those skills in a few chapters.)

Myth No. 3: Guns Keep Us Safe

Often the very instrument that was purchased to protect us ends up taking our life or the life of someone we love. There are fewer than 1,600 verified instances of defensive gun use each year in the US. Compare that to the 118,000 people in any given year who are shot or shoot themselves.[3] For every gun used in self-defense, six more are used to commit a crime.[4] At least one study has shown that guns kept in the home are twelve times more likely to be involved in the death or injury of a member of the household than they are to stop an intruder.[5] Studies of victims who have survived crimes like assaults or burglaries show that they used guns less than 1 percent of the time.[6] More often, they used mace, used a phone (to film or call police), yelled, or ran away. Mace is shown to be just as effective as a gun in stopping a perpetrator. And in cases of sexual assault, having a gun can even be counterproductive.[7]

One study of hundreds of sexual assaults showed that almost none of the victims who survived used a gun. Using a gun in defense of sexual assault did not change the outcome when compared to not using a gun: of those who used a gun, around 4 percent were still physically injured in the assault, and that was about the same percentage of those without guns.[8] Almost two-thirds of the US population live without guns, and there is no evidence that they are more at risk of being robbed, assaulted, or killed than those with guns. Those with guns certainly have much higher rates of being victims of gun violence, murder, or suicide. Having a gun in the home increases the likelihood not only that someone will be shot accidentally but also that someone will die from suicide or murder.[9] This is even more evident when it comes to domestic violence. A gun in the house is twenty-two times more likely to result in a death in one's household or to be stolen and used in a violent crime than it is to be used against an intruder.[10] Over half of all murders of women in the US are by their current or former intimate partner, and guns are the weapon of choice.[11] If there is a gun in the home, abused women are five times more likely to become victims of domestic homicide.[12] A man's access to firearms, even one the woman may have purchased for herself, increases a woman's risk of being killed.

Myth No. 4: The Answer to a Bad Guy with a Gun Is a Good Guy with a Gun

Some folks claim that guns are constantly used for self-defense. We're going to spend some time on this myth because this is a popular one. Hang with us. Those who make this argument usually cite the research of a guy named Gary Kleck, whose study is the poster child for gun enthusiasts because it concluded that there are around 2.5 million defensive gun uses per year.[13] Gun advocates often use his study to say that guns are used 6,850 times per day—once every thirteen seconds—for defense.[14] A Google search shows that it has been cited over one million times. But hold on . . .

According to a Harvard University study, people defended themselves with a gun in only 0.9 percent of crimes from 2007 to 2011.[15] So how did Mr. Kleck convince people of such an inflated number?

Kleck's study has been debunked by multiple impartial experts for several reasons. First, it was not a professional, scientific inquiry. More than half of the "instances" cannot be verified at all, and even those that can are problematic because his research team did not define what constitutes a "use" for self-defense. Shooting in the air or even saying "I have a gun" qualified as defensive uses. The vagueness of his research has been compared to having a "Beware of Dog" sign and saying that your dog kept robbers away. What is clear is that most of the ways people defined "using a gun for defense" did not mean actually shooting an intruder or even pulling out a gun.

As a filmmaker looked further into the study, Kleck said that 54 percent of the defensive uses involved someone verbally referring to the gun. Forty-seven percent involved pointing it at a criminal. And less than a quarter (22 percent) of the defensive uses involved actually shooting the gun (as opposed to waving it). Only 14 percent involved actually shooting at a person. In 8 percent of the incidents, the person defending themselves actually wounded or killed the offender.[16]

The popular statistic that guns are constantly used for defense—every thirteen seconds!—is a fake fact. It's misconstrued. In contrast, the government reports less than three hundred "justifiable homicides" by private citizens in a year.[17] Most of those "justifiable homicides" were in cases of escalating arguments, not from random home burglaries as is often assumed.

Nobody can really know how many lives are saved by guns used for protection. The number will probably vary depending on one's stance on guns. Even those of us who are not fans of guns must concede that there are a certain number of lives saved each year because someone had a gun. But it comes at the expense of thirty-eight thousand lives taken by someone with a gun.[18]

Consider the case of the Las Vegas shooter. No "good guy with a gun" could have stopped a man shooting from a hotel window hundreds of yards away with military-style weapons.

In the case of the mass shooting in Tucson where a man murdered six people and almost killed Congresswoman Gabrielle Giffords, there was an innocent bystander named Joe Zamudio on site with a gun. With the gun still in his pocket, Joe helped another man subdue the shooter and later

Memorial to the Lost

On October 1, 2017, fifty-eight people were killed and 851 others were injured in Las Vegas during a music festival, when a lone gunman fired more than 1,100 rounds from his hotel room. It all happened in ten minutes. He had twenty-four guns in the room with him; fourteen of them were AR-15-style semiautomatic rifles. Many of them were fitted with bump stocks that can shoot ninety rounds in ten seconds. These are the victims who lost their lives.

Hannah Lassette Ahlers, 34
Heather Lorraine Alvarado, 35
Dorene Anderson, 49
Carrie Rae Barnette, 34
Jack Reginald Beaton, 54
Stephen Richard Berger, 44
Candice Ryan Bowers, 40
Denise Burditus, 50
Sandra Casey, 34
Andrea Lee Anna Castilla, 28
Denise Cohen, 58
Austin William Davis, 29
Thomas Day Jr., 54
Christiana Duarte, 22
Stacee Ann Etcheber, 50
Brian S. Fraser, 39
Keri Galvan, 31
Dana Leann Gardner, 52
Angela C. Gomez, 20
Rocio Guillen, 40

Charleston Hartfield, 34
Christopher Hazencomb, 44
Jennifer Topaz Irvine, 42
Teresa Nicol Kimura, 38
Jessica Klymchuk, 34
Carly Anne Kreibaum, 34
Rhonda M. LeRocque, 42
Victor L. Link, 55
Jordan McIldoon, 24
Kelsey Breanne Meadows, 28
Calla-Marie Medig, 28
James Melton, 29
Patricia Mestas, 67
Austin Cooper Meyer, 24
Adrian Allan Murfitt, 35
Rachael Kathleen Parker, 33
Jennifer Parks, 36
Carolyn Lee Parsons, 31
Lisa Marie Patterson, 46
John Joseph Phippen, 56

Melissa V. Ramirez, 26
Jordyn N. Rivera, 21
Quinton Robbins, 20
Cameron Robinson, 28
Tara Ann Roe, 34
Lisa Romero-Muniz, 48
Christopher Louis Roybal, 28
Brett Schwanbeck, 61
Bailey Schweitzer, 20
Laura Anne Shipp, 50
Erick Silva, 21
Susan Smith, 53
Brennan Lee Stewart, 30
Derrick Dean Taylor, 56
Neysa C. Tonks, 46
Michelle Vo, 32
Kurt Allen Von Tillow, 55
William W. Wolfe Jr., 42

revealed that he almost fired at the wrong person.[19] After a mass shooting we are always left wondering how it might have been different if only there had been a "good guy with a gun" present. Well there was, and he almost shot the wrong person. Meanwhile, a person without a gun subdued the shooter.

The same thing happened in Tennessee when James Shaw Jr., armed only with his courage, bravely stopped a mass shooter in a Waffle House. One study shows that the likelihood of injury when using a gun in self-defense (10.9 percent) is almost identical to the likelihood of injury when the victim takes no action at all (11 percent).[20]

It seems safe to say that even if guns work in a small percentage of defensive attempts, they don't work in a whole lot of other attempts. The number of folks who shoot people accidentally crushes any hope for guns saving us, as we can see even in incidents of police killings. And police are professionally trained to use their weapons.

A gun is much more likely to be used in a suicide, a domestic homicide, or an accidental shooting than it is to be used to ward off a criminal.

Myth No. 5: We Don't Need More Laws; We Need to Enforce the Ones We Have

Many gun advocates will say that we just need to enforce the laws that we already have. Hundreds and hundreds of times this argument has been made, citing that there are twenty thousand gun laws on the books. It actually goes back to a 1965 quote by NRA board member John Dingell, who used the twenty thousand number with no source or records. But then Ronald Reagan picked it up. After he was shot in an attempted assassination, he said, "There are some 20,000 gun laws now in the United States," but no one knows where that number came from.[21] Legal experts Jon Vernick and Lisa Hepburn have done the most thorough work trying to count them, and they came up with about three hundred major state and federal laws and a shrinking number of local gun laws, because state laws trump local laws in forty states.[22] Three hundred is a long way from twenty thousand.

So here's a homework assignment: someone compile a list. It would also be interesting to count how many automobile laws there are on the books, as that number might be closer to twenty thousand.

What's more, Ronald Reagan called for a prohibition of AK-47s and military-style weapons, and yet there is currently no law keeping them off our streets.[23]

Myth No. 6: Gun Owners Are the Problem

One of the problems with the political debate around gun control is that people often talk about "gun owners" as one big homogenous group. But they're not.

As we've seen in our quick hike through history, there have been some major rifts in the NRA, and in the gun-owning community in general, over the years. There are many different political persuasions and priorities among gun owners despite the monolithic voice of the NRA that usually dominates the airwaves.

The truth is, most gun owners want to see fewer people die from guns. For many, owning a rifle on the farm or even a pistol for protection does not mean we should have AK-47s on the streets or in our schools.

They may not be the loudest gun owners, but gun owners against gun violence are everywhere.

A recent study by Frank Luntz, who is widely considered to be a reputable, conservative pollster, revealed some stunning things.[24] And other studies have corroborated and reinforced his findings.[25] He polled hundreds of gun owners, distinguishing between NRA members and those not affiliated with the NRA. The study showed how out of sync the NRA is with its own members, and even more so with gun owners in general. Luntz found that 82 percent of the gun owners who were polled (87 percent of the non-NRA members and 74 percent of the NRA members) support criminal background checks for *everyone* purchasing a gun ("universal background checks"). About the same number (80 percent total: 80 percent non-NRA gun owners and 79 percent NRA) think gun retailers should perform background checks on employees to check for criminal records. How about that!

Seventy-eight percent of gun owners (81 percent non-NRA gun owners and 75 percent NRA) said that concealed carry permits should not be given to people who have a history of violent crime such as assault or domestic violence.

An overwhelming majority of gun owners (80 percent total: 84 percent non-NRA gun owners and 74 percent NRA) believe a person wanting to own a concealed carry permit should be required to complete gun safety training.

A significant majority (69 percent total: 74 percent non-NRA gun owners and 63 percent NRA) believe a person should be at least twenty-one years old to obtain a concealed carry permit.

Likewise, an overwhelming majority of gun owners believe someone on the terrorist watch list should not be able to get a gun (76 percent total: 80 percent non-NRA gun owners and 71 percent NRA). And gun owners believe stolen guns should have to be reported to police (68 percent total: 71 percent non-NRA gun owners and 64 percent NRA).

And check this one out: 85 percent of gun owners (83 percent non-NRA gun owners and 87 percent NRA) said that support for the Second Amendment goes hand in hand with keeping illegal guns out of the hands of criminals. In other words, these gun owners are no longer buying into the slippery slope argument or uncompromising stance that has been a staple of the NRA. That's huge. Nearly nine out of ten gun owners in the NRA believe the right to bear arms and public safety don't have to be enemies. An overwhelming majority believe in at least some commonsense gun reforms. That's good news!

There were several other interesting takeaways from this groundbreaking study. One is that a lot of us, including gun owners, don't even realize

Proposals to reduce gun violence
Percent that said "Favor."

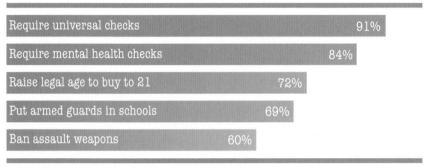

Require universal checks	91%
Require mental health checks	84%
Raise legal age to buy to 21	72%
Put armed guards in schools	69%
Ban assault weapons	60%

Fox News poll of registered voters (whether or not gun owners),
+/- 3% PTS, March 18–21, 2018

how crazy things have become. Over half of gun owners mistakenly believe the statement "Everyone who wants to buy a gun has to pass a background check." Perhaps it should be true, but right now it is not. Another fascinating revelation is that the views of the NRA do not reflect those of its constituency. Sixty-two percent of gun owners said that they feel the NRA is out of touch with them on issues like gun safety and background checks, and only 29 percent said they feel represented by the NRA on issues like these.[26]

This is a major breakthrough. It is a crack in the wall of the polarized gun debate.

This is a small start in trying to really understand the debate on guns and figuring out what's true and what's false. We also want to encourage you to do your own research and to advocate for as much energy and resources as possible to go toward research on gun violence. The more we understand the problem, the more likely it is that we can actually save lives.

seven

KIDS AND GUNS

> If anyone causes one of these little ones—those who believe in me—to stumble, it would be better for them to have a large millstone hung around their neck and to be drowned in the depths of the sea.
>
> —Matthew 18:6

SOME SAY THAT THE SOLUTION to school shootings is not arming teachers but arming kids. Sacha Baron Cohen, political satirist, posed as an Israeli security expert named Colonel Erran Morad (the "Terrorist Terminator"), championing a program aimed at teaching schoolchildren as young as three (yes, *three*) to use firearms, including semiautomatics and basic mortars, to defend themselves in a school shooting. He pitched his idea, creatively named "Kinderguardians," to politicians and gun enthusiasts in the corridors of power. The response was stunning.[1]

Two congressmen, Dana Rohrabacher (Republican, California) and Joe Wilson (Republican, South Carolina), enthusiastically endorse the program on video. Two former politicians, Trent Lott (former Senate Republican leader) and Joe Walsh (former congressman), participate in a promotional video, in which Walsh explains that the Kinderguardians program "introduces specially selected children, from twelve to four years old, to pistols, rifles, semiautomatics, and a rudimentary knowledge of mortars. In less than a month, a first grader can become a first grenader. . . . Happy shooting, kids." The politicians hold stuffed animals called "Gunimals" that have weapons inside them, and teach kids to shoot the "Puppy Pistol," the "Gunny Rabbit," "Dino-Gun," and the "Uzicorn." You can't make this up. At first you laugh, and then you begin to cry.

One of the gun-rights activists in the video, Philip Van Cleave (president of the Virginia Citizens Defense League) actually champions the idea of arming kids as young as four: "Kids haven't quite developed what we called 'conscience,' where you feel guilty about doing something. . . . If they haven't developed that yet, they can be very effective soldiers." Wilson says, "Our forefathers did not put an age limit on the Second Amendment." And Larry Pratt, director emeritus of Gun Owners of America, scorns our prejudice against toddlers having guns: he laughs that the only way to stop a bad guy with a gun is a "good toddler" with a gun. The segment says that the solution to our gun problem is not arming teachers, as some would suggest, but arming the kids themselves, even the preschoolers. That's what we're up against.

■　■　■　■　■　■

I (Shane) had some friends who moved from California to Philadelphia. As they were settling into life in Philly, their six-year-old noticed some of our gun shops, one of which was the Shooter Shop around the corner from us. He asked innocently, "Why are there so many gun shops in Philadelphia when there aren't that many deer to hunt?" Out of the mouth of babes, as they say.

Perhaps it's no surprise that young people are leading the way in the movement against gun violence—from Ferguson to Parkland. The adults have failed them. The politicians have failed them. The young people are rising up.

There is an urgency in their voices because they have seen their friends die. They have hidden in closets as they heard the shots of an AR-15 in their schools. They have had enough.

We need the children to wake up the adults and remind us that kids were not meant to die. And they weren't meant to kill. But it happens all the time in America.

In just a two-week span before I (Shane) participated in a panel discussion on gun violence, the following happened:

- A two-year-old in Milwaukee shot and killed his mother.
- A two-year-old in Indiana killed himself with his mom's gun.
- A four-year-old was killed by her dad with a semiautomatic pistol a few blocks from my house.
- A two-year-old was shot four times on his front porch, less than one hundred yards from where we live.

All those things happened as I was preparing for a panel discussion on gun violence on PBS. Needless to say, it put a fire in my bones for the panel. The killing of children should break our hearts.

In the aftermath of the May 2018 school shooting in Santa Fe, an interview with a student who survived the attack went viral. The emotional, visibly shaken girl was asked by a reporter if she was surprised something so horrific could happen in her school. Her response was an unforgettable "no." Shaking her head, she said, "It's been happening everywhere. I've always felt it would eventually happen here too. . . . I wasn't surprised, I was just scared."[2]

We should never get used to children killing or being killed. The fact is that this is a uniquely American problem. Of all the children (ages zero to fourteen) killed by guns in industrialized countries, 87 percent are US children.[3] Every year, over 2,300 children and teenagers (ages zero to eighteen) are killed by guns, and another 14,500 are injured. Gun violence is the second-leading cause of death among our youth.[4]

A GUN IN THE HOME

"The absence of guns from children's homes and communities is the most reliable and effective measure to prevent firearm-related injuries in children and adolescents."

—American Academy of Pediatrics

Nearly two million kids under age eighteen live in homes with firearms that are both loaded and unlocked.[5]

Sixteen percent of high school students say they've carried a weapon (any weapon, not just a gun) to school in the past month, one 2009 study shows. Another study more specific to guns revealed that, over the course of one month, two out of every twenty-five high school kids nationwide (around 8 percent) carried a gun to school.[6]

It's helpful to reiterate, like the refrain of a song—it doesn't have to be this way. This sort of thing isn't a normal occurrence in other developed countries. There is something wrong when our country has three times more gun dealers than McDonald's. More gun shops than grocery stores.[7]

In my neighborhood we have a food desert; it's hard to get good, nutritious, locally grown food. I'll never forget hearing a young man explain, "It's easier to get a gun in our neighborhood than it is to get a salad." For those of us who are people of faith, we know that our mission in the world is to bring the kingdom of God on earth. Or as we say, we are trying to bring the garden of Eden to North Philadelphia. We want to see God's kingdom come—on earth. On Potter Street. And God's dream is not to see 105 people die every day in the United States from guns, three of whom are kids.

Memorial to the Lost

On December 14, 2012, twenty first-grade students and six school staff were murdered when a man shot his way into the school using a Bushmaster AR-15 assault-style semiautomatic rifle with high-capacity magazines. It all happened in ten minutes. The children killed that day were between the ages of six and seven years old. Here are the names of the children, as well as the school staff who died trying to protect them:

Charlotte Bacon, 6	Grace McDonnell, 7
Daniel Barden, 7	Anne Marie Murphy, 52
Rachel Davino, 29	Emilie Parker, 6
Olivia Engel, 6	Jack Pinto, 6
Josephine Gay, 7	Noah Pozner, 6
Ana M. Marquez-Greene, 6	Caroline Previdi, 6
Dawn Hochsprung, 47	Jessica Rekos, 6
Dylan Hockley, 6	Avielle Richman, 6
Madeline F. Hsu, 6	Lauren Rousseau, 30
Catherine V. Hubbard, 6	Mary Sherlach, 56
Chase Kowalski, 7	Victoria Soto, 27
Jesse Lewis, 6	Benjamin Wheeler, 6
James Mattioli, 6	Allison N. Wyatt, 6

The Kids Shall Lead Them

I (Shane) was talking with a kid in my neighborhood, who at the age of ten had already seen his share of violence and guns and bloodshed on our streets. He bounced into my house after school, as he often did. I could tell he had something he couldn't wait to tell me. He skipped the small talk. "Shane, I figured out who invented the gun," he blasted out, leaving the conversation hanging in silent anticipation for a second, like a comedian waiting to deliver the punch line. I asked the obvious question: "Who?" I'm not sure what I expected him to say. Maybe he was doing a research project? I'll never forget what he said next: "Satan."

He went on confidently, without missing a beat. "Satan wants us to kill each other. God wants us to love each other. Satan invented the gun to make it easier for us to kill each other."

I think my ten-year-old friend may be right, even though it doesn't say that on Wikipedia or in the history books.

In all of our talk about original sin, we sometimes forget about original innocence. I hang out with kids a lot because they have a certain innocence and imagination and defiant hope. It's no surprise that in 2018 the kids in Parkland, Florida, began to lead our country when it comes to gun violence. They have been teaching the politicians what courage looks like.

The prophet Isaiah, the same one who gave us the vision of beating swords into plows, also said that a child shall lead them (Isa. 11:6). He dreams of a time when "the wolf will live with the

Mikel Jollett
@Mikel_Jollett

Right now in America the head of the largest gun manufacturers lobbyist organization is calling children who survived a massacre and want only peace "terrorists."

Newsweek @Newsweek
NRA President Oliver North says Parkland gun control activists are criminal civil terrorists bit.ly/2ryFpXu

2018 **NRA-ILA** LEADERSHIP FORUM

10:06 AM - May 12, 2018

♡ 22.8K ⚪ 11.3K people are talking about this

lamb, the leopard will lie down with the goat, the calf and the lion and the yearling together, . . . the cow will feed with the bear, . . . the infant will play near the cobra's den, and the young child will put its hand into the viper's nest" (Isa. 11:6–8). It's a vision of a world of peace, free of harm and fear. He says, "They will neither harm nor destroy" (v. 9). And, my favorite part, "a little child will lead them" (v. 6). The adults of our world have done a lot of damage. They have created wars and bloodshed and death. We have a lot of politicians who act childishly. And a lot of kids who are wise beyond their years.

The doctrine of original innocence looks like a kid asking, "Why do we have so many guns in Philly when there aren't that many deer to shoot?"

We are not made to kill. We learn to kill. We are taught how to hate. As Nelson Mandela said, "No one is born hating another person. . . . People must learn to hate, and if they can learn to hate, they can be taught to love, for love comes more naturally to the human heart than its opposite."[8]

Before we were sinners, we were creatures that God called "good." We are made in the image of God, every one of us. Every time a life is lost, we lose a piece of the image of God in the world. We are image-bearers of God. It's worth taking a step back and thinking through how we can deconstruct the culture of gun violence, by which we are conditioned to accommodate death.

Violence is a sin that we learn. Violence is taught. It is also caught like a contagion. It is something we form in the imaginations of our children. And it is something we can unlearn. Perhaps the kids will help us.

Politicians and gun profiteers continue to defend the status quo. Companies are designing bulletproof backpacks and talking about arming teachers. But young people have had enough.

They have helped organize some of the largest marches in US history, like the March for Our Lives. They've managed to get some of the largest corporations, like Walmart and Dick's Sporting Goods, to change their policies and make costly decisions like no longer selling assault rifles and setting a minimum age of twenty-one to buy a gun.[9] They've replaced politicians and changed the narrative on gun control. They've helped the new standard for election to become an "F" rating from the NRA and a clean record of refusing NRA money. They've had sit-ins and

walkouts. The young people are rising up. And thank God they are.

Toddlers and Hazelnut Trees

In 2016 RAWtools was at an event in Toledo in partnership with a couple of churches and gun-violence prevention groups. A woman who lost her husband was going to bang on a .22 rifle and participate in helping us turn it into a garden tool. At the end we would take a spade, made from a donated shotgun, to a spot in a community garden and plant a nut tree. The fruit of this tree, along with other produce from the garden, would help provide fresh food to a local elementary school.

The news crew that was on its way to cover the event was pulled to another story—a seven-year-old had unintentionally shot and killed a three-year-old.[10]

When the news crew finally arrived at the end of our event, young children were planting a hazelnut tree with a shovel made from a gun. Unfortunately, the two events that the news crew covered on this day were not quite a coincidence.

Children planting a tree using shovels made from guns

A coincidence would be when two relatable events occur at the same time but hardly ever occur again. Kids are dying too often by gun violence for us to consider this a mere coincidence. Two weeks before the tragedy in Toledo, *USA Today* ran a story in which it found that "minors died from accidental shootings—at their own hands, or at the hands of other children or adults—at a pace of one every other day, far more than limited federal statistics indicate."[11] Every other day we have an opportunity to turn a gun into a tool in a city where a kid died from gun violence. We need to be making garden tools, not burying our children, every other day.

Guns kill three kids per day, over 1,200 per year in the United States, not including the thousands who survive a gunshot.[12] Ninety-one percent of children who die from a gunshot are from the US. This has driven gunshot wounds to be the third-leading cause of death for children in the US, many of which are called accidents.[13] Our medical professional friends tell us, however, that this is wrongly categorized. Such incidents can't be defined as accidents, because that would imply there was nothing that could have prevented them. Children dying because of guns is a preventable problem, not an accident. There are many steps we can take to keep toddlers from gaining access to loaded weapons.

When I (Mike) think about the "least of these" suffering because of gun violence, I think of my own two children. How can I not? And why would I not want to offer myself to be transformed in such a way by a fire that refines me and my neighborhood, moving us toward gardens instead of shooting ranges? The death of a child rocks a community. Ask Pharaoh. After the death of his son, he let the Israelites go, only to retaliate by sending his army after Moses and his people. Scripture tells us Pharaoh's heart was hardened. Pharaoh's heart had not been softened and transformed by fire. When steel is too cold and then struck by a hammer, it cracks. The steel is no longer useful for a tool unless it is welded back together. Pharaoh's heart was cracked at the loss of his firstborn.

We must not let our hearts harden so much that we cannot hear the cries of the children until it's too late and the child is our own. Kids killing kids with guns is directly related to the easy access they have to them, compounded by our ability to carry guns, both openly and concealed, and by our inability to safely store guns. Is our devotion to guns really worth the lives of our kids?

We can change the foundation of how our society solves problems by training the future leaders that a gun is not a problem solver but a problem creator. This is the implication of turning swords into plows. It's a community effort to get rid of weapons, requiring all of us to use other options to solve conflict. The kids need to see the adults be an example of this. Collectively, can your community be this example?

Blacksmith Dane Turpening and Toledo Mennonite pastor Joel Shenk are part of a RAWtools location in Toledo. These images show them gathered around the forge, helping event participants make a garden tool from a gun. As part of their work, they teach youth how to solve conflict nonviolently and how to turn guns into garden tools and other lovely things.

Joel Shenk

eight

ANOTHER DARK SECRET

> Working up the courage to pull the trigger was hard for me. That Smith & Wesson called to me like an old friend who was here to save me. It was time.
>
> —Ben Corey

EVERY THIRTY MINUTES, a person takes their life with a gun. Some 45,000 people die from suicide each year in America.[1] Most people who attempt suicide do not die—unless they use a gun. Access to a gun in a time of crisis is often what makes the difference between life and death.

Suicide is the second-leading cause of death among young people fifteen to twenty-four years old.[2] Of the thirty-eight thousand gun deaths each year, nearly two-thirds are suicides.[3] When access to guns decreases, so do the number of suicides. When access to guns is greater, so is the number of suicides. Just like in war, adding more guns creates more casualties.

In short, guns make it a whole lot easier to commit suicide, and yet suicide is overlooked and neglected in the gun debate. Studies consistently show that suicide attempts by gun almost always end in death: nine out of ten are fatal, compared with 3 percent or less for other more commonly used methods such as overdosing, cutting, or jumping.[4] It's the only method that is anywhere near that high. Studies put suffocation around 25 percent or lower in fatality, and taking poison around 10 percent. When it comes to all the others—jumping, cutting, and other means—the completion rate drops even lower, sometimes showing that over 95 percent of those who attempt suicide survive. The only exception is suicide attempts by gun.[5]

What's more is that 90 percent of the people who survive a suicide attempt do not end up dying by suicide, so surviving the first attempt is monumental.[6] About 70 percent will not attempt suicide again.[7] They get help, counseling, medication, or just rethink their decision to take their life. Just stalling an attempt can stop a suicide, since many suicides, especially by men, are done impulsively or reactionarily. But access to guns makes suicide attempts much more lethal. A gun in the home triples the risk of suicide.

Timing is a critical element when it comes to suicide because so many suicides are impulsive. Many of those who attempt suicide spend less than ten minutes deliberating before the attempt. Suicide expert Jill Harkavy-Friedman of the American Foundation for Suicide Prevention stresses how critical the time element is when it comes to suicide.[8] She points out that a crisis often seems less hopeless with time. Time opens up the opportunity to get help, which is why limiting the access to guns is so important. If the first attempt can be prevented, or even survived, then the life is almost always saved. Guns make that nearly impossible.

And guns make the impulsivity so much easier. Seventy percent of suicides happen within an hour of consideration, and nearly a quarter (24 percent) happen within five minutes.[9]

THE ECHOES OF GUN VIOLENCE

I (Mike) lost my mom to suicide. She didn't use a gun, but I found out years later that guns have an impact on how first responders engage with suicide calls (and other special circumstances). I can't speak to all calls, but in our case it was standard practice for law enforcement to have to clear the scene of firearms prior to a paramedic entering the house or property, whether or not they knew of the presence of a gun. There is no way for us to know if that ten minutes or so made a difference for my mom, especially since we lived in a more rural location at the time. I certainly don't blame first responders for not rushing into the house immediately; there is good reason for their practiced caution to be in place—tragedies have occurred and continue to occur. At some point first responders became endangered by the possibility of guns being in a home, and a new practice was put in place—for the sake of losing fewer lives and harming fewer people. This is an echo of gun violence that many of us don't know about. It's also a practice of gun safety. Firefighters and EMS crews are being outfitted with tactical gear because of mass shootings. Are we willing to trade EMS response time and public funds for unfettered access to guns?

It's one of the reasons that states with higher gun ownership have more suicides, especially among kids. Eighty percent of kids who commit suicide with a gun use a family member's firearm. Veterans are especially at risk: two-thirds of veteran suicides are by gun (and twenty veterans commit suicide by any method each day, which is 22 percent higher than the civilian population).[10]

Meanwhile, some states, like Florida, have written into law a provision that prohibits doctors from asking patients or parents if there is a gun in the home, including patients that they may be worried are considering taking their lives. The NRA has said that asking this is unacceptable and beyond the reach of what a doctor should do. The NRA's chief Florida lobbyist said, "We take our children to pediatricians for medical care—not moral judgment, not privacy intrusions."[11]

Memorial to the Lost

Each year, over 21,000 Americans take their own life with a gun. There are too many to mention by name, but we honor their memories and the loved ones they left behind.

Fortunately, some of Florida's doctors sued to stop this ridiculous law, and they prevailed in court. It is one more reminder that guns are a public health issue, and a doctor's job is to do no harm.

Programs that limit access to guns have been effective in decreasing suicides. We don't have much data on that in America, since getting data is one of the problems, but other parts of the world are way ahead of us on reducing suicides and the role that guns play. A promising program was implemented in Australia.

After a mass shooting on April 28, 1996, where thirty-five people were killed and twenty-eight wounded, Australia said, "Never again." Over the course of the next year, Australia launched one of the most vigorous gun buyback programs in history. They collected roughly 650,000 privately held guns. One study says that this was 20 percent of the guns in the entire country. Australia's prime minister, John Howard, knew the campaign would not be easy. He even wore a bulletproof vest on occasion as the process unfolded.[12]

Here's what's so important about what happened next: not only did firearm homicides drop by 42 percent, but the suicide rates also dropped dramatically. Firearm suicides dropped by 57 percent in the seven years after the gun reforms. As the number of firearms dropped, so did the number of suicides. As Australia bought back 3,500 guns per 100,000 people, there was a 74 percent drop in gun suicides and a similar but less precise effect on homicide rates (difference between averages for 1990–1995 and 1998–2003).[13] Without a doubt, lives were saved, and the United States has a lot to learn from the courage of Australia. In the two decades since these shifts, there has only been one mass shooting in Australia. Firearm suicides continue to drop (and suicides by other means have not increased to compensate). It is clear: *we can save lives if we want to.*

Another study, done in Israel, related to the suicide rate of soldiers, 84 percent of which were gun suicides. Israel enacted a policy to decrease the

"IT'S A FACT THAT GOD LOVES YOU"

Benjamin Corey is a mutual friend who has worked with us in a variety of ways. He is a military veteran who found himself in a dark and lonely place and nearly pulled the trigger one night.

> Working up the courage to pull the trigger was hard for me. There were so many mixed emotions that I couldn't explain, yet I so desperately wanted to follow through. However, something inside me kept getting in the way—so I decided I'd go to the store to grab something to drink and take the edge off, before coming home to finish the job once and for all. . . . Upon returning home, I sat back down on my black couch amidst a dark and gloomy living room whose shades hadn't welcomed daylight in weeks. I looked at the pistol staring back at me as if it wanted me to pick her back up and click the safety to "off." I again began to sob as I looked around the room and saw how badly things had spiraled out of control . . . especially when I saw the bottle of sleeping pills beside me which I had been abusing for quite some time, taking a few in the morning to make me sleep all day and a few at night to ensure I was only a prisoner to my thoughts for the shortest amount of time possible. I was rarely "with it," and when I was, that Smith & Wesson called to me like an old friend who was here to save me. It was time.

Ben Corey at the anvil

Something beautiful happened to Ben on his trip to that store. On the way there, he repeatedly asked God if God loved him. While there, a woman walked by and placed a piece of paper in his hand, which he put in his pocket without looking at it. When he got home, he remembered and pulled it out to look at it. At the top it read, "It's a fact that God loves you."

This saved Ben's life.

He later took that Smith & Wesson and made a garden tool out of it. He also had a disabled German Mauser from World War II that he obtained while stationed overseas. We got a little artsy with that one and kept it in one piece, but with the barrel turned into a garden tool. Its bayonet also made a good little weed shovel.

Ben with his finished garden tool

proliferation of guns, especially among soldiers. They stopped letting soldiers take their weapons home with them on weekends. And suicides dropped by 57 percent among Israeli soldiers. Because where fewer guns are present, there are fewer suicides.[14]

It's clear—when it comes to homicide and when it comes to suicide, we can save some lives . . . if we want to.

Suicide Guns

As we've seen, the suicide rate among soldiers and veterans is astronomical, twice that of the general population.[15] Twenty veterans or active military service members take their life every day.[16] Our friend Ben Corey could have been one of those numbers, but he beat his gun into a plow. And we are so glad he did. Our hearts grieve for every life lost to suicide and rejoice with every life that is spared.

Not all stories end like Ben's. In the time RAWtools has been operating, we have received many inquiries from folks about what to do with a gun they don't want to keep or sell because a loved one used the gun to complete suicide. It is often the case that after investigation is finished, police are required to return the gun to the family. Sometimes they offer to destroy it, but they first have to notify the family to give them the choice. It's hard enough to live through the trauma and days following a suicide; the gun being returned further tips the scales of grief.

One gun donation to RAWtools was from a family whose teen played Russian roulette with guns he had found. Some had bullets and some didn't. The police confiscated most of the guns, but for some reason one rifle was left behind. A friend of the family

Veterans
commit suicide at twice the rate of nonveterans.

Source: US Department of Veterans Affairs, "VA National Suicide Data Report, 2005–2015," June 2018, https://www.mentalhealth.va.gov /docs/data-sheets/OMHSP_National_Suicide _Data_Report_2005-2015_06-14-18_508 -compliant.pdf.

saw what that gun represented to the family and offered to take it off their hands. Now it's become a few garden tools cultivating life from Florida to Oregon.

Another donated gun was from a friend whose dad completed suicide decades before. Like many others, he held on to it because it carried meaning, having belonged to his dad. But it had become tainted by also being the means by which he lost his dad. A family heirloom gun carries a lot of weight. In many cases the gun provided food and memories from traditional hunting and camping trips that have nothing to do with a culture of violence (unless you're the deer) and everything to do with familial bonds and experiences. So when tragedy strikes in the form of suicide, families are placed in a predicament. The gun has taken on a new identity because of this tragic part of its history. So now what?

Healing Hearts and Minds

Love compels us to care for those who struggle with mental illness or thoughts of suicide. Beating swords into plows means protecting lives—including preventing the harm someone might inflict on themselves.

States and countries that reduce access to guns see fewer people take their own lives. What if we could save even a few lives by making guns a little less accessible? Wouldn't it be worth it? "Red flag" laws are being introduced across the country. They would allow law enforcement to temporarily confiscate a gun when someone is a risk to themselves. The gun would be returned when a medical professional cleared the individual as mentally fit for gun ownership.

Interrupting a person's suicide attempt is the best way to prevent suicide and further attempts. It's part of what drives advocacy for three- to seven-day holds on gun purchases. If the country wanted to curb gun violence, two-thirds of which is suicide, education on what to do when a friend or loved one exhibits signs of suicide and mental illness should be a large part of a comprehensive approach.

Guns in a house are more likely to be used on someone residing in the home than on an intruder. Suicide is a part of this, as well as murder-suicide (killing one or more persons before killing oneself). A lot of folks know someone who lost their life to suicide or have had suicidal thoughts themselves. Are there measures we can take to remove the most productive form of completed suicide from a home when the conditions merit this? Can we do this without stigmatizing the mentally ill? Part of the problem is our failure to recognize mental illness as a legitimate illness. But if we really believe in protecting people more than protecting guns, this should matter to us.

Every one of these lives matters to God.

nine

DUDES AND THEIR GUNS

Consider your man card reissued.

—Bushmaster assault rifle advertisement

A FEW YEARS BACK there was a massive controversy around a sporting game in Las Vegas called Hunting for Bambi, which described itself as "over thirty women ready to be chased down like dogs." Men would pay $10,000 to shoot paintballs at women who were running across a field and wearing nothing but sneakers. The women were to receive $1,000 to participate and $2,500 if they avoided getting shot. The event was to be taped so that the men could watch it at home afterward. After the "hunt," the men would have the option of "mounting their prey"—meaning they could pay to have sex with the woman they just shot. It turned out to be a hoax, but we're convinced that the men who created the idea intended to move forward with it, if not for impending legal action. And the fact that national news outlets and the general public couldn't figure out whether to take it seriously or see it as a hoax is part of the point. We live in a world in which this idea could even be conjured up. Was anyone surprised that it *could* be real? It came from a dark place. It never turned into something real, but where it came from was real. Hunting for Bambi never materialized, thank God. But toxic masculinity is still very real, and it often expresses itself in the form of gun violence.[1]

Men own guns at triple the rate of women in the US: 62 percent of men compared to 22 percent of women. Men also commit 89 percent of murder-suicides, and 85 percent of all homicides. Of the ninety-six mass shootings since 1982, all but two were committed by men (and most were white men).[2]

Guns are not strictly a male problem. Obviously, there are women who love guns and violence, and there are men who hate violence and have beautiful hearts of love and compassion. One of the reasons Jesus came to earth was to show us what God is like, and another reason was to show us what it looks like to be perfectly human. I once heard a female theologian say, it makes sense for God to have come as a man (in Jesus) to show us what a redeemed male looks like, to assure us that men can be loving and gracious and caring like God. Many of our dominant metaphors for God reinforce the violent theology that God is a warrior or that God sanctifies violence and war. My (Shane's) friend, award-winning author Lauren Winner, once said, "You may have driven past some church called Church of the Good Shepherd to get here tonight, but I'm reasonably confident that none of us drove past a Church of the Mother Hen."[3] Both are biblical images of God. But sometimes we've allowed our masculinity to change how we understand God rather than allowing God to change how we understand our masculinity. We'll take a closer look at some of this militant theology later in the book, and I have written extensively on this in *Jesus for President* and *Jesus, Bombs, and Ice Cream*, as well as other books.[4] Certainly one of

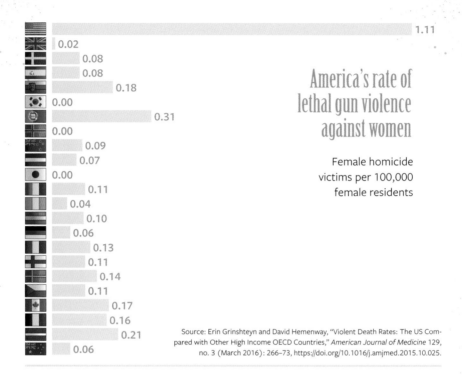

America's rate of lethal gun violence against women

Female homicide victims per 100,000 female residents

1.11
0.02
0.08
0.08
0.18
0.00
0.31
0.00
0.09
0.07
0.00
0.11
0.04
0.10
0.06
0.13
0.11
0.14
0.11
0.17
0.16
0.21
0.06

Source: Erin Grinshteyn and David Hemenway, "Violent Death Rates: The US Compared with Other High Income OECD Countries," *American Journal of Medicine* 129, no. 3 (March 2016): 266–73, https://doi.org/10.1016/j.amjmed.2015.10.025.

the things we need in the world right now is men who are healthier and less prone to commit acts of violence and abuse. We need men, and women, who are more like Jesus.

We dudes have done some serious damage to the world, especially when it comes to the shedding of blood. Perhaps it's not a coincidence that the inaugural murder of Cain killing Abel was a man killing a man. And many of the murders in the Bible, the wars throughout history, and the mass shootings in America have been done by men.

While all humanity is fallen, we can especially see that violence is one of the demons that a lot of us men in particular need to exorcise from our souls.

Each day in the US, at least three women are killed by their boyfriends or husbands. Domestic violence takes the lives of two thousand people per year, with 70 percent of those being women.

Studies show that roughly a quarter of women who are killed are killed by a spouse or ex-spouse and nearly another quarter by a boyfriend or girlfriend. An additional 19 percent are killed by another family member. **And in 72 percent of spousal murders, guns are the weapon of choice.**[5] It is one more reminder that even though we are conditioned to think that guns protect us from an armed stranger, most people are killed by someone they know—and often someone they know well.

People with a history of committing domestic violence (predominantly men) are five times more likely to subsequently murder an intimate partner (predominantly women) when a firearm is in the house.[6] A man's access to firearms increases a woman's risk of being killed. Not surprisingly, when Canada tightened some of its gun laws, homicide rates for women dropped by 40 percent.[7] We've seen the same thing happen here in the US.[8] Some local governments in the US are currently trying to make it hard for someone convicted of domestic violence to get a gun. And they have faced huge resistance, even lawsuits, from gun extremists, even though a majority of gun owners want to prevent domestic abusers from gun ownership.

As we have seen in recent mass shootings, domestic violence is often a warning sign. It's one of the consistent early indicators for mass shooters. Studies have shown that in murders and murder-suicides, a stunning number of them have a history of domestic violence. Simply put, people who are violent at home, with the people they know most intimately, are likely to be violent outside the home.[9] Prior domestic violence is by far one of the clearest risk factors. Past criminal history in general is not nearly as reliable or predictable as domestic violence is. People who beat their wives or girlfriends often end up killing them—with a gun.[10]

All of this is one more reason that taking action to remove guns from domestic abusers is a good move, even though states like California, where such measures have recently been taken, will likely face lawsuits for attempting to do so.

From its earliest days, the gun industry has targeted both men and women in specific ways. Marketers have preyed on the need for men to protect their families and be in control. And they have used fear and vulnerability as a selling point for women. There was the "boy plan" that aimed to reach 3.4 million boys aged ten to sixteen.[11] In the early 1900s, Winchester began a prominent ad campaign that claimed that "every real boy" wants to have a Winchester. Gun marketers even talked of the need to "win over the parents," who were seen as the obstacle to selling a gun to a twelve-year-old.[12]

Then there were the attempts to market to women, like guns that match any outfit, made in different colors. There were ads with beautiful women that said a gun can make you even more beautiful. One could argue that such an ad was also targeting men and encouraging them to make sure they find a woman who also likes guns.

But the women were resistant. All the way back to the earliest mass marketing of guns, mothers have led the resistance. And groups like Moms Demand Action still are. During the ambitious "boy plan" attempt to market guns to kids, one retailer complained, "I could sell a thousand rifles to boys if it weren't for their parents."[13]

For men, guns became more than just a product or a tool. They became a totem of manhood or an instrument of adoration. Guns became more than a symbol and were a physical manifestation of power and control and, as in one Bushmaster ad, a "man card."

Vadim Kozlovsky / shutterstock.com

We've made heroes out of men with guns—from Rambo and Clint Eastwood

Bork / shutterstock.com

to characters in old Westerns and mafia movies. For those of us who seek to be like God, we look to Jesus, not to Hollywood, to see what it means to be a man—and to be human. The gun industry has recently tried to challenge even that, making a bumper sticker that says, "If Jesus had a gun he'd still be around."

Men headed up most corporate enterprises in the nineteenth century, so it's not that surprising to see how male-heavy the gun industry was. Women didn't even have the right to vote while the Second Amendment was being debated and guns were scattering across the country.

The business of death undoubtedly took a toll on everyone, whether they realized it or not. Just as soldiers talk about the "moral injury" of the cost of war on their conscience, we can see some of the same scars on the conscience of the trademark names of the gun empire. Colt's own brother committed suicide, and the family tree of the gun market—Winchester, Colt, Remington, Smith & Wesson—carried a lot of heavy baggage from the family business. After all, their names were becoming colonized by the gun empire, synonymous with weapons that were taking a pretty bloody toll on the world. What must happen when your family name becomes associated more with death than with life? Perhaps the women felt it most acutely.

The Gun Fortune's Effect on Women[14]

Sarah Winchester was the wife of William Wirt Winchester, who was the only son of Oliver Winchester. She became the matriarch of the Winchester dynasty. The legend is that she was haunted by the souls lost to guns from which her family gained their fortune.

Sarah was rumored to have dipped into Spiritualism, a fusion of religious beliefs in which ideas like karma and mysticism connect, which was very popular at the time, especially among wealthy women. The Spiritualist movement made some strong statements about racism, violence, and the degradation of the earth. There was a value for life and a desire to connect with the spirits of those who had died. Spiritualist leaders saw the universe as a profoundly interconnected web of life, which one leader described as a "most sensitively attuned harp." Your actions had reactions in the spiritual realm. Here's how one Spiritualist guru put it: "All that has been wrong, must be atoned for. We must, in some way, make atonement for every thought, word, and deed which has wounded, wronged or injured."

With her Winchester fortune, Sarah moved about as far from the gun empire as she could—from her home in Connecticut to California. And she began building a house for herself on a plot of land known as Llanda Villa. It wasn't just any house. It's one of the most perplexing houses in the world, not because it is ritzy and luxurious but because it was confusing and compulsively built. The mansion, built over a period of thirty years, has 200 rooms, 7 stories, 10,000 windows, 2,000 doors, 47 fireplaces, 150,000 panes of glass, and over 7 miles of sprinklers. Worth $130 million in today's money, it was the most expensive residence in the country.

Sarah Winchester

The house was a maze; much of it is still around. Staircases lead to dead ends at ceilings. Doors open into walls. There are trap doors and spy holes. It was built incessantly. As soon as something was finished, Sarah would tear it down and rebuild. It wasn't that she didn't like it—she simply was obsessed with building and tearing down and building again.

Sarah wore a black veil and was a mysterious woman. Folks who knew her were clear—she was not "crazy," she was haunted. She was not insane, she was tormented.

We may never know with certainty what haunted her, but I think we can take a guess.

In the ghost story of Sarah Winchester, she was haunted by the spirits of those killed by Winchester guns. She built her home as a maze to trick and confuse the spirits. She is said to have told a friend, "They must never be able to find their way through my house. . . . Each year I will add new rooms so that the spirits will go weary of trying to get to me."

It may be that the "moral agnosticism" and the absence of conscience so evident in the men involved in the business of guns all fell on her shoulders, just as the stocks did. Having a moral conscience may not have been a part of the world of selling Winchesters, but it was a part of the world of Sarah Winchester.

Author Pamela Haag does a magnificent job juxtaposing the madness of Sarah with the madness of the gun business. As Sarah was obsessively building her enormous mansion, businesses were obsessively building their gun factories. In the darkness of the night, twenty-four hours per day, you could hear the hammers in California and in Connecticut. One was a massive compound for war; the other was a massive attempt to bring peace and to calm the spirits of the dead. Haag says that Sarah could have built a university, but instead she built the mansion. She could have built a church like the Colt family did.

Sanseven / Shutterstock.com

Winchester estate

But that would only "morally whitewash" the blood fortune and try to convert it into something "impeachable." Maybe she didn't want it to yield something good. Maybe she just wanted to expose the insanity of it all. In the words of Haag, "Maybe she did not want to rehabilitate the fortune but to show instead the immutable deformity at its heart."

These are the words of Sarah Winchester: "War is now a sad reality . . . although it seems more remote from me than from my eastern friends." She could not escape the spirits of the dead, but she did manage to leave the business of guns and death far behind.

At one point, the gun enthusiast (and president of the United States) Theodore Roosevelt expressed a desire to pay Sarah a visit in 1897. Unsurprisingly, she did not accommodate his visit but is noted as saying that she was not one to have guests in her home.

Sarah Winchester exposes a collision in America between male ambition and female conscience. Who was truly pathological? Sarah spent her life trying to find peace, while her family business made wars possible. Perhaps she was eventually comforted after all her penance, and the Winchester businessmen are now the ones who are haunted.

A cross adorned with guns at the Colt church

In the words of Pamela Haag, "It is feasible to poise (male) ambition and (female) conscience against each other along a fault line of American character."[15]

Incidentally, Elizabeth Colt had a very different response to her gun fortune—she built a church. It seems like a reasonable way to try to redeem and reconcile money amassed from gun sales, but it is an eerie thing to see. I (Shane) went to visit it a little while ago. On the front door, the columns are lined with guns sculpted into the cement. The cross is surrounded with guns. As you take a close look at a beautiful stone flower sculpted into the door, you see that

Elizabeth Colt's gun sanctuary

the center of the flower is the barrel of a revolver. The fusion of faith and guns is everywhere in America, but nowhere as explicitly as guns carved into the architecture of a place where people worship the Prince of Peace. I'm not sure which is more disturbing: Sarah Winchester's haunted mansion or Elizabeth Colt's gun sanctuary.

Wounded Healers

Just as guns were a man's business and have become the "man card" for a kind of toxic masculinity in America, women have been at the heart of the resistance. Over and over, women have used their wounds to expose the pain caused by gun violence, and women have used their tears as a balm to prevent further pain.

Laurie Works

Laurie Works is a resilient woman who has used her wounds to help heal the world of violence. On Sunday, December 9, 2007, Laurie and her family started their day like many others. They drove from Aurora to Colorado Springs to attend New Life Church. After the service, they were walking to their van, trying to figure out where they would eat lunch. As they were getting into their van, Matthew Murray began shooting at them. It later came to light that Murray was also the shooter at a Youth With A Mission (YWAM) campus earlier that morning.

Murray's bullets struck Laurie's dad, David, who survived, and took the lives of two of Laurie's sisters, Rachel and Stephanie (Laurie's twin). Laurie often recalls thinking in the midst of it all, "I'm going to need counseling." That moment was the beginning of her journey toward becoming a wounded healer.

Laurie Works

When the family's pastor suggested that they meet with the parents of the shooter, they were prepared to do so (in large part because of the family's previous exposure to restorative justice). The meeting happened just a few months after the shooting.

Laurie marching at Demand the Ban

Years later, Laurie penned a poem written to Matthew Murray highlighting how similar they were, two sides to the same coin. One beautiful portion of the poem reads:

> Mettle isn't about bullets and bridges
> It's about meeting the darkness and naming it holy
> So instead of a bridge I'm building an altar
> To both the sides of this same coin
> To believing in my own darkness as fiercely as I believe in your light
> To the complexity of being human[16]

Just as we speak of seeing the image of God in one another, Laurie alludes to seeing our own capacity for darkness as well. Like seeing God in others, we must also be aware of our capacity to hurt. Laurie gives us a window to see this. She explored getting a concealed carry permit and completed the classes, but when it came time to decide if she wanted to own a gun, she ultimately decided she couldn't put someone else through what she has battled since she lost her sisters.

Sadly, this wasn't the only shooting Laurie has been connected to. She knew people in the theater in Aurora when a man opened fire during a midnight showing of *The Dark Knight Rises*. She found herself taking food and water to first responders after the Planned Parenthood shooting in Colorado Springs. She lived in the neighborhood where a man openly carried an AR-15 and killed three people: two women on a porch, and a military vet riding his bike who came out of the alley at the wrong time. She lived in an apartment where a neighbor would randomly fire his gun at night, even to the point that one night she left because his shooting began to hit the apartment building.

So when Laurie thought about counseling the day she lost her sisters, she was right. She did need a lot of it for herself, which she speaks of in a TEDx talk she delivered in Jackson, Wyoming.[17] But it also set her on a journey to completing her master's degree in counseling from the University of Colorado–Colorado Springs. She has developed a trauma-informed yoga class and has led several victim support groups for other shooting and trauma survivors.

Laurie has written a letter to Congress urging commonsense gun reform. She's also written blog posts offering advice after mass shootings, both for victims and for their communities. She sheds light on how the media takes advantage of tragedy and abandons one when the next one happens. One of her core messages is to be present. Be with each other.

Sharletta Evans

It was the winter of 1995, just before Christmas. Sharletta Evans had her two sons with her as she drove to a relative's house to pick up a grandniece after a drive-by shooting in their neighborhood the previous night. She left the kids in the car with her twenty-one-year-old cousin and seventeen-year-old niece and went inside to pick up her grandniece. While she was inside, the shooters came back. Bullets rained down on the car and the house. After the shooters left, Sharletta went back out to the car to find that the bullets missed her six-year-old son, Calvin, but one hit her three-year-old son, Casson, in the head.

Sharletta held her son and walked on the sidewalk. She talked to him. "You can make it. Hold on big guy." Her dress was covered in blood from her collar to the hem. As the ambulance arrived, Casson took his last breath in his mom's arms. Attempts to revive him at the hospital were unsuccessful.

Casson Evans, killed in a drive-by shooting in December 1995

What happened next Sharletta can only describe as an act of God. She heard a voice asking her if she would forgive the people who did this. By the power of the Spirit, Sharletta said she forgave them.

Seventeen years later she would be the first person to participate in a pilot program with the Colorado Department of Justice, the High Risk/Impact Victim Offender Dialogue. The victim-based restorative-justice program makes it possible for victims to meet with their offenders. There's a long process of counseling on both sides that prepares the victim and the offender to explore every possible outcome from such a unique and weighted conversation.

Raymond Johnson was one of three teenagers in the drive-by car, and it was determined that he was the one who fired the bullet that killed Casson. At the time in Colorado, juveniles could be sentenced to life without an opportunity for parole, as Johnson was.

As reporters explained about the program, "Beyond a sheer willingness to participate in restorative justice, the offender has to meet a three-part test for acceptance based on demonstrating accountability, genuine remorse and willingness to repair harm. Johnson met all the criteria, though on the last count the only reparations he could offer were honest answers to a mother's unanswered questions."[18]

"There were so many questions," Sharletta said. "When it came to every emotion, [my facilitator would] ask me where was I at. What did I want to say to him? I really had to dissect every emotion so there were no surprises."

After each of them had prepared for their meeting, Sharletta and Raymond spent time asking each other questions and recalling that night seventeen

Memorial to the Lost

Using two sawed-off shotguns, a TEC-DC9 semiautomatic handgun, and a 9mm semiautomatic carbine rifle, two students took the lives of twelve other students and a teacher on April 20, 1999. The shooting influenced many subsequent shootings. Here are the names of the lives lost that day:

Cassie Bernall, 17

Steven Curnow, 14

Corey DePooter, 17

Kelly Fleming, 16

Matthew Kechter, 16

Daniel Mauser, 15

Daniel Rohrbough, 15

William David Sanders, 47

Rachel Scott, 17

Isaiah Shoels, 18

John Tomlin, 16

Lauren Townsend, 18

Kyle Velasquez, 16

years prior. Since their meeting, the Colorado Supreme Court struck down life sentences without parole for juveniles, and Sharletta has actively testified for Raymond to get a new sentence with an opportunity for parole. Sharletta actively advocates for victim-offender dialogue and juvenile sentencing reform. She has testified numerous times for restoration.

In 2009, three years prior to their meeting, Raymond sent Sharletta a Mother's Day card and asked if she would be his mother. She didn't answer until their meeting. It was hard for her to consider. Their meeting lasted eight hours. At the end, she held his hands and prayed over him. She also brought the card he sent and told him, "Yes, I will be your mother."

In 2016 Sharletta was able to meet with the driver of the car through restorative justice.

Sharletta's story of forgiveness and extensive work to offer the opportunity for restitution and restoration for offenders is awe-inspiring. It's an example of what it looks like to no longer learn how to make war. It's what we're called to do when we choose to carry a plow instead of a gun. We have to recognize the trauma in our community and support the people like Sharletta who are working so hard, telling us to see the face of God in others.[19]

It's Time

Beyoncé is onto something with her call for women to get in formation and "run the world." Oprah announced at the Golden Globes last year to men who abuse and sexually assault women: "Your time is up." The movement to end gun violence is largely led by women—like Shannon Watts of Moms Demand Action and Lucy McBath (mother of gunshot victim Jordan Davis). Some of the largest marches in US history are happening right now and are led by women—the Women's March is a movement shaping US history. Women are calling for an end to violence in all its ugly forms. The #MeToo campaign has been sweeping our country, calling for an end to the violence of sexual assault. All of this is an expression of women who are calling out and taking on the toxic masculinity that is destroying so many lives. And gun violence is one aspect of it. We have a bit of a woman-power revolution happening—and it's about time. If Sarah Winchester were alive today, instead of being locked away in the loneliness of her mansion perhaps she would be marching in the streets with the women who are saying, "Your time is up."

One can hope.

Ten

THE SECOND AMENDMENT AND THE SERMON ON THE MOUNT

> Liberty may be endangered by the abuse of liberty.
>
> —James Madison

FOR SOME FOLKS, the Second Amendment is as holy as the Great Commandment. So it warrants a closer look. But it is important to note from the outset that for those of us who consider ourselves Christians, the final authority for life is not the Constitution. It is the Bible, and it is Jesus. We believe that the Bible is divinely inspired in a unique way that the Constitution and other human documents, as important as they may be, are not. David Anderson often says, "We are better at protecting the Amendments than the Commandments,"[1] one of which is "Thou shalt not kill."

For many of our international readers, this chapter will be particularly disturbing, since your governments most likely do not guarantee the right to bear arms as a human right. And yet even for the most patriotic US citizens among us, there are unmistakable complications with reading the Second Amendment as a blank check for gun ownership with no limitations or regulations, something that even the folks who wrote the amendment did not permit. During a video call with youth in Afghanistan, we noticed that, with their questions, they were trying to comprehend why our laws needed the Second Amendment at all. After all, war is a constant presence in their lives, and so why would a country lawfully introduce it into its neighborhoods and defend it in its courts?

Second Amendment author James Madison wrote these words: "Liberty may be endangered by the abuse of liberty as well as by the abuses of power. The former rather than the latter is apparently most to be apprehended by the United States."[2]

One person's freedom can become another person's oppression. One person's right to bear arms can infringe on another person's right to life, liberty, and the pursuit of happiness. When the Constitution was written, freedom for white men included the right to own slaves, but we eventually came to see that if all people are created equal, then no one can own another person as property or be counted as three-fifths human.

One person's right to drink alcohol can impose on another person's safety on roads, and so the invention of cars led to new regulations that horses and buggies did not have. And as technology evolved, with cars able to go over one hundred miles per hour, so did the laws that govern them. When smoking tobacco was proved to be detrimental to public health, we adopted rules about where people can and can't smoke. Fireworks are seen to be a safety hazard, are illegal in many places, and have limits on how powerful they can be even in the places where they are legal. And when it comes to owning guns, it is quite apparent that one person's right to bear arms can encroach on another person's right to live. Sometimes the problem is not just the abuse of power but the abuse of liberty.

We have been better at protecting guns than protecting people. Is one person's desire to own a military-style assault rifle that can shoot one hundred rounds per minute so important that we will continue to allow hundreds of lives to be lost in mass shootings where these are the weapon of choice?

"A Well Regulated Militia"

These are the words of the Second Amendment: "A well regulated Militia, being necessary to the security of a free State, the right of the people to keep and bear Arms, shall not be infringed."

It is interesting that it begins with the words "well regulated." That seems to be the last thing some gun owners want, but it is right there in the Constitution.

Rather than a "well regulated Militia," one might even suggest a rewrite to the Second Amendment to more accurately describe what we have today in the US: "A poorly regulated mass of armed individuals."

It is striking that the NRA posted only half of the Second Amendment at their headquarters in Sacramento, California. It reads: "The right of the people to keep and bear arms, shall not be infringed." They left out that half about "well regulated" and "militia."

One might guess there would be fifty militias in the United States, one per state, and that they would be well regulated. But one would be wrong. The lines between militias and armed hate groups like those that marched on Charlottesville and that took over the wildlife refuge in Oregon get blurred. The Southern Poverty Law Center listed more than five hundred armed militias and hate groups in 2010, and the number of armed militias grew as much as 245 percent in one year (2009).[3] Some of our worst domestic terrorists, like Timothy McVeigh, have been linked to militia groups.

It's clear that what the authors of the Constitution had in mind by "militia" is radically different from the gun-toting extremist fringe groups that exist today, such as the Bundy gang, who took over the federal land in Oregon, or the white supremacists who marched in camo in Charlottesville.

What the militias have evolved into over the past two hundred years is a uniquely American phenomenon. They often pride themselves on being "patriots," but the irony cannot be missed. These militia groups are often made up of individuals who are compelled by conspiracy theories and deep distrust of the government. To be fair, we believe that a certain amount of distrust of power is a good thing, perhaps even patriotic. But the irony is that these highly armed people who are often draped in American flags and call themselves patriots are prepared to go to war with our own military and, if necessary, to kill hundreds of our own military service members. They are the 3 percent of gun owners who own half of the three hundred million guns in America. They are the ones who send death threats and march in the streets in full camo while holding semiautomatics. They are the folks who think it makes sense to arm four-year-olds. They are not the majority of gun owners, but they are a forceful, intimidating minority. Some of them are terribly violent, aggressive, and racist, such as the folks who showed up in Charlottesville with torches.

We don't want to paint them all with the same brush. Some militia groups are white supremacists, like those who threatened protesters in Ferguson and marched in the neo-Nazi rally at Charlottesville. But modern-day militias are not all filled with Timothy McVeighs. Some of them simply have a distrust of the government and have tried to stand alongside the oppressed in struggles like Standing Rock, where Native Americans blocked the oil pipeline. It is not uncommon for militias to protect vulnerable people from government and corporate forces that threaten to run over them, and they usually bring their guns and body armor.

Dana Gould ✓
@danagould

The pro AR-15 argument comes down to "preventing state tyranny."

In other words, "I need an AR-15 because one day I might have to mow down a bunch of U.S. soldiers. Don't get me wrong, I support the troops. I just want to be ready to murder as many as possible if necessary."

5:37 PM - Feb 23, 2018

♡ 48.7K ○ 18.3K people are talking about this

They may have different stripes, but what is consistent is that they don't trust the government and that they believe in arming themselves in case the need should arise to fight the government itself. Can you think of other industrialized countries where the people live in such constant suspicion of their government that they are actively preparing to use bullets instead of ballots to change things?

The backdrop for the Second Amendment was the armed citizenry of each state that existed before there was a large, stable federal military like the one we have today. They were sort of like state armies or state national guards, like the Kansas militia or the Michigan militia. It is important to note that one of the duties of the original state militias was to serve as slave patrols. States like Virginia wanted to make sure that the slave masters were able to shoot runaway slaves, squash slave revolts, and keep other slaves subservient. It may not have been the only purpose of the state militias, but it was certainly a major one. And now this amendment written at least in part to allow the armed oppression of slaves continues to keep us in chains.

The real dilemma with the Second Amendment was what to do once the "united states" had a unified army. What role do the militias have now? And do we really need fringe militia groups when there is a federal army, national guard, and armed police units in every municipality in the country?

The question became this: Does the Second Amendment guarantee the collective right to own guns, like in the case of the militias, which still need regulation, or is it an individual right not contingent on any affiliation to a group? That is the million-dollar question.

And the Supreme Court has ruled on this one. For two hundred years the courts interpreted "the right to bear arms" as a collective or state right, but in 2008 it became crystal clear (in *District of Columbia v. Heller*) that the right to bear arms is an individual right, and states cannot block it.

But what the court also made clear is that the Second Amendment is not unlimited. Here are the words of one of the most conservative justices, the late Antonin Scalia: "Like most rights, the Second Amendment right is not unlimited. It is not a right to keep and carry any weapon whatsoever in any manner whatsoever and for whatever purpose. . . . The Court's opinion should not be taken to cast doubt on longstanding prohibitions on the possession of firearms by felons and the mentally ill, or laws forbidding the carrying of firearms in sensitive places such as schools and government buildings, or laws imposing conditions and qualification on the commercial sale of arms."[4] In short, individuals have a right to guns, but those rights are not unlimited. They are subject to rules, regulations, and restrictions. The jury may still be out on whether that is true in practice.

> Most of our tension on guns comes from these two dueling rights, both guaranteed by the Constitution:
>
> | The right to keep and bear arms. | And the right to live in communities free of violence, the assurance of "domestic tranquility." |
> | --- | --- |

The 90 percent of Americans, including gun owners, who wanted to see change happen after Sandy Hook could probably figure this out, but here's where things get dicey: there are a few gun extremists who have held the conversation—and the politicians—hostage. That's 10 percent or less who believe in limitless guns with no restrictions, something that not even the writers of the Second Amendment believed in.

The irony is that white gun extremists once fought for strict gun control when it came to Native Americans and African Americans owning guns. White gun enthusiasts were the pro-gun-control force behind two of the most prominent regulations of weapon sale: prohibiting the sale of arms and ammunition to "hostile Indians" after Little Big Horn in 1867 and prohibiting gun ownership by African Americans after the Colfax massacre. Clearly, we've been selective in how we interpret the Second Amendment, written by white men, for white men.

Guns were proliferating in the US at the precise time that the Dred Scott case declared that African Americans have "no rights which the white man was bound to respect," which obviously included the right to guns. White folks loved gun control when it meant controlling black and brown and native people and preventing them from accessing guns.

Native Americans were quite wealthy compared to many rural white folks in the 1800s. Their success at trading fur and other valuables made it conceivable that they could out-arm white folks if there weren't some regulation on sales.

Then, some African Americans began to embrace guns. As we saw earlier, guns had some celebrity endorsements from African Americans like journalist Ida B. Wells, who bought a pistol after witnessing a lynching and said, "The Winchester rifle deserves a place of honor in every Black home."[5] With celebrity endorsements from black heroes like Wells, some black folks started to see the gun as an "equalizer," and white folks got worried.

In the landmark 1876 case *US v. Cruikshank*, the Supreme Court ruled that it did not have the power to control states, which effectively meant that the racist agenda of disarming African Americans would be permitted. The ruling, celebrated by the NRA, supported gun control to limit African Americans trying to access guns for their protection in states like Louisiana that didn't want black folks to have guns.

What all this shows is that some of our first battles over the Second Amendment were about keeping Natives and African Americans from having guns. The NRA believed in gun control when it meant preventing people of color from acquiring guns.

When we think about the Second

"They had no rights which the white man was bound to respect; and . . . the negro might justly and lawfully be reduced to slavery for this benefit."

Dred Scott v. Sandford, 60 U.S. 393, 417, 450–451 (1857), majority opinion written by Chief Justice Roger B. Taney

Amendment, it is important to remember the historic context. Slavery was legal. It was written before guns were able to shoot more than one bullet at a time. It was also written at the same time as the "Three-Fifths Clause" (in 1787), which declared black folks to be three-fifths human. Times change, and societies evolve and advance. Slavery is no longer legal. Hopefully all of us agree that black folks are 100 percent human, even though some of our social institutions may still be catching up. Maybe it is also time to rethink the Second Amendment. In 2018, in response to the hundreds of marches happening across the country related to gun violence, the ninety-seven-year-old retired Supreme Court justice John Paul Stevens made national news doing exactly that—calling for a repeal of the Second Amendment, a "relic of the 18th century."[6] He also says the court made a wrong decision back in the 2008 ruling that the right to bear arms was an individual rather than a collective right.

It is helpful that the Supreme Court has ruled that the right to bear arms is not unlimited and does not prohibit all regulations of firearms. In light of the court's ruling, there have been several suggestions to repeal the Second Amendment and replace it with a Twenty-Eighth Amendment. The new version might go something like this: "A well regulated State National Guard, being helpful to the safety and security of a State in times of need, along with the strictly regulated right of the people to keep and bear a limited number of nonautomatic arms for sport and hunting, with respect to the primary right of all people to be free from gun violence . . . this shall not be infringed."[7] It's worth considering.

When the Second Amendment was written, we had this in mind.

Not this.

Freedom for All

One person's freedom can become another person's bondage.

For we also know that the Declaration of Independence declares the right to "life, liberty and the pursuit of happiness." We also have the right to live. We must also protect the right *not* to bear arms.

There's a beautiful passage in Paul's letter to the Galatians, in the New Testament, where he says, "You, my brothers and sisters, were called to be free. But do not use your freedom to indulge the flesh; rather, serve one another humbly in love. For the entire law is fulfilled in keeping this one command: 'Love your neighbor as yourself.' If you bite and devour each other, watch out or you will be destroyed by each other" (Gal. 5:13–15).

We cannot focus just on the legal and political battle. As important as it is to change laws, no law can change the human heart. You can't legislate love and vote to abolish fear. There is some serious heart work that we need to do as well. So let's think about the contrast between the Second Amendment and the Sermon on the Mount.

Every Christian must concede that the Bible is a higher moral authority than the Constitution, and that the Golden Rule—do to others what you would have them do to you—is a greater commandment than the Second Amendment. In fact, Jesus's command to "turn the other cheek" flies in the face of the NRA's command to "stand your ground."

Here are a few stories that cast a vision for a world where the cross is mightier than the sword. They offer us an alternative to the "live by the sword, die by the sword" dead-end road of gun violence.

When we heard that the man who killed Trayvon Martin was going to auction his gun, our imaginations began to turn. Do we make a bid so we can destroy it? How much money would we need for that (rumors say it sold for upward of $200,000)? Instead, we decided to ask for surrogates. Beyond the amount of money, there was something awry with funding a person who killed another. So, what if we put out a call for 9mm handguns like the one used to kill Trayvon Martin? With the help of Benjamin Corey (whose story is shared in chapter 8), we asked for folks to give up their guns. We called

Memorial to the Lost

During the Sunday service on November 5, 2017, a man opened fire on the congregation at the First Baptist Church using an AR-15-style semiautomatic rifle. Twenty-six people died in the shooting including an unborn child. Here are the names of those killed that day:

Keith Allen Braden, 62

Robert Michael Corrigan, 51

Shani Louise Corrigan, 51

Emily Garcia, 7

Dennis Neil Johnson Sr., 77

Sara Johns Johnson, 68

Emily Rose Hill, 11

Gregory Lynn Hill, 13

Megan Gail Hill, 9

Carlin Brite "Billy Bob" Holcombe, unborn child of Crystal Marie Holcombe

Crystal Marie Holcombe, 36

John Bryan Holcombe, 60

Karla Plain Holcombe, 58

Marc Daniel Holcombe, 36

Noah Holcombe, 1

Haley Krueger, 16

Karen Sue Marshall, 56

Robert Scott Marshall, 56

Tara E. McNulty, 33

Annabelle Renae Pomeroy, 14

Ricardo Cardona Rodriguez, 64

Therese Sagan Rodriguez, 66

Brooke Bryanne Ward, 5

Joann Lookingbill Ward, 30

Peggy Lynn Warden, 56

Lula Woicinski White, 71

this campaign "Sow Your Ground" and ended up with half a dozen 9mm handguns, as well as a few others.

One was from a youth pastor in the Midwest who had just successfully convinced his church leadership *not* to have armed guards at their church, despite some recent threats. He put on the table a Bible opened up to the New Testament and asked them to show him where armed guards fit in with the message of Christ.

Another was from a man who once self-identified as a "gun-toting liberal." He had purchased his gun to protect LGBTQ friends who had felt threatened from recent legislation passed by his state's lawmakers, not unlike politically left-leaning groups that arm themselves as a means of protecting the protestors. Even before our "call *out* of arms," he had decided to simplify his life and rid himself of useless items. When he thought about his handguns, he realized they were more of a hindrance than a help. He also didn't feel comfortable selling them, and so he was stuck, until he saw our request for gun donors.

RAWtools also contacted pastors to see if they would help us disable guns from donors. This usually meant meeting with us and a gun donor in the church parking lot: we were asking pastors if it was okay to bring a gun onto their property. The pastors would often consult with their elders and discern a way forward—if they agreed, we would arrange this unorthodox "meet and greet." Sometimes we'd share a meal. Donors bring the guns and we bring the chop saw. Have anvil, will travel.

These donors exercised their Second Amendment right to own a gun. Eventually they decided that that right looked more American than it did Christian.

They chose something else.

They chose a different posture.

Instead of "stand your ground" they chose "sow your ground." We then sold a tool made from the guns and gave that money to the Trayvon Martin Foundation.

It's the good ole WWJD moment, isn't it? How can you read the Sermon on the Mount and think it is congruent with open or concealed carry? Unless you believe Jesus was talking about a Colt .45 revolver when he said "Blessed are the peacemakers," there is no other connection. The gun that "won the West" is not strapped to Peter standing guard at the pearly gates. He learned his lesson when Jesus put an ear back on a centurion. You know, the ear Peter was so eager to lop off.

For many of Jesus's followers who needed to feel emboldened, perhaps the next step in their journey was to take up weapons and go after their oppressors. Jesus knew that many of the people he was speaking to were walking a fine line between being oppressed and trying the role of oppressor for once. In fact, many of them were hoping Jesus would be the one to lead them in some sort of revolt.

In Jesus's Sermon on the Mount, just after the Beatitudes, we see Jesus creating a shift in creative imagination by moving beyond an eye for an eye and into loving enemies and turning the other cheek. Loving enemies can hardly happen with the threat of some sort of quick draw; it certainly would lack depth and have a sort of emptiness to it. Are we listening when Jesus tells us, "If you love those who love you, what reward will you get? Are not even the tax collectors doing that? And if you greet only your own people, what are you doing more than others?" (Matt. 5:46–47). If only our politicians would have ears to hear this.

In the Sermon on the Mount, Jesus is asking us to do far more than just reach across the aisle. That is the first step, but beyond that it means carrying our enemy's backpack for more than a mile, more than is asked and legally required of us. Many of us can caveat stories from our past with "when I didn't know better," implying that now we know better. We know better because we recognize the consequences and understand why a law or rule is in place. We no longer have any excuse for gun violence: we know better. How much gun violence will it take for us to change our rules? If a law or the lack of a law (or even a house rule) is not serving us well, shouldn't we go another mile and alter it?

What if we blended Jesus's call to turn the other cheek with the stand-your-ground laws in our country? In turning the other cheek, we realize we are standing our ground. For Jesus's audience, being hit on the right cheek meant that you had been backhanded, something administered to an inferior, not an equal.[8] Giving them the other cheek was a way to say to the person who slapped you, "No, if you are going to hit me, hit me on this cheek with a fist like an equal, and not with a back hand on that cheek like I am inferior." This was a creative way of exposing a rule, and it either made a person treat the other as equal or exposed the oppressor for who they were.

Stand-your-ground laws in our country today make it legal to physically injure, and even kill, another person if you feel threatened. This is why Trayvon Martin's killer was found "innocent," or "just," in the eyes of the law (he was a neighborhood watch volunteer).

We propose enacting the sow-your-ground tactics. As farmers know their land, so should neighbors know their neighborhood. Farmers have taken time to prepare the land for harvest. We and our neighbors should plan and be in relationship in order to prepare for the needs of each season.

It's in sowing your ground that you are made aware of the needs and behavior of your community. You react to situations in ways that keep your community not just alive but also thriving. This is a central message of the Sermon on the Mount. Jesus repeatedly referenced laws in his "you've heard it said, but I say" directives. It's as if Jesus saw a people paralyzed by a set of rules that kept them from imagining an alternative.

These sets of rules kept them from seeing the effect those laws had on a community. Communities looked more like the empire of Rome than the kingdom of God. Jesus offered alternative ways to engage these laws that stretch our understanding of engaging with the world. Walter Brueggemann calls this the prophetic imagination.[9] It's the imagination that Micah and

Isaiah were invoking when they spoke of turning swords into plows. It's the kind of imagination we all are capable of using. It doesn't come without risk, but neither does farming.

The 2017 church shooting in Sutherland Springs, Texas, reignited this conversation. Should churches be gun-free zones? If they are, should it be announced? Most folks against gun-free zones claim that it's advertising to bad people with guns that a building is full of "soft" targets—that is, the people in the building are easy to shoot.

The Beatitudes in the Sermon on the Mount were about soft targets—blessed are the meek, the merciful, the peacemakers, the hungry, and those who thirst for righteousness. These are the soft targets. When metal is introduced to the forge, it softens. The Beatitudes talk about people who haven't really chosen to be soft targets, though nevertheless they are. Jesus is telling us their lives are what we are to strive for. Jesus tells us they will inherit the kingdom because they are living as if they are in it. The kingdom is a gun-free zone, full of soft targets, and Jesus calls it blessed.

One could argue that Jesus entered the world as a soft target. But no one is going to argue that Jesus is a softie. He's courage with skin on. He modeled for us what the "greatest love" looks like, and there is no greater love than laying down our life for others. But in Jesus, God entered the world in the most vulnerable way—as a child, a refugee. Jesus was born with a target on his back in Herod's violent world, as children were being killed. And, of course, he died on a cross with love on his lips. He shows us that there is something more courageous than violence: love.

The soft targets are the people who rejected the notions of power and might and militarism. Pacifism does not mean passivity; nonviolence is simply a refusal to use violence to get rid of violence. It insists that we would rather die than kill. That's the love that we see in Jesus and that we are called to emulate. We would rather be soft targets than have hardened hearts. We would rather die with a cross in our hands than a gun.

Remember what we said about heat and the forge and Pharaoh? Hard, cool metal cracks under pressure and is not able to adapt to change. Soft, heated metal can be shaped into life-giving tools. If we rely on guns as the tool that brings safety, freedom, and happiness, it's harder to imagine alternative tools that also offer those human rights.

Some of us don't get to choose to be softened in the forge. Life is heated as it is. Those of us who haven't experienced the heat of life may be fortunate but can also be oblivious to the struggles of others. But the forge is calling us. The heat of life is not something to avoid. We must be present with others in the midst of the heat. The heat is where God is working. If Jesus is "God with us," we must also be God to others, including our enemies and neighbors. How can this happen when our neighbors are at the other end of the gun barrel?

Perhaps this speaks to ministry-outreach models, but the church in America cannot miss the opportunity to show how the vulnerability that Christ showed on the cross is also the vulnerability that can form neighborhoods that value plows over swords.

Imagine if every Christian in America took their commitment to Jesus as seriously as gun owners take their commitment to the Second Amendment. We wouldn't be in the mess we're in. Can we really carry a cross and a gun? When Jesus said to love your enemies, isn't it safe to assume he meant that we shouldn't kill them?

Allowing thirty-eight thousand lives to be lost each year falls short of what love requires of us. Love protects, as 1 Corinthians 13 says. And love sacrifices. Love is patient and kind. It isn't self-centered or easily angered. It delights in truth and doesn't return evil for evil. It doesn't boast, and it isn't proud. In short, love looks like Jesus. It is willing to die but not to kill.

We remember that Jesus laid down his "rights"—he became the victim of violence to heal us from our "right" to kill. He loved his enemies so much that he died for them.

CONSIDER *This*

LAYING IT ALL OUT THERE

I (SHANE) WAS AT A FRIEND'S HOUSE hanging out with their kids, and we grabbed the *Guinness Book of World Records* off the bookshelf. Flipping through the pages, we laughed at all the amazing feats, gawked at the most bizarre tattoos and piercings, and joked about what record we'd like to try to break. Then I flipped to another page. Most guns. It listed the countries with the most civilian-owned firearms. And, of course, number one was the United States with 270 million guns, or about ninety guns per one hundred people. At the time, the number two country for most guns was India with 46 million, or about four guns per one hundred people. I wasn't expecting that fact amid all the wild and wonderful things that filled those pages. And this was an old copy of the *Guinness Book of World Records*.[1]

It's not a record we should be proud of. Nor should we be proud to lead the developed world in number of homicides. We hold that record too. Per capita, America has six times as many firearm homicides as Canada, and nearly sixteen times as many as Germany. The US has 29.7 homicides per million people. Switzerland is second with 7.7. Germany has 1.9. Australia 1.4.

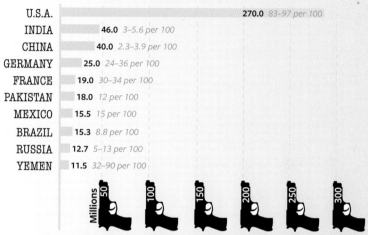

Source: *Small Arms Survey 2007: Guns and the City* (Cambridge: Cambridge University Press, 2007), http://www.smallarmssurvey.org/publications/by-type/yearbook/small-arms-survey-2007.html.

Gun murder rates in the US per one thousand people are 17 times higher than Australia, 35 times higher than Germany, 37 times higher than Spain, and 355 times higher than Japan. We are an anomaly, and we'd be wise to take some tips from around the world.[2]

America has 4.4 percent of the world's population but almost half of the world's civilian-owned guns. There are 644 million guns in the world: we have around 42 percent of those in the US.[3]

■ ■ ■ ■ ■ ■

After the Sandy Hook massacre in 2012, many Americans and politicians said, "Never again." But it keeps happening. Again. And again. In the intervening five years since Sandy Hook, there have been over 1,600 mass shootings.[4] On average, there is one mass shooting every day in America.[5]

Almost half of Americans (44 percent) say they personally know someone who has been shot, either accidentally or intentionally.[6]

More guns equals more violence. States with more guns have more gun deaths. It's true not only in the United States but around the world. Developed countries with more guns have more gun deaths.

States with tighter gun control laws have fewer gun-related deaths. Economist Richard Florida took a look at gun deaths and other social indicators—like population density, stress, diversity, immigrant populations, and other factors—none of which correlated with more gun deaths. But he did find one correlation. States with tighter gun control laws have fewer gun-related deaths.[7]

America's biggest gun problem is suicide, not homicide. Gun homicides (like all homicides) are declining. The majority of gun-related deaths in the US are suicides.[8] It is one of the most compelling reasons for reducing access to guns. Greater access to guns dramatically increases the risk of suicide.

Guns allow people to kill themselves much more easily. One study showed that 90 percent of suicide attempts by gun end in death, whereas only 10 percent of suicide attempts by other methods end in death.[9] Guns are much deadlier than alternatives like cutting or poison. Just stalling an attempt makes it less likely to result in death.

Where there are more guns, there are more police officers killed by civilians and more civilians killed by police officers. On average, there are
around one thousand people killed by police every year, many of those
victims unarmed. Several websites track each shooting, noting details such
as whether the victim was armed, whether video footage is available, and
the circumstances that led to the shooting.[10]

Guns are by far the leading cause of death of police officers killed on duty.
Ninety percent of all homicides of law enforcement officers are committed
with a gun.[11] What's more, in states with more guns and less restrictions on
those guns, more police officers are killed on duty. One fifteen-year study
shows that almost one officer per ten thousand is killed each year in high-gun
states, and every 10 percent increase in firearm ownership correlates with ten
additional officers killed in homicides.[12] This also explains why there are so
many police-involved shootings in these same areas and why so many more
citizens are killed by the police in the US than in other developed countries.
So whether we are concerned about black lives or blue lives or all lives, we
should care about reducing the proliferation of guns.

Though the debate on gun control seems incredibly polarized and di-
vided, there is a stunning amount of support from both sides on specific
policies, even from gun owners. Check out these numbers:

Policy	Percent of Americans Who Favor
Preventing the mentally ill from purchasing guns	89 percent
Background checks for private sales and at gun shows	84 percent
Creating a federal database to track gun sales	71 percent
Banning assault-style weapons	68 percent
Banning high-capacity magazines	65 percent

Source: Kim Parker et al., "America's Complex Relationship with Guns," Pew Research Center, June 22, 2017, http://www.pew
socialtrends.org/2017/06/22/americas-complex-relationship-with-guns.

Although Americans want to protect the right to bear arms, they're very much supportive of many gun policy proposals—even more contentious ideas like more background checks at gun shows and banning semiautomatic and assault-style weapons.

Empirical evidence shows that more guns mean more violence. Americans support policies that reduce access to guns, but the fact is, we've been better at protecting guns than protecting people. This is the situation we find ourselves in.

Winchester's dream of "scattering our guns as much as possible"[13] has become our nightmare. We manufactured an average of 9,458,172 guns annually in the US from 2012 to 2015. That's 25,912 per day. That's 1,079 per hour. That's 17.9 per minute. That's 1 gun every three seconds.[14]

We need a new approach to reducing gun violence. Rather than demonizing gun owners, perhaps we should focus on cutting funds from the gun profiteers. Instead of concentrating on the issue of *rights*, maybe we should approach it as an issue of *conscience*.

Eleven

IN GUNS WE TRUST

> Violence is the ethos of our times. It is the spirituality of the mod-
> ern world. Violence is thriving as never before in every sector of
> American popular culture, civil religion, nationalism, and foreign
> policy. Violence, not Christianity, is the real religion of America.
>
> —Walter Wink

J. WARREN CASSIDY, a former NRA executive, once said that we should approach the NRA as one of the world's great religions.[1] It promises safety, power, control, freedom, and security.

Many may bristle at the word *idol*, since it feels old-fashioned and overly dramatic, but stay with us. In the ancient story of the Israelites melting their gold and forming a golden calf (Exod. 32), most scholars don't think the Israelites set out to make an idol or worship another "god." They didn't think they were doing anything wrong and were convinced that their golden calf was compatible with their God. Moses had been gone for a long time, and they got anxious and started taking things into their own hands. We know how that ended—a couple of smashed tablets from Moses, a stern rebuke from God, and a gold cow that was thrown into the forge. Maybe they made a couple of gold plows out of it?

> "You would get a far better understanding if you approached us as if you were approaching one of the great religions of the world."
>
> —J. Warren Cassidy, former executive vice president of the NRA

Idols are the product of us creating gods in our image, and that image becoming our fascination, rather than us remembering that God created us in God's image. Somewhere along the way we have grown comfortable ignoring the image of God in each other in exchange for the idea that the image we have of ourselves is more valuable than the image we have of others. We must protect our image at all costs. It's a long way from a place on the cross, where a man died because he saw the image of God in his neighbors and decided to protect them at all costs.

Idols and false gods do not belong just to primitive societies thousands of years ago. They change and evolve with every generation. We put our trust in new things that are not God. We sacrifice lives to things that make empty promises that they cannot fulfill. Idols never go out of style. They just evolve.

Idols are things we put our trust in. They are not God, but we treat them like they are. They take on a transcendent, magical character. We hold them with a sacred reverence that should only be given to God. We are willing to die for them and kill for them and sacrifice our children for them.

We give them life, even though they take life from us. From the earliest days, gun marketing made some huge claims. Colt advertised its pistol not just as an instrument for protection but as your "one true friend, with six hearts in his body."[2]

Guns are doing damage not just to our bodies but also to our souls. They are something we begin to put our trust in, our faith in. We believe they will save us in times of trouble, deliver us from evil, take out our enemies—everything that the Bible promises us God will do for us.

In 1998 Charlton Heston, president of the NRA, after being given an antique musket, held it up like Moses holding his staff up to part the Red Sea (well, he did play Moses) and then said, "Sacred stuff resides in that wooden stock and blue steel . . . when ordinary hands can possess such an extraordinary instrument."[3] People in the audience erupted with excitement. The gun is not just a tool. It is an object of reverence and devotion.

Some May Trust in Chariots

In our world today, we take it even further than reverence; we actually have faith in our guns to save us. The word *faith* is an interesting one. When it was used in the ancient Roman Empire by the early Christians, it was very controversial because *faith* was a word reserved for Rome and Caesar. The Latin word for faith is *fides*, which is also where we get our notion of fidelity. It is about loyalty, like we would say, "He's a faithful husband." We tell people to have faith in us, to trust us. Faith has everything to do with trust, allegiance, and where our hope lies.

In fact, the early Christians were actually first called "atheists" because they did not put their faith in the emperor or the chariots and horses of the empire.[4] They had lost all "faith" in Caesar and his empire. Their faith in God and God alone was a subversive claim. After all, Rome took great pride in its wealth and power and might. Every time the Christians said "Jesus is Lord," they were also declaring "Caesar is not." You can see why they got killed and jailed for insurrection.

One of the reasons we create idols is that they are visible, concrete, tangible. It's hard to trust in something invisible, like God. The Bible even recognizes this complexity, saying that's why we talk so much about "faith."

Faith is believing in something we cannot see, but what we believe is just as real as—or even more real than—the stuff we can see. Hebrews 11:1 puts it this way: "Now faith is confidence in what we hope for and assurance about what we do not see."

It's hard to trust that God is our "refuge" and "deliverer" and will protect us from harm, as the Bible promises over and over, since we can't see God. It's much easier to think that our handgun will protect us. Guns become idols that we put our trust in—in part because we can see them. We can touch them. They feel more real than God, and we can end up trusting our guns more than we trust our God. *But does God need our guns?*

As the psalmist says, "Some trust in chariots and some in horses, but we trust in the name of the Lord our God" (Ps. 20:7). One of the constant themes in the Bible is that God is our deliverer—and the battle is God's, not ours. "Vengeance is mine," says the Lord (Deut. 32:35 ESV). Another way of putting it: "Vengeance is not yours." Only God can be trusted with ultimate power. It's why God seems to really like working through our weakness rather than our strength. It is poisonous to our soul to begin to think that we have power and control over our lives, over others, over the world.

There's a story in the Bible of an army commander named Gideon who went forth to fight the Midianites (Judg. 7). Like any good commander in chief, he rallied the troops—thirty-two thousand of them, to be exact. But God told Gideon, "You've got too many," and ordered him to send some away so that he wouldn't be tempted to think it was his own strength and might, or the power of his arsenal, that saved him. So twenty-two thousand head off, leaving him with ten thousand. God speaks to him again, telling him it's still too many. Gideon then whittles the army down to three hundred—from over thirty thousand to three hundred. It's not much of a force to be reckoned with against the mighty Midianites, but that is precisely the point. When we are too strong and armed, we tend to lose our faith in God to deliver us. We rely on our guns and bombs, the idols that are easier to see and trust in than an invisible God who can at times feel distant. That's why living an unarmed life takes faith, and courage, and trust in God.

Think about the other folks God appointed to lead. Consider the fact that God chose a shepherd boy to be king. When Samuel was on his quest to find the one who was to be king of Israel, Jesse brought out his sons—all except David, whom he didn't even consider a candidate. Samuel said to him, "Are these all the sons you have?" And Jesse replied, "There is still the youngest. . . . He is tending the sheep." Jesse brought David in from the field. Upon his arrival, the voice of the Lord said, "Anoint him; this is the one" (1 Sam. 16:11–12). The anointed David would go on to be the young man who killed the giant Goliath, who was not only a big dude but an "uncircumcised Philistine," the enemy of God's people. But if you know the story, you'll recall he didn't do it with mighty weapons. He didn't have an AR-15. No big guns at all.

The Scriptures say that even as everyone was preparing for the big fight, David was going back and forth to care for the sheep. And he couldn't even walk with the armor they tried to put on him. Saul, familiar with violence (an understatement), loaded David up with armor and a sword, ready for battle. But David said, just like a child, "I cannot go in these" (1 Sam. 17:39). He took them off, grabbed a few stones, and headed into battle to face the nine-foot embodiment of power. He looked into the face of Goliath with his five-thousand-shekel armor and his spear, whose "iron point weighed six hundred shekels" (17:7). The story is much more a critique than an endorsement of power and violence. As with many Bible stories, it is a subversive text. Little David toppled the giant with a slingshot. That's God's power at work, in our weakness. Not through our weapons or might or firepower.

There's a pattern in Scripture that continues to mirror that same thing—God's power is shown in our weakness, not in our strength. In Sarah, a barren elderly woman becomes the mother of a nation. In Moses, a stuttering prophet becomes the voice of God. A shepherd boy becomes a king who defeats a giant with a slingshot. A homeless baby is the one who leads us home. God's power is revealed in weakness. God uses the foolish to confound the wise, and the weak things to shame the strong. That's pure gospel.

But it also flies in the face of our culture, where it seems naive to trust in a God who doesn't always seem to show up the way we think God should.

Even Peter, when faced with the existential crisis of armed soldiers coming to arrest Jesus, picked up a sword. He stood his ground. He pulled the sword off one of the men confronting Jesus and cut the guy's ear off.

Jesus responded by scolding Peter, telling him to put his sword away. "All who draw the sword will die by the sword" (Matt. 26:52). And then Jesus picked up the ear of the wounded persecutor and put it back on, healing the man. The message is crystal clear. The gospel of Jesus, and the way of Jesus, is nonviolence. Even toward those who are violent to us.

The early Christians understood the message. Early church father Tertullian said that Christ, in disarming Peter, disarmed every soldier.[5] If ever there were a case to be made for justifiable violence, Peter had it. In light of Jesus, there is no such thing as redemptive violence, even to protect the Messiah himself. Jesus shows us another way—a way that we can interact with evil without becoming evil. It may cost us our lives, but we know "to live is Christ and to die is gain" (Phil. 1:21). We have nothing to lose and nothing to fear. Even Peter ended up being executed, hung upside down on a cross. Many of the early Christians were killed. But they insisted that when we remain faithful to Jesus, even in our deaths, God's love prevails. In the blood of the martyrs is the seed of the church, Tertullian once wrote.[6] The early Christians insisted on this: for Christ we can die, but we cannot kill.[7]

Peter learned, and any of us who dare to follow Jesus must learn, that we cannot carry a cross in one hand and a weapon in the other. We cannot serve two masters.

Becoming Like What We Worship

Idols change us. They possess us. They capture our hearts. They require an uncompromising allegiance. They take on a false authority. They make promises they can't keep. They ask more and more of us and constantly let us down.

Author Andy Crouch says that idolatry is seductive because at first it seems to work. But over time the idols give less and demand more. Some have compared it to alcoholism. You drink one sip, then another, and before long the alcohol is your master. You are its tool. What seemed to offer you control is now in control of you. Crouch puts it this way: "All idols begin by offering great things for a very small price. All idols then fail, more and more consistently, to deliver on their original promises, while ratcheting up their demands. . . . In the end they fail completely, even as they make categorical demands." Psychiatrist Jeffrey Satinover memorably says, "Idols ask for more and more, while giving less and less, until eventually they demand everything and give nothing."[8]

We can see that we have made idols of guns by the inability of so many to admit that guns can do anything wrong. "Guns don't kill; people kill" expresses that well. We don't claim the same about cars. Cars kill people. We know that. Sure, there is a driver behind the wheel (at least until recently!), but if that person had been riding a bicycle instead of driving a car, the accident would not have been fatal. Similarly, if the Las Vegas shooter had been armed only with rocks to throw, not as many people would have been killed.

Historian Garry Wills describes our gun idolatry this way: "The gun is our Moloch. . . . Like most gods, it does what it will, and cannot be questioned.

Its acolytes think it is capable only of good things. . . . Its power to do good is matched by its incapacity to do anything wrong. . . . If it seems to kill, that is only because the god's bottomless appetite for death has not been adequately fed."[9] We just don't have enough guns yet. And so here we are buying tons of guns to protect ourselves from people who are buying tons of guns. You can only have a lack of guns, not a surplus.

Again, we are willing to die for idols, kill for them, and sacrifice our children to them.

Think of all the promises a gun pledges to its owner—power, control, safety, protection, deliverance, self-confidence, self-determination, ridding the world of evil. If a gun were actually able to keep all its promises, then we would be like God.

That may sound familiar. It goes all the way back to the garden of Eden. Amid all the organic, non-genetically-modified-or-artificially-pesticided trees full of fruit, there was one tree that the first humans were not supposed to touch—the tree of the knowledge of good and evil. God warned Adam and Eve that if they ate of its fruit, they would discover something called "death." God warned them that they could not be immortal and know good and evil at the same time.

Along came a slick little serpent who convinced them that if they ate the forbidden fruit, they would be like God—quite an alluring proposition. They'd be the judges of good and evil, of what is beautiful and what is ugly. They would rule

themselves and control their own destinies. We all want to be like God, right? They decided they couldn't live without the knowledge of good and evil. Apparently death was a small price to pay for the possibility of god-like knowledge. And so they ate.

Most of the ugliness in the human narrative comes from a distorted quest to be like God. To know good and evil and to rid the world of evil.

In the Gospel of Matthew (13:24–30), Jesus talks about how the wheat and the weeds all grow together in this world, and we often want to rip up the weeds—or take out the "bad guys." But that is not ours to do. Only God can do that.

Murder often begins with a hunger for justice, lust with the recognition of beauty, gluttony with our enjoyment of the delectable gifts of God.

THE WHEAT AND THE WEEDS

The kingdom of heaven is like a man who sowed good seed in his field. But while everyone was sleeping, his enemy came and sowed weeds among the wheat, and went away. When the wheat sprouted and formed heads, then the weeds also appeared.

The owner's servants came to him and said, "Sir, didn't you sow good seed in your field? Where then did the weeds come from?"

"An enemy did this," he replied.

The servants asked him, "Do you want us to go and pull them up?"

"No," he answered, "because while you are pulling the weeds, you may up-root the wheat with them. Let both grow together until the harvest. At that time I will tell the harvesters: First collect the weeds and tie them in bundles to be burned; then gather the wheat and bring it into my barn." (Matt. 13:24–30)

It's important to note that the greatest seduction is sometimes not the "anti-God" but the "almost-God." Poisonous fruit can look delectable, which is why it's so dangerous. Even things like "freedom" and "peace" and "justice" can be deadly pursuits if they are not rooted in Jesus. It's beautiful things that tempt us. It's beautiful things that we die for and kill for. And it's beautiful things that we market, exploit, brand, and counterfeit. Nations fighting for peace end up perpetuating the very violence they seek to destroy.

Memorial to the Lost

The Washington Navy Yard shooting occurred on September 16, 2013, when a lone gunman fatally shot twelve people and injured three others at the headquarters of the Naval Sea Systems Command (NAVSEA) inside the Washington Navy Yard in southeast Washington, DC. The attack lasted just over one hour and ended when the shooter was killed by police.

It was the second-deadliest mass murder on a US military base. These are the names of the victims lost that day:

Michael Arnold, 59	Mary Francis Knight, 51
Martin Bodrog, 53	Frank Kohler, 50
Arthur Daniels, 51	Vishnu Pandit, 61
Sylvia Frasier, 53	Kenneth Bernard Proctor, 46
Kathy Gaarde, 62	Gerald Read, 58
John Roger Johnson, 73	Richard Michael Ridgell, 52

It may well be that the difference between murderers and saints is that murderers think the evil of the world is outside of themselves, while saints think the evil of the world is inside of themselves. Most of the folks who have done terrible things in the world were convinced they were ridding the world of evil—but they only added evil to the world.

True worship is when we let God change us and make us more like God. Idolatry is when we try to change God and make God more like us.

The things we worship and adore and love change us. We begin to act like them. That's why heroes and role models are so important. If we raise our kids to admire people with guns—like Samuel L. Jackson in *Pulp Fiction*, Bruce Willis in *Die Hard*, Clint Eastwood in *Dirty Harry*, and more recently the Punisher, Iron Man, Matt Damon as Jason Bourne, Liam Neeson in *Taken*, and Charlize Theron in *Atomic Blonde*—then our kids will start to act like the heroes they adore. This is why saints are so important. They are the heroes of the church. They show us what God is like, and you won't find many gun lovers among the saints. One old saying says, "It behooves us to be careful what we worship, for what we are worshiping, we are becoming." What dominates our imaginations begins to determine our character.

For Christians, Jesus is the one we adore and worship and hopefully begin to act like. And the great saints are simply people who remind the world of Jesus, who have been transformed by the one they worship and who give off the fragrance of Jesus in the world.

What's just as important as whether or not we worship God is the character of the God we worship and what our worship of God does to us. Does it make us more loving, more concerned about life, more compassionate for the marginalized? Or does it make us more aggressive and angry and self-righteous and violent?

I (Shane) met someone a while ago who told me he was an atheist. As he described to me the God that he didn't believe in, I told him, "I don't believe in that God either."

We believe in a God who would rather die than kill. We believe in a God whose last words are grace and forgiveness for the people who are killing him. We believe in a God who interacts with evil without becoming evil, who exposes our violence to heal our violence, who endures death to save us from death. We are atheists to the god of war and believers in the Prince of Peace.

If the NRA is a religion, as J. Warren Cassidy suggests, then we want nothing to do with the god they worship.

Addicted to Violence

It's been said that America's original sin is racism. Perhaps we could even name it white supremacy. The fruit of that sin is violence. Racism and violence go hand in hand. When we stop seeing the image of God in other human beings, they become disposable. We call them savages or animals or three-fifths human. And violence always follows. We can see that from the earliest days of this nation. The blood still cries out to God from the ground.

Dehumanization can lead to violence, kind of like how lust can lead to rape, or how greed can lead to exploitation. We saw the violence and racism in Charlottesville, and we see it in obvious and subtle ways all over the country. Even our national anthem is a war song—bombs bursting in the air. Given our nation's track record with violence, it is not that surprising that respectfully kneeling during the anthem as a public lament of the loss of black lives can still be called unpatriotic or anti-American.

We are addicted to violence. We are infected by it like a disease. And it can't go untreated.

Right now, the US spends over $600 billion per year on the military. No other country is even close to that expenditure: the US spends more than the next seven countries combined.[10] We spend over $20,000 per second on defense. Fifty-three cents of every discretionary federal dollar goes to the military (compared to fifteen cents helping to alleviate poverty).[11]

A lot of countries have military bases, and a few have bases in other countries besides their own. Russia has eight bases in other countries. Britain has seven in other countries. France has five. The United States has 662 military bases outside the United States, in thirty-eight other countries.[12] Ninety-five percent of foreign military bases are from one country—more than any country or empire in the history of the world.[13] And there are still politicians whose number one priority is strengthening the military.

The Pentagon spends more in three seconds than the average American makes in a year. The Pentagon budget consumes 80 percent of individual tax revenue.[14]

BEATING PLOWS INTO SWORDS

Of the thirty-one aircraft carriers in the world, nineteen belong to the US. In fact, the USS *New York* (a transport ship that holds military vehicles and troops) is a story opposite of changing swords to plows. The government took metal from the World Trade Center and made the ship's bow stem, along with the bow stems of the *Somerset* and *Arlington,* from it. One ship for each 9/11 crash site. If only there were something else we could have used that steel for.

USS *New York*

The US military spends over half a billion per year on advertising.[15] In a four-year stretch, it paid $6.8 million to professional sports teams to honor soldiers, including staged patriotic events.[16] Paying for solemn moments of remembrance—from tax dollars.

There are twenty-seven thousand people employed in recruitment, advertising, and public relations for the military.[17]

When it comes to weapons of mass destruction—the big guns—check out these numbers. There are roughly fifteen thousand nuclear bombs in the world. Only nine of the 196 countries of the world have nuclear weapons.

Ninety-three percent of them are owned by two countries: the US and Russia. About half of all the nukes in the world are owned by one country alone: the US.[18] We have nearly seven thousand nuclear bombs, and there is only one country that has ever used a nuclear bomb on people. It was us. And we did it twice in one week, killing one hundred thousand instantly and tens of thousands more in the weeks that followed. Just like our guns, our bombs keep getting bigger and bigger. We now have bombs that are eighty times stronger than the Hiroshima bomb. Cumulatively, our nuclear arsenal is equivalent to fifty thousand Hiroshima bombs.[19]

Fifty nuclear bombs could kill 200 million people (the combined populations of Britain, Canada, Australia, New Zealand, and Germany).[20] We have 6,800 of them. How many times do we need to be able to blow up the world?

It's like something off that *Hoarders* reality show where folks stockpile things—like ketchup packets or toilet paper or cats—only this is worse. It is a national epidemic.

We have a problem. We have a pathological, spiritual illness. We are addicted to violence. And our weapons have become our idols. Our nation has more guns than any other nation. Spends more money on its weapons. Sells more weapons. We're the only country that's killed one hundred thousand people in one blast, and it can feel like we'd do it again.

If we don't do something, it is going to kill us. It is going to erode our soul.

When you hoard anything, it starts to create a toxic environment. Especially when what you are hoarding is dangerous to begin with. It weighs us down: $17.2 billion per year just to maintain the stockpile of weapons we have.[21] We are wasting money and lives.

Experts estimate that gun violence is costing the US economy over $100 billion per year.[22] The World Health Organization puts that number even higher, at closer to $155 billion annually.[23] That's just paper money. The human toll has no price tag.

Hoarding—whether that means stockpiling guns or stockpiling bombs—turns us into something we do not want to be, something we don't even recognize. Something that is not good for the world.

More guns and more bombs are not making the world safer. Saying more guns will solve our gun problem is sort of like a drunk saying he just needs more whiskey, or like thinking that the solution to a flood is more water.

We end up creating a world that we do not want to live in. "The doors of hell are locked on the *inside*," C. S. Lewis said.[24]

As you can see, the gun problem runs deep. We have said from the beginning that what we have is not just a gun problem but also a heart problem. No matter how good our laws are, no law can heal a human heart filled with hatred or racism. No government, even the best one, can solve the human predicament of sin and the way it so often expresses itself in violence.

Violence is killing us. Over and over we have picked up the sword and died by the sword. The US is fighting wars in seven countries as of March 2018.[25] And in one year (2016) we dropped over twenty-six thousand bombs. Listen to that again: in one year we dropped 26,171 bombs. That's seventy-two bombs per day, or three per hour.[26] We have made the world a very fragile place.

It's easy to see why Martin Luther King Jr. became so passionate about nonviolence and spoke so powerfully against the big guns of war: "A nation that continues year after year to spend more money on military defense than on programs of social uplift is approaching spiritual death." King called America the "greatest purveyor of violence in the world today."[27] He said that every time he told young people that violence would not solve their problems, they asked why the government kept using violence to solve its problems. He had to speak consistently against violence, whether it was being used by protestors in the streets or politicians in the Pentagon. King also noted that every time a bomb goes off overseas, we feel the second impact of it here at home—as schools go bankrupt, kids go without health care, veterans die on our streets, and entire blocks of our cities look like war zones of abandoned factories and houses. President Dwight Eisenhower nailed it: "Every gun that is made, every warship launched, every rocket fired signifies, in the final sense, a theft from those who hunger and are not fed, those who are cold and are not clothed. This world in arms is not spending money alone. It is spending the sweat of its laborers, the genius of its scientists, the hopes of its children."[28]

If we live in a nation that idolizes its weaponry, we must recognize that we are the ones who are suffering—from our idols and from our fears. We are killing ourselves, and the soul of the nation is at stake. The lives of our children and grandchildren are at stake. It's time to name our love affair with guns and violence as a form of idolatry. We've trusted in something other than God and the promise that love will cast out fear.

The good news is, it is never too late to repent.

The word *repent* may also sound extreme or antiquated, but we like it since it really means to "rethink" how we are living and where we are headed. In the words of GPS systems, we need to "recalculate" where we are and where we are going so that we can arrive safely at our destination—or in this case, our destiny.

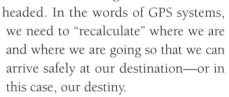

"Every gun that is made, every warship launched, every rocket fired signifies, in the final sense, a theft from those who hunger and are not fed, those who are cold and are not clothed."

Dwight D. Eisenhower

Twelve

EXORCISING DEMONS

> For our struggle is not against flesh and blood, but against the rulers, against the authorities, against the powers of this dark world and against the spiritual forces of evil in the heavenly realms.
>
> —Ephesians 6:12

WE'VE SPENT A LOT OF TIME on the physical reality of guns, and there is something amazing about seeing actual metal transformed. We also want to see streets transformed. And a world transformed.

The battle against violence is not just about guns. We could get rid of all the guns in the world, but people would still find ways to kill. There is a spiritual dimension. No matter how thorough our gun laws become, no law can change a human heart. That's why this is not just a political battle.

Just as there is a spiritual dimension to our adoration of guns that is a form of idolatry, there is also a spiritual side to violence and our obsession with it. We want to suggest that it is literally a form of demonic possession. Hang with us.

It's hard to think about violence as only a physical reality in the world we live in, though it is surely that. We want to suggest that there is something happening in the spiritual realm, what the Bible calls the "authorities" and "powers" and "spiritual forces of evil" (Eph. 6:12). Maybe that kid who said Satan invented the gun is more right than we thought.

You may not be a person who thinks much about things like angels and demons. You may not even think that you believe in them. You may think of them like you think about dragons or fairies. But when you look at these mass shootings—Columbine, Aurora, Sandy Hook, Pulse, Las Vegas—there is something so hauntingly evil, it goes beyond anything we can rationally understand. Maybe you move a little closer to acknowledging that there are "spiritual forces of evil" that can compel us to do unreasonable things. Perhaps it is not too far-fetched, even for the skeptics, to consider that the Charleston shooter was compelled by a dark, evil spirit. We are not going to let him off the hook or make an excuse for the evil he did. We are not trying to explain it away; rather, we are trying to show how dreadfully enigmatic it is.

If some of the forces that we are up against are spiritual, then changing laws alone is not enough. We're thinking specifically of Pastor Larry Wright. During one of the worship services at his church in North Carolina, an armed man came in, carrying a gun and ammo. Pastor Wright fearlessly invited him to the altar, and the armed man surrendered the gun to a deacon. Then, Pastor Wright invited the man to stay for the rest of the service and went on to finish his sermon. At the end the pastor gave an altar call—an invitation to come to the altar for prayer, where people can commit their lives to Jesus. The man came forward for prayer that night.

Memorial to the Lost

On July 20, 2012, a lone gunman opened fire on an audience at a movie theater's midnight showing of *The Dark Knight Rises*. Multiple weapons were used, including an AR-15-style semiautomatic rifle, a .40 caliber handgun, and a 12-gauge shotgun. Twelve lives were lost and many others injured. The incident lasted less than ten minutes. Here are the names of those who died that night:

Jonathan T. Blunk, 26

Alexander J. Boik, 18

Jesse E. Childress, 29

Gordon W. Cowden, 51

Jessica Ghawi, 24

John Thomas Larimer, 27

Matthew R. McQuinn, 27

Micayla C. Medek, 23

Veronica Moser-Sullivan, 6

Alex M. Sullivan, 27

Alexander C. Teves, 24

Rebecca Ann Wingo, 32

GATHERING AROUND THE FORGE

When RAWtools transforms guns, we often have an entire worship service with prayers and songs and testimonies. We realize that the battle against gun violence is not just about policies and legislation; it is also about healing hearts. Walter Brueggemann says, "Bringing pain to speech creates energy; not bringing pain to speech brings violence." We invite people to consider the hostilities that exist in their own  hearts—whether they own a gun or not. One of the things we've done is invite people to write the hostilities of their own hearts on paper and throw them into the fire. Sometimes we even use "flash paper"—a special combustible paper used by magicians and circus performers that burns up without leaving a trace. It's pretty fun. It's also deep. Guns are just the outward manifestation of a much deeper illness—they're the symptom of the disease.

"I saw in his eyes hopelessness, hurt, pain, despair," explained Pastor Wright. "I came down and prayed with him and we embraced. It was like a father embracing a son."

The man was escorted by police to a facility for treatment. Eventually he returned to the church to apologize, perhaps even to worship and feel the love. It turns out that he is a veteran who has struggled with PTSD and mental illness and has had trouble affording his medication. He was also a convicted felon who was given a gun.[1]

We don't want to conflate mental illness with demon possession. Nor do we think other church shootings could have been prevented by prayer in the same way.

What is clear, though, is that there are some deep forces at work. As the writer of Ephesians says, we are up against principalities and powers, and spiritual forces. There is a physical side of the principalities and powers that works in our governmental systems and structures. Policies and politicians can oppress people and create obstacles to the kingdom of God and human flourishing. Things like not having access to needed medication or veterans services are the results of those.

And there is also a spiritual force at work, something that takes many different shapes. In the Gospels, there is a story about a man named Legion. The story happens in "the region of the Gerasenes," which consisted of ten cities (known as the Decapolis) near the Sea of Galilee, under Roman occupation and plagued by violence. It was a hub for much of the Roman military, and Gerasenes was known as a place where many Roman veterans with benefits were given land to dwell in, a veteran's settlement of sorts. As Jesus passed through the area, he met a man who could not be subdued because he was "possessed" by an evil spirit, a word loaded with meaning, especially to Galileans whose land was occupied by armed soldiers (Mark 5:1–20). They were controlled by an evil outside force. So was the man. Violence held them in its possession.

The evil spirit had made the man unclean by forcing him to live among the graves, which was a violation of the Hebrew holiness laws (Isa. 65:4) and just a rough place to live in general. He could not get the death out of his mind or body. The demon occupation led him to hurt himself, beating himself with hands possessed by violence. His own life, and perhaps the lives of others, was in danger. Demon possessed or violence possessed—there wasn't much distinction. Maybe not for us either.

Jesus asked the man his name, and he replied, "Legion," the same word for a division of Roman soldiers. Scholars note that a legion consisted of around two thousand troops, and there would have been several legions around the Decapolis.[2] It's interesting that in the story, after Jesus tells the demons to leave the man, they beg to stay in the area. Nearby was a band of pigs, *band* being the same word used for a group of military cadets.[3] They too were unclean. The demons asked to be sent among the pigs. (Jews did not touch pigs.) Jesus summoned the Legion to enter the pigs. And the pigs, specifically numbered at two thousand, "charged" into the sea to their deaths. And the man lived!

None of the listeners could have missed the subversive symbolism in the story, remembering Pharaoh's army that charged into the sea, where they were swallowed up and drowned (Exod. 14). Jesus healed people who had been made sick by a violent world. The story ends with the people asking Jesus to leave—after all, his message is controversial, and they lost a lot of pigs. Everyone was pretty upset, except for the man formerly known as Legion. He was free.

Principalities and Powers

When you challenge guns, some people want to kill you with their guns. Many of the leaders in the movement to reduce gun violence receive death threats regularly. We've seen some mean stuff. At one point, our entire website at Red Letter Christians (the organization Shane leads) was hacked and redirected to a gun site. But it helps to remember that the forces we are up against are not just "flesh and blood"; spiritual forces are at work.

We learned this at the vigils we did at the local gun shop, the Shooter Shop. As we prepared for one of our vigils, we got word that some progun people had announced a counterprotest. They posted some pretty nasty stuff online, including calling us names. No big deal. But then we read one post where they told people to bring their guns because they might need them. They went on to say, carry your guns; don't leave them in the car—it's a "sketchy" neighborhood and someone could steal them.

We moved forward with our vigil—prayerfully, centered in nonviolence, in Jesus, in love, even for those who might oppose us. We took a pledge of nonviolence and had a briefing about the likelihood of the counterprotest. And they did show up. There were not many of them, but they were loud, intimidating, and angry. They had as many American flags as they had people, and they waved them proudly. They hurled names and insults. They called me (Shane) a pedophile (perhaps for bringing kids from my block to the vigil) and told me to cut my hair. They had a point on that last one; it had been about ten years since I'd cut it. But on we went.

Jamie Moffett

Vigil at the
Shooter Shop

As folks shared their firsthand experiences of being shot by stray bullets and losing their kids and parents to guns, the counter-protesters began shouting over them. As one fellow in a wheelchair shared, they yelled over him, interrupting him: "He's probably illegal." "Get a job." And worse.

It really did begin to feel evil.

There was a point where we decided not to try to overpower them. Maybe it was one of those "third way" moments—neither fight nor flight, we just kept our vigil going, rising above the polarizing binaries of "us" and "them" and carving out a new way to relate. It was hard as they yelled and spat insults at us. **Sometimes the "third way of Jesus" looks good on paper, and then you have folks waving guns and flags in your face.**

We had a permit, a sound system, and a stage, but we didn't want to try to outyell them. We really did want to disarm their hatred. We tried to talk with them. We asked them to join us. We insisted that we were not there against them—we were there to save lives, including the lives of people they love.

We paused as they chanted, "USA! USA!" And then, in a move that felt led by the Spirit, our group of pastors and activists and victims of violence began to quietly say the Lord's Prayer together. As our voices cried out in a gentle unity, "Thy kingdom come, Thy will be done, on earth as it is in heaven . . ." the counterprotesters began to sing "God Bless America" at the top of their voices. Needless to say, it was eerie.[4]

When I got home, we debriefed the whole event with some of the teenagers. They had all kinds of wise things to say, takeaways from the day. One of them said he caught a glimpse of what Martin Luther King Jr. and others felt as people spat on them and insulted them, and of why nonviolence was the only answer to violence. Another young man mentioned how important it was to ground ourselves in prayer before we went so that we were spiritually prepared to face such hatred. And all of them mentioned how it felt like we were not fighting people but something much deeper—we were fighting a spiritual battle, not against just flesh and blood.

Several weeks later, the owner of the Shooter Shop ended up in the hospital, and we reminded ourselves that he is made in the image of God too. He is not our enemy. We sent him a gift and let him know he was in our prayers.

Not long ago, the Shooter Shop closed down. It has now been converted into affordable housing for formerly homeless veterans. One more little example of changing swords to plows.

Thirteen

CHRISTIANS WITH GUNS

Do we really want peace? Then let's ban all weapons so we don't have to live in fear of war.

—Pope Francis

"BIBLE QUIZZING" used to be a big deal for lots of us Bible nerds, especially in the Bible Belt. It was a competition, with teams and rules and referees, to see who knew the Bible the best. And you had to know verses word for word, without pausing. But listen to this story that shows just how badly we miss the point, even when we know the Bible cover to cover.

I (Shane) was researching a story about a man who allegedly lost a Bible-quoting contest and killed the man who beat him—tragically shooting his opponent in the face. The story appears to be true.[1] But even more disturbing is that in my research I discovered many other news stories of people who had killed someone because of an argument over the Bible. Most noteworthy is the story of a twenty-year-old college student killed after a heated argument about what the Bible has to say about forgiveness. He was shot twice in the head by a longtime friend.[2]

These stories embody so much of what has gone crazy in this country of God and guns. It doesn't matter how much of the Bible you have memorized; if your instinct is to kill someone who knows more than you, you missed the point.

You can see the bizarre, eerie interplay between Christian faith and guns from the earliest days of guns in America. Charles Adams, great-grandson of the second president, said, "We have a Mission; it is the distinct call of the Almighty. [The clergymen] want to go out, and have this Great Nation [export] the blessings of Liberty and the Gospel to other Inferior Races, who wait for us as for their Messiah—only we must remember to take with us lots of shotguns."[3]

The earliest gun marketers were called "missionaries." Colt had a revolver called the Peacemaker, undoubtedly winking at Jesus's blessing of the "peacemakers" who will be called the "children of God." And as mentioned, Colt's wife, Elizabeth, used her gun fortune to build a church, which had guns carved into the entrance—a church branded with guns instead of a cross.

Some guns have Bible verses etched into them. A Florida gun manufacturer designed an assault rifle called the Crusader, engraved with the words of Psalm 144:1: "Blessed be the LORD my Rock, who trains my hands for war, my fingers for battle." The safety selector that controls the trigger has three settings: "Peace," "War," and "God Wills It." Yours for only $1,580.[4]

How is there a market for a Psalm 144 gun? Because too many Christians, including popular TV preachers and bestselling authors, love their guns. This is especially apparent when you look at the stats on gun ownership and note that white evangelicals own tons of guns. A Pew Research Center survey showed that 41 percent of white evangelicals—almost half—own a gun. Compare that to the 30 percent of the general population who own a gun. The demographic with the highest rate of gun ownership is white, evangelical Christians. The followers of the Prince of Peace are packing heat. Praise the Lord, pass the ammunition.

A mixed message

(And other Christians are not much better: 29 percent of black Protestants, 33 percent of white mainline Protestants, and 24 percent of Catholics own guns.)[5]

After the San Bernardino shooting, where fourteen people were killed and twenty-two others injured, Jerry Falwell Jr., the president of Liberty University, one of the largest Christian colleges in America, told his student body that "if more good people had concealed carry permits, then we could end those Muslims before they walked in." He stuck his hand in his back pocket, indicating that he had a gun, and said, "If the people in that community center had had what I got in my back pocket right now . . ." A video of the event shows the student body responding with applause.

It gets worse. Falwell invited Liberty students to attend a free course offered on campus to acquire concealed carry permits and concluded by saying, "Let's teach [Muslims] a lesson before they show up here."[6]

I (Shane) am an evangelical Christian. In fact, I have spoken at Liberty University, to this same student body. I have been hopeful that Liberty is moving beyond the culture wars of the 1980s, and my hunch is that many of the students and faculty are doing just that, reclaiming a Christianity that looks more like Jesus again.

I know Jerry Falwell Jr. represents some of the most distorted and confusing versions of Christianity out there, but there are many Falwell-light expressions of God-and-gun theology.

The Jesus I worship did not carry a gun. He carried a cross. Jesus did not tell us to kill our enemies; he told us to love them.

Christians often refer to Jesus as the Lamb of God. Lambs don't hurt anybody.

Early Christians understood that Jesus's words to Peter ("Put your sword back in its place," Matt. 26:52) were meant to disarm every Christian. No longer could any Christian legitimately justify violence toward anyone—even enemies. There is not a single Christian in the first three hundred years of the faith who justifies violence or makes a case for self-defense.[7] Instead, history records the opposite. Early Christians insisted that for Christ we can die, but we cannot kill. We can die on behalf of others, but we cannot kill for them. Jesus had abolished the sword once and for all.

So what can Christians do? We can lay down our lives. We can put our bodies in the way of violence. It was Jesus who said, "Greater love has no one than this: to lay down one's life for one's friends" (John 15:13). We can die in the name of Christ, but we dare not kill in the name of Christ. As the saying goes, grace has the power to dull even the sharpest sword.

It's hard to imagine Jesus enrolling in the concealed carry class at Liberty University or anywhere else. And it is even harder to imagine Jesus approving of the words of Falwell as he openly threatened Muslims.

The venue where Falwell gave these comments makes them even more troubling. Liberty isn't just a struggling little fundamentalist Bible college. Liberty is one of the largest Christian universities in the United States. Liberty has over one hundred thousand students.

One year later, almost to the day, Falwell announced that Liberty University would be opening a state-of-the-art shooting range on campus featuring pistol, rifle, and shotgun facilities. It's a $3 million project on five hundred acres of land, backed by the NRA. At thirteen thousand square feet indoors and thousands more outside, it is one of the most expansive and expensive shooting ranges in the country—and it's on the campus of one of the largest

Memorial to the Lost

On December 2, 2015, a man and a woman opened fire on
a holiday party for the San Bernardino County Department
of Public Health. Three semiautomatic rifles (an M&P15, a
.223 caliber DPMS model A-15, and a Model 64F .22 caliber)
and two semiautomatic 9mm handguns were used to murder
fourteen people on that day. Here are their names:

Robert Adams, 40

Isaac Amanios, 60

Bennetta Betbadal, 46

Harry Bowman, 46

Sierra Clayborn, 27

Juan Espinoza, 50

Aurora Godoy, 26

Shannon Johnson, 45

Larry Daniel Kaufman, 42

Damian Meins, 58

Tin Nguyen, 31

Nicholas Thalasinos, 52

Yvette Velasco, 27

Michael Raymond
Wetzel, 37

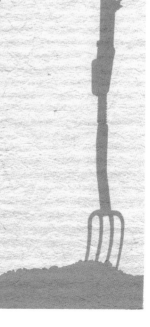

"Christian" universities in America. And there is a free course for those students who want a concealed carry permit. More than 1,600 people have taken it. "We have a very pro-Second Amendment student body," Falwell said.[8] Liberty opened the shooting range in 2018—and had the grand opening the week of Easter. Nothing says "Christ is risen" like a gun range.

Jerry Falwell Jr. publicly represents a version of "Christianity" that looks more like the gospel of the NRA than the gospel of Jesus. The gun and the cross offer us two very different versions of what power looks like. One is willing to kill. And one is willing to die.

If we want to know what perfect love looks like, we look at Jesus on the cross, who loved his enemies so much that he was willing to die for them—for us.

Whom Shall You Serve?

We are troubled by militant Christianity. Just as we grieve for Muslims around the world as they have their faith distorted by ISIS, we are grieved by Christian extremists who pervert the faith.

There's a verse in Galatians that talks about folks who come proclaiming a "gospel" different from the gospel of Jesus. "I am astonished that you are so quickly deserting the one who called you by the grace of Christ and are turning to a different gospel—which is really no gospel at all. Evidently some people are throwing you into confusion and are trying to pervert the gospel of Christ" (Gal. 1:6–7).

We cannot sit idly by when a fellow Christian makes open threats to Muslims, or anyone else, especially when he does so in the name of the Prince of Peace.

Christians are meant to remind the world of Jesus—not just with our words but by the way we live. We are not to conform to the patterns of this world but to live in ways that confound the patterns of this world.

The idea that the church is to be the body of Christ is not just a pipe dream or empty rhetoric. It's not something to read about in theology books and leave for scholars to pontificate about. We are to become the literal body of Jesus in the world—to make God's love manifest, visible, real.

Christians are to be little Christs— people who put flesh on Jesus in the world today. It's what we remember as we partici-

HOLY IMAGINATION

I (Shane) was speaking on this topic once, and a questioner raised his hand to ask what I would do if an intruder were threatening my family. I answered him honestly: "I don't know what I would do, but I hope I would manifest the fruit of the Spirit." That should be a response on which all Christians agree.

pate in the Eucharist, or Holy Communion—we are eating and drinking the body and blood of Jesus, praying that it will transform us. We are pledging our allegiance to a victim of violence who rose above violence and refused to become violent.

As we do it, we say we are doing it in "remembrance"—we are re-membering Jesus. The body of Christ made up of many members is becoming one. There's the saying "You are what you eat." That's what Communion is about—being transformed into Christ's body, so that Jesus lives in us and through us. We become the body of Jesus. We are willing to pour out our lives for the world. We are even willing to shed our own blood to "take up our cross."

There's a beautiful image in Scripture that we are to "clothe" ourselves with Christ (Col. 3:12–17). The basis for living out the ethics of Jesus in this world is not that it works but that this is the way God is. We are not promised that everything is going to turn out perfect. Look at the cross. Look at how the story ends for the apostles. It is ugly. If there is anything we can learn from our history, as William Barclay says, it's that we are to be "completely fearless, absurdly happy and in constant trouble."[9] We mock death with our fearless love—or at least we should.

In an age of violence and terror, it's important not just to live well but to die well. We are not called simply to live like Christ; we are called to die like Christ. And he died loving. The heroes of our faith (folks like John the Baptist, the apostles, Stephen, Ignatius, Maximilian Kolbe, Polycarp, Dirk Willems, Rufus and Zosimus, Perpetua and Felicitas, all the way down to contemporary folks like Óscar Romero, Dorothy Stang, and the Nag Hammadi Coptic Christians of 2010) are not war heroes but martyrs. They did not die with guns in their hands. They died carrying a cross, faithful to the nonviolent Christ.

Martyr means "witness," and the ripples that the martyrs' deaths made are part of what spread the gospel of grace. They are not people who died killing but people who died loving and were slaughtered as they looked into the face of evil people and said, "God loves you."

In the South, we have a saying: "You are the spittin' image (of someone)." One theory says that it's shorthand for "spirit and image." *Spittin' image* means more than just that you look like that person. It goes beyond just appearance to include character and temperament. It means that you remind people of that person. You have their charisma. You do the same things they did. In the truest sense, Christians are to be the spittin' image of Jesus in the world. We are to be the things he was. We are to preach the things he preached and live the way he lived. We are to follow in the footsteps of our rabbi so closely that we get his dust on us. We are to remind the world of Jesus. The criterion for whether something is a manifestation of the kingdom of God is the person of Jesus. Does it look like him? "Be imitators of God" (Eph. 5:1 NRSV)—that word *imitate* derives from the same word as *mimic*, like a mime.

When you put metal in the forge, it starts to take on the character of the fire. Outside of the fire it is cold, dark, and hard, but as it draws near to the fire, it begins to get warm and to soften. It even begins to glow. Eventually you can hardly distinguish between the metal and the fire—they both burn bright orange. If you remove the metal from the flame and it gets too far away from the fire, it starts to turn a dull gray and grow cold. But as soon as it nears the fire, it lights up again. So it is with us. We are to stay near to Jesus, the light of the world, so that we begin to glow as he glowed. And we dare not stray too far from the source, or our hearts will grow cold. If we draw near to the light of the world, we begin to glow as Jesus glowed.

Coe Burchfield

Oh Lord, oh Lord, keep your
hand on that plow, hold on

Oh Lord, oh Lord, keep your
hand on that plow, hold on

Oh Lord, oh Lord, keep your
hand on that plow, hold on

—"Gospel Plow," American folk song

Fourteen

UNLEARNING VIOLENCE

8,000: Murders seen on TV by the end of elementary school
200,000: Violent acts seen on TV by age eighteen
79: Percent of Americans who believe TV violence precipitates
real-life mayhem[1]

THE TOYS WE PLAY WITH growing up include guns. The games we play include battle games—cops and robbers, paintball, laser tag, Nerf battles. Childhood movies and games and sports events, even comic books, are shaping how we think about violence and how to live in a world full of violence.

Those who say "guns don't kill; people kill" often say we need to place the blame on Hollywood films and violent video games and all the ads and stories that shape our imagination in the way of violence. We think they are on to something.

Even the news has a certain bias toward violence. As journalists often say, "If it bleeds, it leads." Or as one reporter put it, "We don't cover landings at the airport."[2] News covers the tragic stories, the murders, the crashes, the hate crimes. But we need some journalists to tell the good stories, to remind us how many planes landed safely at the airport, not just how many crashed.

It's not just the news. Pretty much all of the top-grossing pay-per-view events of all time are fights—Mayweather vs. Pacquiao earned $400 million.[3] In 2009 the video game *Call of Duty: Modern Warfare 2* made $310 million in one day, setting the record for video game sales—and it is a game designed to mirror the physical realities and horrors of war.[4]

Violence sells, in a million different genres, including sports, video games, movies, and breaking news. Ninety percent of movies, 68 percent of video games, and 60 percent of TV shows depict some violence.[5]

The first movie I (Shane) can remember seeing in the theater was *Poltergeist* (my mom has apologized profusely for this). I remember watching *Rambo: First Blood Part II*—and getting a giant Rambo knife with a saw, compass, and waterproof matches inside its hollow handle. At ten years old, I was ready to take on the world like Sylvester Stallone. I couldn't convince my mom to get me the RPG-7 missile launcher, so I had to settle for the knife. Some of the first television shows I remember watching were reruns of the Wild West classic *Bonanza* and the war classic *M.A.S.H.* I watched them while sitting on my grandfather's lap. Later on it was *Miami Vice* and *The A-Team*. And on and on. Though they vary in style, television shows from every decade have guns in common. We are inundated with violence and are trained to fear.

No matter what era or generation, the heroes of our childhoods always had a gun. The new-school heroes, in movies from *The Fast and the Furious* to Denzel Washington's *The Equalizer* to the Marvel comic-book movies to even the beloved *Pirates of the Caribbean*, almost always have a weapon. Even the most well-made, inspirational movies like *Wonder Woman* and

Black Panther can endorse the myth of redemptive violence. The good guy or gal wins, but there is always blood.

Things are even crazier now. We have video games like *Goldeneye 007* and *Grand Theft Auto* in which you actually see blood splatter on streets and walls. In *Grand Theft Auto* you can earn points for things like assaulting an old woman or running over a prostitute. In *Dead Rising 2*, the killer-hero of the game guzzles booze to restore his health and vomits it up if he drinks too much. That's what we are up against.

THE LANGUAGE OF VIOLENCE

big shot, on a hit list, shell shocked, hit the bull's-eye, gun shy, standoff, a trigger, shotgun wedding, troubleshooter, son of a gun, going postal, we have a shot, pull the trigger, fast as a speeding bullet, shoot for the moon, hotshot, you call the shots, target audience, right on target, smoking gun, blew me away, she's a pistol, notch in the belt, dodged a bullet, went ballistic, shoot from the hip, it's a long shot, give it my best shot, lock, stock, and barrel, trigger happy, don't jump the gun, pistol-whipped, stick to your guns, sure shot, politician under fire, shoot for the top, wrong end of the barrel, straight shooter, he's the big gun, take a shot in the dark, bite the bullet, who's riding shotgun, blew his brains out, blown to smithereens, explosive personality, arm like a cannon, bring out the big guns, shoot down an argument, fire away, got flak over it, shooting blanks, outgunned, shooting for gold, ammunition for my argument, shot it from every angle, we killed them, shoot me an email, look down the barrel of a gun, it's a blast, bombed it, nuke 'em, nuclear option, I'll cover you, bombarded, this is a land mine, let's get fired up, I'll kill you, aim to kill, fire when ready, straight shot to the city, it's a booby trap, got you in the crosshairs, duck and cover, the silver bullet, rapid-fire questions, knock 'em dead, plan of attack, don't shoot the messenger, took potshots, fry him, no magic bullets, shotgun approach, take a knife to a gunfight, more bang for your buck, young gun, bombs away, loose cannon, welcome to the gun show, I got ambushed, overshot the driveway, shoot yourself in the foot, I'm shot, got a good shot at it, drink a shot, open season, our plans blew up, kill the bill, he blew up, shooting duck, shooting gallery, killing time, my foot is killing me, dead or alive, stand your ground, blow this joint, shoot to kill

We are obsessed, addicted. More than twenty-five billion hours have been logged on the video game *Call of Duty*.[6] That's 2.85 million years. In fact, *Call of Duty* players collectively log some 1,300 years of gameplay every day. Imagine the generative things that could be done with 1,300 years' worth of time every day.

We even have a president who said, "I could stand in the middle of Fifth Avenue and shoot somebody and I wouldn't lose voters."[7] The craziest thing is, he is probably right.

Violence is a disease. It does something to us. It changes the way we act and talk.

It may seem like a stretch, but just think about the way our epidemic of gun violence seeps into our language, like a cancer. It might not be something we even notice without really deconstructing things. Many of our metaphors and verbs and images are shaped by it.

The Power of Language

Our words, our tongue, even our virtual language of tweets and Facebook posts, have power, for good or bad. Language has the power to heal or to wound. A comment can build someone up or tear someone down. Just as metal can be crafted to make a gun or a plow, words can bring life or destroy it. Words can comfort or hurt. They can disarm a situation or aggravate a conflict. They can open minds or they can close them. They can reveal truth or hide the truth. They can stop wars and they can start them.

The Bible talks about taming the tongue (James 3) and says it can be used as a weapon. Jesus points out the power of language—and that we speak out of the overflow of what is in our heart (Luke 6:45). He goes so far as to say that if we call our neighbor "Raca," a fool, then we have committed murder in our heart (Matt. 5:22). That's pretty serious. So as we think about gun violence, it is important to think about not just the external forms of violence but also the internal forms. Just as when you look at a tree or an iceberg, what you can see with your eyes is only a little part of the whole thing. There's much more going on underneath the surface. So it is with violence.

Guns are not just a political problem but also a heart problem, and our exposure to guns begins early.

Language experts have some important insight into the way culture shapes language—or, perhaps more often, the way language shapes culture.[8] In English, when things are working normally, we say, "It's running fine." Your watch is running. The car is running. You've got to run to a meeting. The general pace of life reflects that language (we move fast). In Spanish, when things are working normally, the word used is *walking*. Your clock is walk-ing. Your meeting walks well. Latino culture walks instead of runs. Similarly, English stands alone in the amount of violent language it uses in everyday speech. Many languages do not employ phrases like "I'm so mad, I could *kill* her." It would be offensive and unthinkable.

The experts are adamant—violent media has an effect on us. Studies consistently show that violent media leads to violent behavior.[9] Our young people often learn to shoot a virtual gun in a video game before they shoot a real one. Their imaginations are trained to see shooting someone as a way to solve a problem. And the things they imagine in their minds begin to have real-life effects. Just look at interviews with mass shooters in America. People often learn to kill virtually before they kill in reality. Even the military uses video games to teach the use of real weapons in real conflict zones. And it does something to us: it desensitizes us.

Other parts of the world are much more appalled by violence than we are in the US. When Americans think of X-rated films, we think of sex. In other places, X ratings also include pornography and sexual content but are just as much used to indicate violence. It's worth noting that what we find explicit and intended only for adults is generally sexual. Many folks

Memorial to the Lost

On February 26, 2016, after firing at multiple people in traffic, a gunman arrived at his workplace at Excel Industries and opened fire on other workers in the building using an AK-47-style semiautomatic rifle and a Glock 22 semiautomatic handgun. Three people lost their lives and multiple others were wounded. Though it is not one of the most well-known mass shootings, or the most deadly, it is a reminder that mass shootings are frequent, though they don't all make the news. Many of them affect small rural towns like Hesston. Shane spoke about gun violence in Hesston just a few days before this shooting, talking about how gun violence is not just an urban problem. The town has a large Mennonite population (Mike's denomination) that cared for the families of the victims and of the person responsible, to heal the wounds of the tragedy. Here are the names of those who died:

Renee Benjamin, 30   Brian Sadowsky, 44
Josh Higbee, 31

around the world find violence just as toxic and offensive as pornography. Americans are more disturbed by sex than by killing. We don't want our kids exposed to sex prematurely, but we often have no reservations about exposing them to violence.

One grandmother made her ten-year-old grandson return *Grand Theft Auto*. She was irate about the sexual content but apparently totally numb to the violence.[10] I (Mike) played this game in college, and it's the game that made me realize I'd gone too far. It's a game where you play a car thief among rival groups of friends and enemies; you can also play in an open mode where you wander around town stealing cars. And you have weapons. You can get on a rooftop, and if you aim just right and fire, the head will fall off/disappear from your victim. If that victim happened to have weapons, you can now approach and possess them, accumulating your arsenal. Sometimes, if you don't kill these people in the video game, they chase you and wound you. One of the ways to get "healthy" is to steal a car and drive until you find a woman dressed as a prostitute and pull alongside her. She would get in, the car would shake, and your "health" would improve so you could go on stealing cars and shooting people. Again, this was in a game mode where you were free to explore the city, steal cars, shoot people and cars, and drive recklessly, with zero regard for other drivers or pedestrians (there was incentive to hit pedestrians). Rockstar Games released a new version in June 2017, and in the promo video they say, "You want to make real money? A dirty little secret: it's in arms!" and "Look up new and exciting ways to terminate people, then make a tiny profit and do your country proud."

At one point, the video game development company Electronic Arts linked to gun manufacturers' websites on their video game websites. You were essentially two to three clicks away from playing with a gun on the screen to buying a real-life version. These links have since been removed, but the rise of online gaming and online shopping still keeps the two connected by only a few clicks. First-person shooter games are doing blockbuster business. In 2017, *Call of Duty* earned half a billion dollars in a single day.[11]

Violence is something we learn.

And it is something we can unlearn.

It is something we are conditioned in.

America may differ from the Roman Empire in many ways, but the two share the idea that power comes from weaponry and that freedom is maintained by violence. War is still the way of the world, but it's not the way of Jesus. In the empire's attempt to make disciples of us, we are taught the way of the sword rather than the way of the cross, and we are persuaded to kill our enemies rather than love them. We become convinced that violence is the only way to defeat the "bad guys" and right the wrongs of the world.

Not everything is as obvious as video games and war movies, but the logic of power and might is prolific, and the allure of violence is everywhere. In his book *America and Its Guns*, James Atwood points to the sports arena. We don't have the gladiatorial games today, but we do have the Super Bowl and professional wrestling and mixed martial arts (UFC). When you look at the things that entertain us, they often involve pain, conflict, and the possibility of someone getting hurt. We have a fascination, obsession even, with violence.

Even the names for our sports teams are revealing, in contrast to the iconic image of Jesus as a lamb. You won't find a professional sports team whose mascot is a lamb. It doesn't exude power, might, or victory. The NFL has Lions, Titans, Bears, Bengals, Broncos, Jaguars, Raiders, Buccaneers, Chiefs, Vikings, Cowboys, Giants, and Redskins . . . but no Lambs.[12]

Faith is crucial in a world so full of violence. The writer of Romans says, "Do not conform to the pattern of this world, but be transformed by the renewing of your mind" (Rom. 12:2). It is not only metal that needs to be made new.

We need to be made new.

EARLY CHRISTIANS ON VIOLENCE

We ourselves were well conversant with war, murder and everything evil, but all of us throughout the whole wide earth have traded in our weapons of war. We have exchanged our swords for plowshares, our spears for farm tools. . . . Now we cultivate the fear of God, justice, kindness, faith, and the expectation of the future given us through the crucified one. . . . The more we are persecuted and martyred, the more do others in ever increasing numbers become believers.

—Justin Martyr, *Dialogue with Trypho* 11.3, 11.4

"And they shall beat their swords into ploughshares . . ." In other words, they shall change into pursuits of moderation and peace the dispositions of injurious minds, and hostile tongues, and all kinds of evil, and blasphemy. . . . Christ is promised not as powerful in war, but pursuing peace.

—Tertullian, *Against Marcion* 3.21

Evil ought not be repaid with evil. . . . It is better to suffer wrong than inflict it. . . . We should rather shed our own blood than stain our hands and our conscience with that of another.

—Arnobius, *Against the Pagans* 1.6

We cannot endure even to see a person put to death, though justly. . . . To see a person put to death is much the same as killing them. . . . How, then, . . . can we put people to death?

—Athenagoras, *A Plea for the Christians* 35

Renewing Our Minds

For the early church and Christians today, baptism is one of the signs that we are being washed from all the pollution of sin and violence, and we rise from the waters of baptism as a new creation. "The old has gone, the new is here" (2 Cor. 5:17). We are a new creation—our old life, our old ways, and our propensity to violence and resentment and revenge are being transformed. And it is a process. As Scripture says, we are working out our salvation "with fear and trembling" (Phil. 2:12).

If we are enjoined then to love our enemies, . . . whom have we to hate? If injured, we are forbidden to retaliate lest we become as bad ourselves. . . . Better to be slain than to slay.

—Tertullian, *Apology* 37

The Creator puts his prohibition on every sort of man-killing by that one summary precept, "Thou shalt not kill."

—Tertullian, *On the Spectacles* 2

To us it is not lawful either to see or to hear of human slaughter.

—Minucius Felix, *The Octavius of Minucius Felix* 30

He nowhere teaches that it is right for His own disciples to offer violence to anyone, however wicked.

—Origen, *Against Celsus* 3.7

Stephen . . . did not ask for vengeance for himself, but for pardon for his murderers.

—Cyprian, *On the Good of Patience* 16

The whole world is wet with mutual blood; and murder, which in the case of an individual is admitted to be a crime, is called a virtue when it is committed wholesale. Impunity is claimed for the wicked deeds, not on the plea that they are guiltless, but because the cruelty is perpetrated on a grand scale.

—Cyprian, *To Donatus* 6

The early Christians were radically committed to nonviolence in every form. Ron Sider has collected many of the writings of early Christians in a great book called *The Early Church on Killing* that displays how strong and consistent the first Christians stood against violence. Some of them were violent people before they got dipped in the baptismal waters and washed in the blood of Jesus.[13]

This transformation of our minds and souls doesn't just happen on its own. A gun doesn't just turn into a plow. It has to be formed, molded, shaped. Transformation takes time and patience, and it must endure the flames of the forge.

Jesus used the word *disciple* purposefully, as it shares the same root as the word *discipline*. "Whoever wants to be my disciple must deny themselves and take up their cross and follow me" (Matt. 16:24).

We have to work out our soul muscles just like we work out our physical muscles, or else our hearts become unhealthy, physically and spiritually. Our muscles can atrophy, and so can our compassion.

We need holy habits for our spirits just like we need healthy habits for our bodies. Jesus isn't the only one trying to make disciples out of us; the NRA and Wall Street and Hollywood are battling for our minds too. So are the gun profiteers who want to add 3 million guns each year to the arsenal that already plagues our streets.

The Scriptures tell us, "Set your minds on things above, not on earthly things" (Col. 3:2). A lot of pastors interpret that to mean that we shouldn't listen to secular music or watch R-rated movies. We used to burn our cassette tapes and CDs, and now we delete our media from the cloud. But it's much deeper than that. This is about putting good things into our minds so that good things come out of us. Like Jesus said, "A good man brings good things out of the good stored up in his heart, and an evil man brings evil things out of the evil stored up in his heart. For the mouth speaks what the heart is full of" (Luke 6:45).

When we pray and practice the other spiritual disciplines—like Sabbath keeping, solitude, simplicity, and fasting—we begin to purge ourselves of the toxic stuff of earth and fill ourselves with the holy stuff of heaven, sort of like when we stop eating junk food and eat real food.

Part of renewing our mind is filling it with stuff that is not violent. As the apostle Paul wrote to the Philippians, "Finally, brothers and sisters, whatever is true, whatever is noble, whatever is right, whatever is pure, whatever is lovely, whatever is admirable—if anything is excellent or praiseworthy— think about such things. . . . And the God of peace will be with you" (Phil. 4:8–9). We can begin to put this into practice by simply asking God to fill us with the fruit of the Spirit, the things that Scripture says God is like: love, joy, peace, patience, kindness, goodness, faithfulness, gentleness, and self-control.

Once when I (Shane) was speaking at a military school on the subject of discipline, I addressed the discipline of nonviolence and how it is something we learn and practice and train ourselves in. I ended by inviting each cadet to pray that the fruits of the Spirit would live inside of them and flow through them into the world. I said each one of them slowly. Afterward, one of the cadets came up to me with tears in his eyes. He said, "As you said each of those, I realized how foreign they are to the military world. . . . That is not what they are teaching us and training us to be." He went on to say he wasn't sure that he could continue to be in the military, as his commitment to Christ seemed to be colliding with his military service. He wasn't sure that he could love his enemies and simultaneously prepare to kill them. Could he carry a cross in one hand and a gun in the other?

Just as violence is something that we learn, so is nonviolence. And just as violence is something we absorb, even unintentionally, such absorption also happens in the church.

It's why we surround ourselves with saints, hoping they will rub off on us and inspire us to live in countercultural ways.

It is also why we surround ourselves with people who are nonviolent. Community is key. Jesus once said, "Where two or three gather in my name, there am I with them" (Matt. 18:20). We are called to live in community, and it is one of the ways we can resist the dominant forces in this world that teach us fear and prejudice and violence. Community, and spiritual community in particular, is how we create positive peer pressure.

Teenagers always hear about peer pressure as a bad thing, and it can be. But it can also be a good thing. We can surround ourselves with people who remind us of the kind of person we want to be, and they rub off on us. When we surround ourselves with a critical mass of people who create a gravity that moves us toward God and toward our best self, we are unstoppable.

Just like coals of a fire—or a forge—keep each other warm, so do we. The deeper, longer, and more dense the coals are, the hotter the fire is. And everyone knows the way to put a fire out is by scattering the coals. We can't keep the fire alive inside of us without staying near to the source of the fire and by staying near to others who fan the flame in us.

God said it's not good to be alone. Jesus lived in community, sent the disciples out in pairs, and said whenever two or three of us gather in his name, he is with us. We are better together. Community is about realizing that others can make us better, that we can do more together than on our own. The good news is that we are not alone in the world.

So if you want to be more courageous, hang out with courageous people. If you want to be more generous, hang out with generous people. On the other hand, if you want to be more narcissistic, hang out with self-absorbed folks and watch reality TV. That too will rub off on you.

If you want to be less violent, hang out with folks who are nonviolent.

Surround yourself with people who remind you of Jesus—and they will move you closer to him.

CONSIDER
This

MATTHEW 5

Now when Jesus saw the crowds, he went up on a mountainside and sat down. His disciples came to him, and he began to teach them.
He said:

"Blessed are the poor in spirit,
for theirs is the kingdom of heaven.
Blessed are those who mourn,
for they will be comforted.
Blessed are the meek,
for they will inherit the earth.
Blessed are those who hunger and thirst for righteousness,
for they will be filled.
Blessed are the merciful,
for they will be shown mercy.
Blessed are the pure in heart,
for they will see God.

> Blessed are the peacemakers,
> > for they will be called children of God.
> Blessed are those who are persecuted because of righteousness,
> > for theirs is the kingdom of heaven.

"Blessed are you when people insult you, persecute you and falsely say all kinds of evil against you because of me. Rejoice and be glad, because great is your reward in heaven, for in the same way they persecuted the prophets who were before you.

"You are the salt of the earth. But if the salt loses its saltiness, how can it be made salty again? It is no longer good for anything, except to be thrown out and trampled underfoot.

"You are the light of the world. A town built on a hill cannot be hidden. Neither do people light a lamp and put it under a bowl. Instead they put it on its stand, and it gives light to everyone in the house. In the same way, let your light shine before others, that they may see your good deeds and glorify your Father in heaven.

"Do not think that I have come to abolish the Law or the Prophets; I have not come to abolish them but to fulfill them. For truly I tell you, until heaven and earth disappear, not the smallest letter, not the least stroke of a pen, will by any means disappear from the Law until everything is accomplished. Therefore anyone who sets aside one of the least of these commands and teaches others accordingly will be called least in the kingdom of heaven, but whoever practices and teaches these commands will be called great in the kingdom of heaven. For I tell you that unless your righteousness surpasses that of the Pharisees and the teachers of the law, you will certainly not enter the kingdom of heaven.

"You have heard that it was said to the people long ago, 'You shall not murder, and anyone who murders will be subject to judgment.' But I tell you that anyone who is angry with a brother or sister will be subject to judgment.

Again, anyone who says to a brother or sister, 'Raca,' is answerable to the court. And anyone who says, 'You fool!' will be in danger of the fire of hell.

"Therefore, if you are offering your gift at the altar and there remember that your brother or sister has something against you, leave your gift there in front of the altar. First go and be reconciled to them; then come and offer your gift.

"Settle matters quickly with your adversary who is taking you to court. Do it while you are still together on the way, or your adversary may hand you over to the judge, and the judge may hand you over to the officer, and you may be thrown into prison. Truly I tell you, you will not get out until you have paid the last penny.

"You have heard that it was said, 'You shall not commit adultery.' But I tell you that anyone who looks at a woman lustfully has already committed adultery with her in his heart. If your right eye causes you to stumble, gouge it out and throw it away. It is better for you to lose one part of your body than for your whole body to be thrown into hell. And if your right hand causes you to stumble, cut it off and throw it away. It is better for you to lose one part of your body than for your whole body to go into hell.

"It has been said, 'Anyone who divorces his wife must give her a certificate of divorce.' But I tell you that anyone who divorces his wife, except for sexual immorality, makes her the victim of adultery, and anyone who marries a divorced woman commits adultery.

"Again, you have heard that it was said to the people long ago, 'Do not break your oath, but fulfill to the Lord the vows you have made.' But I tell you, do not swear an oath at all: either by heaven, for it is God's throne; or by the earth, for it is his footstool; or by Jerusalem, for it is the city of the Great King. And do not swear by your head, for you cannot make even one hair white or black. All you need to say is simply 'Yes' or 'No'; anything beyond this comes from the evil one.

"You have heard that it was said, 'Eye for eye, and tooth for tooth.' But I tell you, do not resist an evil person. If anyone slaps you on the right cheek, turn to them the other cheek also. And if anyone wants to sue you and take your shirt, hand over your coat as well. If anyone forces you to go one mile, go with them two miles. Give to the one who asks you, and do not turn away from the one who wants to borrow from you.

"You have heard that it was said, 'Love your neighbor and hate your enemy.' But I tell you, love your enemies and pray for those who persecute you, that you may be children of your Father in heaven. He causes his sun to rise on the evil and the good, and sends rain on the righteous and the unrighteous. If you love those who love you, what reward will you get? Are not even the tax collectors doing that? And if you greet only your own people, what are you doing more than others? Do not even pagans do that? Be perfect, therefore, as your heavenly Father is perfect."

Fifteen

THE THIRD WAY OF JESUS

> The Christian ideal has not been tried and found wanting. It has
> been found difficult; and left untried.
>
> —G. K. Chesterton

CATHOLIC PRIEST DANIEL BERRIGAN is a legendary peace-maker. Among other things, he helped launch the Plowshares movement, where people of faith take tools and symbolically disarm nuclear weapons, enacting the prophecy of Micah and Isaiah that inspires us. I (Shane) had the chance to be with Dan on several occasions before he passed in 2016. One of Dan's many great lines is, "The making of peace is at least as costly as the making of war—at least as exigent, at least as disruptive, at least as liable to bring disgrace and prison and death in its wake."[1] Dan often said, of Jesus's call for us to suffer and die, "If you want to follow Jesus, you had better look good on wood."[2] His life taught me a lesson: it's not that we have tried the way of the cross and it has failed us, but that we never really tried the cross. We have found it impractical, or maybe we think it is a great idea for individuals to aspire to, but it's unrealistic to think we can really "love our enemies" in a world of ISIS and mass shooters. Let's take a moment to consider the narrow way of Jesus that leads to life.

Scientists say that our brains develop in ways that have predictable patterns.[3] Some of the responses are involuntary, like blushing when we are embarrassed or tearing up when something moves us. Even what moves us to tears can be developed and shaped by our experiences and memories. But what's interesting is that some of our brain tissue actually forms in ways that determine our responses to situations. It may be why kids are so imaginative and older folks often have a hard time doing something different than how they've done it for thirty years.

I heard one scientist say that it's kind of like our brain develops "ruts" and we are conditioned to stay in the ruts, to act in predictable ways. In fact, one mark of intelligence is the ability to think outside the box, to solve problems in innovative ways.[4]

Criminologists say that one of the quickest ways to diffuse violence is with surprise. Those who commit violence depend on the predictability of their victims. They are mentally prepared for their victims to respond in one of two ways—fight or flight. They are expecting the victim to try to run or to fight back. But when victims do something unconventional that surprises them, it throws the whole plan out of whack, and they are caught off guard. In many cases, the surprise response creates a liminal space that allows just enough psychological wiggle room for miracles to happen—or, some would contend, a perfectly reasonable, scientific mental response.[5]

It's often called "the third way of Jesus."

Michael Nagler, in his excellent book *Is There No Other Way?*, gives example after example of creative ways people have reacted to violence or assault that has disarmed the aggressor or saved their lives. Some of them are not that intentional or complicated. For example, one woman was so petrified and startled by a burglar that her first response was to ask him what time it was. It threw him off, and by the time he answered her, she had already started lecturing him about how he was better than what he was doing, could have just asked her for help, should have never broken the window, and was rude for coming in the middle of the night. Before long, she had cooked him a meal and sent him on his way. Now, not all the stories end like that. But there are lots of stories where folks have been even more intentional and remained steadfast in their faith and committed to the way of the cross—and amazing things happened.

Author and professor Walter Wink does brilliant work demonstrating the creativity Jesus has in his teaching in the Sermon on the Mount with the familiar "turn the other cheek" verse. Wink points out that Jesus was not suggesting that we sadistically let people step all over us. Jesus taught enemy-love with imagination. He gave three specific examples of how to interact with our adversaries. In each instance, Jesus was pointing us toward something that disarms others. He taught us to refuse to oppose evil on its own terms. He invited us to transcend passivity and violence by finding a third way.[6]

First, when hit on the cheek, turn and look the person in the eye. Do not cower down, and do not punch them back. Make sure they look into your eyes and see your sacred humanity, and it will become increasingly harder for them to hurt you.

This relates to a second example. Only the poor were subject to such abuse. If a poor person was being sued and had nothing at all, they could be taken to court for their outer garment (Deut. 24:10–13), which was not uncommon to peasants who had lost everything to wealthy landlords and tax collectors. So here Jesus was telling impoverished debtors, who had nothing but the clothes on their backs, to strip naked and expose the greed of the repo man. Nakedness was taboo for Jews, but the shame fell less on

the naked party and more on the person who looked on or caused the nakedness (Gen. 9:20–27). In essence, "You want my coat? You can have it.
You can even have my undies, but you cannot have my soul or my dignity."

Here is another instance of dealing with the troubles of everyday life: "If
anyone forces you to go one mile, go with them two miles" (Matt. 5:41). This
may seem like a strange scenario, but for first-century Jews it was a common
occurrence to be asked to walk a mile with a soldier. With no Humvees or
tanks, soldiers traveled by foot and carried large amounts of gear, so they
were dependent on civilians to carry their supplies. Plenty of zealots were
probably listening to Jesus and shook their fists in the air when he asked
them to walk with a soldier. Roman law specified that civilians had to walk
one mile, but that's all. In fact, going a second mile was an infraction of the
military code because one mile was the limit (not to mention that it was
simply absurd for a Jew to befriend an occupying soldier and want to walk
an extra mile with him). It is a beautiful scene to imagine a soldier asking
for his backpack but the person insisting on another mile. This would force
the soldier to get to know them, not as an enemy, but as a person. The Jew/
Christian could talk with them and woo them into the movement with love.

In each of these instances, Jesus is teaching the third way. It is here that
we see a Jesus who abhors both passivity and violence; the third way is
neither submission nor assault, neither fight nor flight.[7] But all of this only
makes sense when we realize that Jesus is not talking about the best ways
to successfully win the age-old battle to restrain evil. He redirects this urge
by saying, "Do not resist an evil person"; he has an entirely different way of
viewing evil (Matt. 5:39). This third way teaches that "evil can be opposed
without being mirrored . . . oppressors can be resisted without being emu-
lated . . . enemies can be neutralized without being destroyed." This is the
prophetic imagination that can interrupt violence and oppression.[8]

If the peculiar people of God are to transform the world through fascination, it seems these amazing teachings should work at the center of it. Then

Memorial to the Lost

On November 5, 2009, a soldier entered a medical treatment building on base and opened fire using a 5.7mm semiautomatic pistol. Most of the victims who died that day were unarmed service people. Here are the names of the thirteen men and women who lost their lives in the shooting:

Michael Grant Cahill, 62

Libardo Eduardo Caraveo, 52

Justin Michael DeCrow, 32

John P. Gaffaney, 56

Frederick Greene, 29

Jason Dean Hunt, 22

Amy Sue Krueger, 29

Aaron Thomas Nemelka, 19

Michael S. Pearson, 22

Russell Gilbert Seager, 51

Francheska Velez, 21 (and her unborn child)

Juanita L. Warman, 55

Kham See Xiong, 23

FORT HOOD MILITARY POST, KILLEEN, TEXAS (APRIL 2, 2014)

Less than five years later, it happened again at Fort Hood. A lone shooter opened fire on colleagues on base on April 2, 2014. The weapon used was a .45 caliber semiautomatic pistol. By the end of the spree three men had lost their lives and several others were injured. Here are the names of those who died that day:

Daniel M. Ferguson, 39

Timothy W. Owens, 37

Carlos A. Lazaney-Rodriguez, 38

we can look into the eyes of a centurion and see not a beast but a child of God, and then we can walk with that child for a couple of miles. Look into the eyes of tax collectors as they sue you in court, see their spiritual poverty, and give them your coat. Look into the eyes of the ones who are hardest for you to like, and see the One you love. For God actively loves all people and sends rain to water the fields of both the just and the unjust (Matt. 5:45). That's why enemy-love is the only thing Jesus says that makes a person like God—perfect.

I (Shane) have a friend who was on a train and had a knife pulled on her. The man said, "Here's the deal: you're going to give me your bag, get off at the next train station, and not say a word."

He picked the wrong person. My friend, a petite woman, may have looked like the perfect target. But he didn't know who he was messing with. She is a spitfire activist from Brazil whom I've seen tell off police officers when they were acting out of line. She looked back at this man trying to mug her and introduced herself. She told him about the photos and addresses of her loved ones in Brazil, the contents of the bag he had rudely demanded. She went on to tell him there was nothing of value to him in the bag, and he most likely wanted money instead of photos. So then she said, "In my pocket is $20, which I am glad to share with you. I will give it to you, and then you can get off at the next stop and not say anything." And so it went.

I (Mike) have a friend who was living by herself when a man broke into her house. She got out of bed and, in her best teacher voice, sternly told the man, "Get out of my house. You do not have permission to be here." And he left.

Another friend arrived home after a church event, expecting his wife, who drove separately, to be just behind him. He heard a knock on the door. Thinking his wife's hands were full, he opened the door only to find a man with a gun and a fake police jacket who immediately put him facedown on the floor with a gun to his head. Another man entered and began searching the house. My friend told them he had no weapons and that he was not a person of violence. After not finding what they were looking for, they left. It turned out to be a case of mistaken identity. The person they were after parked his car between two houses, and they picked the wrong one. Had my friend's instinct been to react with violence, it's more than likely he wouldn't be here today. His wife arrived soon after the men had left. **De-escalation is an undervalued nonviolent skill.**

Such stories can be frightening to imagine. And it's scenarios like these and other what-ifs that motivate many gun owners. But we must not let these scenarios occupy our imaginations to a degree that is out of proportion with their actual occurrence. There is nothing wrong with being concerned about keeping yourself and your family safe. But we need to refocus our imagination on what that might look like. This is what the prophets are talking about when they say we train for war no more and we no longer learn how to make war. We plot for peace. We engage in the practice of de-escalation of everyday interaction and do not plan violence for the intruder who may possibly be hurting our grandma. We can train for those situations too, but let's not obsess over them. De-escalation of the small things helps keep the big events from happening. We are training our hearts and our brains in the way of Jesus, in the way of nonviolence. The saints must start small with peacemaking, by loving those right next to them and treating their critics like they would like to be treated themselves.

I (Shane) recently heard another story from some of my friends at Christian Peacemaker Teams, who train in nonviolence, learning to de-escalate situations, observe, and respond to crises in some of the most troubled conflict zones in the world. One place they work is Hebron, where the Israeli military has established checkpoints that disrupt the lives of local Palestinians. One day, a Palestinian man was passing through a checkpoint with Israeli soldiers. They began to physically abuse him. He was pushed to the ground, and it looked like he could be beaten to death. A young Palestinian woman interrupted the scene, yelling at the man on the ground. "You forgot the baby. Here. You must take him. This is your baby." She put the baby in his arms and left abruptly. The man sat stunned, holding the child in his arms, and the soldiers did not know what to do. Eventually, they stormed off, muttering under their breath. The man sat there in the street with the baby, too weak and stunned to move. My friends hung around long enough to see the woman return and retrieve the baby. She approached the man and he gently lifted the baby into her arms as they laughed with relief. They had never met, but that woman's courage and creativity may have saved his life.

We get another glimpse of extreme love in the musical *Les Misérables*, in which a priest allows a vagrant, Jean Valjean, to stay in his home, only to get knocked unconscious and robbed. The next day, the authorities catch Valjean and drag him before the priest. When they say Valjean claimed that the priest had given him the silver goods in his bag, the priest instinctively, beautifully, says, "I am so thankful you have come back, as you forgot the candlesticks." As the guards release Jean Valjean, the priest whispers in his ear, "With this, I have ransomed your soul."

Sounds good (musicals can do that for you), but it's not that easy. When someone stole a power drill from my (Shane's) community in Philadelphia (and we all knew who), we didn't run after the person with the drill bits saying, "Hey, my friend, you forgot these." We wanted to teach the person a lesson of justice rather than a lesson of love.

We can learn from other examples. We have to seek out these heroic, creative stories of compassion: they don't often make the news. Our kids aren't playing video games that teach de-escalation and conflict resolution. But we need these redemption stories. We think of the kids in Rwanda who lived through the genocide. In one of the most violent genocides in modern history, Hutus were killing Tutsis—nearly one hundred thousand per day. A group of Hutus entered one of the schools and asked the kids to separate—Hutus on one side, Tutsis on the other. The kids refused, held hands, and said, "We do not have Hutus and Tutsis. . . . We only have sisters and brothers." They lived through that fearsome event.

Of course, not all stories end that well.

This kind of love takes courage—it's willing to risk death rather than take someone's life. This love is not sentimentality but the kind of love Dorothy Day spoke of, saying that it is such a harsh and dreadful thing to ask of us, but that it's the only answer.[9] The only thing harder than hatred is love. The only thing harder than war is peace. Until the courage that we have for peace surpasses the courage that we have for war, violence will continue to triumph and imperial execution rather than divine resurrection will have the final word.

Pope Francis says it well: "How I wish that all men and women of good will would look to the Cross if only for a moment! There, we can see God's reply: violence is not answered with violence, death is not answered with the language of death. . . . The uproar of weapons ceases and the language of reconciliation, forgiveness, dialogue, and peace is spoken."[10]

It would be irresponsible not to be very clear that when you follow Jesus and the way of the cross, you might get killed. But you also might get killed owning a gun. The important thing is to stay faithful. And we know, thanks to the martyrs, that our death—if we die as Christ did, loving even our enemies—can be as much a witness to our faith as our life. As Tertullian once wrote, in the blood of the martyrs is the seed of the church.[11] Whenever a Christian is killed, ten more are born.

The same can be said of terrorism or violence—when we return violence for violence, we add fuel to the fire. One soldier in Iraq said he went into the military to fight terrorism but ended up realizing that they were creating it. He said that every person killed made the fire of rage and violence even stronger. Martin Luther King Jr. said, "Darkness cannot drive out darkness; only light can do that. *Hate cannot drive out hate; only love can do that.*"[12]

It is possible to look at history and argue that violence works. You can also look at examples in history where it looks like nonviolence has worked and others where it seems nonviolence has failed. The question for those of us who follow Jesus is this: Which looks the most like Christ?

Ron Sider said it well when he spoke at the Mennonite World Conference in 1984:

> Unless we are prepared to risk injury and death in nonviolent opposition to the injustice our societies foster, we don't dare even whisper another word about pacifism to our sisters and brothers in those desperate lands. Unless we are ready to die developing new nonviolent attempts to reduce international conflict, we should confess that we never really meant the cross was an alternative to the sword. Unless the majority of our people in nuclear nations are ready as congregations to risk social disapproval and government harassment in a clear call to live without nuclear weapons, we should sadly acknowledge that we have betrayed our peacemaking heritage. Making peace is as costly as waging war. Unless we are prepared to pay the cost of peacemaking, we have no right to claim the label or preach the message.[13]

His words helped give birth to the Christian Peacemaker Teams, who are doing some of the most daring and redemptive work when it comes to this third way of Jesus.

Imagine what would happen if we had as much courage for peace as we have had for war? What if we had as many monuments and holidays designated for the heroes of peace as we have for the heroes of war? What if we channeled all our incredibly gifted minds to devise ways to de-escalate violence rather than crafting new drones and bombs and guns? What if we were as willing to die for the cross as we have been willing to die for the sword? What if . . .

sixteen

LOVE CASTETH OUT FEAR
(AND FEAR CASTETH OUT LOVE)

Love is more powerful than all the weapons in the world.

—Mural in Afghanistan

IN ALL OUR TALK ABOUT ORIGINAL SIN, sometimes we forget original innocence. By that we mean that every human is created in the image of God. We have love in our DNA. There is something in almost every person that recognizes that killing is wrong. That's why violence is something we have to learn. In the military, folks are trained to desensitize. But in all of us there is an inherent resistance to killing. One study of folks in war has shown that only 15 to 20 percent of the individual riflemen in World War II fired their weapons at an exposed enemy soldier—because there was an internal resistance to killing.[1]

Soldiers experience a "moral injury," or an injury of conscience. Undoubtedly, it is part of why the suicide rate of soldiers and veterans is so high (twenty per day) and why many of our veterans suffer from mental illness, are homeless, and are overrepresented on death row.[2] One veteran told me (Shane), "When you kill someone, it does something to the one holding the gun too." We are the victims of our own violence. When we take a life, something inside of us dies. Thank God that mercy and grace and all the beautiful things of the Spirit are big enough to heal the wounds of violence. God is healing both the victims and the perpetrators.

James, a RAWtools gun donor, event host, gun disabler, and conspirator for nonviolence, wasn't always that way. He grew up angry and fearful, which turned into violence. He enlisted in the military and came home in shambles, suffering from PTSD. It wasn't until he was introduced to the red letters (Jesus's words) in the New Testament that he became focused on loving instead of hating. His PTSD episodes dropped significantly after this lifestyle change. Sadly, he lost a friend and brother who couldn't overcome the effects of war. His friend used a pistol to take his life. We turned it into a garden tool.[3]

It is interesting to see how the evolution of violence has included a buffer for our conscience. We've moved from sword fighting, to muskets that shot one hundred yards, to guns that can shoot five miles. Obviously part of that is for the safety of the shooter, but there's no doubt that part of the evolution of weapons has been our aversion to killing up close. When it comes to the death penalty, anonymity and distance are important in the execution of human beings. Firing squads even to this day (the last firing-squad execution in the US was in 2010) have a blank bullet, called the "bullet of conscience," in one of the guns of the shooters.[4] It really would take only one shooter to execute someone, but having multiple shooters, one of which has a blank bullet, gives the conscience its needed wiggle room.

Now we have snipers and sharpshooters and drone operators. Disturbing new research shows the moral injury suffered by drone operators, those who can do remote-control killing and then go to Starbucks for coffee.[5] The effect that it has on one's soul is immeasurable. I (Shane) have heard drone operators talk about what it did to them, including how their brains had a difficult time discerning reality from fantasy. One drone operator even told me that the language they use for the kills has evolved. "We no longer call them casualties; we call them 'splats,'" because it looks like a fly being squashed on the computer screen. What must it be like to be responsible for hundreds of "splats"? It all does something to our souls. We just aren't meant to kill.

A FEAR-FILLED PEOPLE

- Nearly half of Americans are afraid that our nation will end up in a nuclear war with North Korea.
- Forty percent—almost half!—of Americans are afraid they will be a victim of a shooting.
- About 75 percent of Americans admit they fear government corruption under the current Trump administration.
- More than 70 percent of Americans fear that robots will take over their lives.

We are a fear-filled people.

Original sin is just as real as original innocence. Inside each of us is a sinner and a saint at war with each other. And each day we get to choose who we want to be. Just as our gifts and skills can be used for life, they can also be used to take life. And our imaginations continue to devise new ways of taking lives.

Fear and Love

We might instinctively think that the opposite of love is hate. But maybe the opposite of love is fear, which the Bible has a lot to say about. Pastor Rick Warren has said that God encourages people to "fear not" 365 times in the Bible, one for each day of the year.[6] That number might be disputed, but what is not is that "fear not" is one of the most reiterated commandments in Scripture. There are hundreds of verses about fear.

Love does not have room for fear. And fear does not make space for love. Just as love casteth out fear, fear also casteth out love. We can see all

Isaiah 41:10
Jeremiah 1:8
Jeremiah 30:10
Exodus 14:13
Psalm 27:1
Psalm 56:3
Psalm 56:4
Psalm 56:11
Psalm 118:6
Proverbs 3:24
Zepheniah 3:13
Zechariah 8:13
Zechariah 8:15
Matthew 1:20
Matthew 10:31
Matthew 17:7
Matthew 28:5
Matthew 28:10
Luke 1:13
Luke 2:10
Luke 1:30
Luke 5:10
Luke 8:50
Luke 12:4
Luke 12:32
John 12:15
John 14:27
Acts 18:9
Micah 4:4
Acts 27:24

"THERE IS NO FEAR IN LOVE. BUT PERFECT LOVE DRIVES OUT FEAR." [1 JOHN 4:18]

around our country what happens when a society is driven by fear rather than love. Fear leads to violence. When we create policies out of fear rather than love, we do really terrible things to people. We build walls and ghettos and prisons and defense shields. We rip apart families of immigrants and refugees, and threaten to send young people back to countries they have never lived in, all because of fear. Let's stop there. One of the most dangerous things in the world is powerful people who are afraid.

When fear drives us, we often turn to our guns. Some of our laws, like the stand-your-ground laws, do not even require an actual threat in order to justify taking someone's life—they require only a perceived threat. Perceived fear is actually a legal defense in court. The color of someone's skin may be enough to create fear. Jordan Davis, an African American teenager in Florida, was killed by a white man who said his music was too loud while he was in his car at a gas station. The man who killed Jordan said he feared for his life. Jordan was unarmed of course, as was everyone in the car with him. Though in this case the man was found guilty, presumption of fear is nevertheless a legitimate legal defense in several states.

Jordan is not alone. We know the names of the victims of gun violence, racial violence, and police violence.

A Parable for Our Time

There's a story Jesus told that has everything to do with the world we live in, and it is a reminder that violence is not a new thing, even though guns may be the newest expression of violence. It's a story that may be familiar to some and new to others. Try to hear it with fresh ears and allow it to speak into our current context.

It comes from the Gospel of Luke (10:25–37). The backdrop for the bit we will read is that a very religious man, an "expert in the law," is trying to "test" Jesus, so he asks what someone must do to "inherit eternal life." Jesus

MEMORIAL TO BLACK BODIES

This is a list of only some of those killed by law enforcement officers with guns. There are others who were killed without guns, such as Sandra Bland, Eric Garner, and Freddie Gray.

Michael Brown
Tamir Rice
Philando Castile
Alton Sterling
Kathryn Johnston
Walter Scott
Jordan Edwards
Terence Crutcher
Rekia Boyd
Laquan McDonald
Akai Gurley
Eric Harris
William Chapman II
Samuel Dubose
Jeremy McDole
Ricky Ball
Jamar Clark
Keith Lamont Scott
Anthony Lamar Smith
Sylville Smith
John Crawford III
Dontre Hamilton
Rumain Brisbon
Ezell Ford
Botham Shem Jean

Shane Claiborne

Michael Brown memorial

_____ (for the new victims that are being added constantly)

answers in characteristic Jesus style. He tosses the question back and says essentially, "You tell me" (we're paraphrasing a little bit). After all, the man is an expert in the law. The man replies by saying that we need to love God and love our neighbors. Jesus says, "Exactly." Part of the point seems to be that sometimes we know what we need to do—we just don't do it.

The man goes on. "Who is my neighbor?" Perhaps he is also wanting to know who is exempt from love and compassion. Who is he not required to love or care for?

Then comes our story.

In reply Jesus says:

A man was going down from Jerusalem to Jericho, when he was attacked by robbers. They stripped him of his clothes, beat him and went away, leaving him half dead. A priest happened to be going down the same road, and when he saw the man, he passed by on the other side. So too, a Levite, when he came to the place and saw him, passed by on the other side. But a Samaritan, as he traveled, came where the man was; and when he saw him, he took pity on him. He went to him and bandaged his wounds, pouring on oil and wine. Then he put the man on his own donkey, brought him to an inn and took care of him. The next day he took out two denarii and gave them to the innkeeper. "Look after him," he said, "and when I return, I will reimburse you for any extra expense you may have."

Which of these three do you think was a neighbor to the man who fell into the hands of robbers?

The story has some beautiful treasures of wisdom, especially in relation to our conversation here about guns and violence.

The religious folks do nothing in response. They pass by on the other side of the road. Perhaps they offered their "thoughts and prayers" as they passed by. Maybe they were late for a trustee meeting or for a worship service. Maybe they were scared, as the bandits could have still been around. Maybe they were just timid.

Then comes the Samaritan—who by every definition was a social outcast. Samaritans were shunned for many reasons. They were a mixed-race people and were frowned on for that reason. They didn't have orthodox religious beliefs about how and where you worship God. Good religious folks didn't even associate with Samaritans, and they went out of their way to avoid them. But here the Samaritan is the one who responds—the unlikely hero. The text actually says he was moved with *compassion*, a word that we have made too fluffy. It meant that you were stirred in the deepest part of your gut, moved in the innermost part of your being. A better translation might be "gut-wrenched." And so he goes to great lengths to take care of the man, at great cost and perhaps grave risk to himself. The point is clear—the people who you think would respond, the quintessential religious folks, are apathetic (just as many of our politicians and preachers are today). And the hero is someone we might least expect. He may not have had all the right beliefs, but he had the right compassion. He may not have had everything right in his head, but he had things right in his heart. The true test of our faith is how it moves us in compassion for the most vulnerable people in our world. And don't forget, it was an expert in the law trying to test Jesus that provoked the story to begin with.

It's also noteworthy that we don't know much about the person in the ditch, the victim of violence. The two major ways of identifying his cultural or social identity have been stripped away. He is naked, so any clues his clothing could offer about his origin or religion are gone. And he is unconscious, so his dialect, language, or accent couldn't help either. That seems to be part of the point. All that we know is that the person is human. He is a child of God made in the image of God. We don't know his politics or theology or social status or sexual identity. To put it in today's terms, he could be a Republican or a Democrat, a conservative or a liberal, a Muslim or a Jew, a Nazi or an anti-fascist. He could have been a saint or a rival gang member. But his life matters. He is made in the image of God.

Memorial to the Lost

This shooting took place in Shane's neighborhood, around the corner from where he lives. It happened during the writing of this book. Two men armed with a military-style assault rifle and a handgun opened fire, shooting more than thirty bullets in less than one minute, killing twenty-three-year-old Anthony Torres and thirty-eight-year-old Jose Vega.

These two men died less than fifty yards from where Shane had been writing this book about ending gun violence. This memorial is to them and to all the people who are alive right now but whose lives will be cut short by gun violence in the days ahead unless we take action.

Shane Claiborne

Finally, the story also reminds us that we need to walk the streets where people get beat up. The story would have never happened if people had not been walking the Jericho road. Some of us have moved away from the streets where people get beat up. We need to lean into the places of pain and draw closer in proximity to the suffering of our world. It's possible to live our lives unaffected by violence because we have insulated ourselves from the suffering of the world. The story also reminds us that people get beat up at inconvenient times. No doubt, the Samaritan was on his way somewhere, just like the religious folks, but the Samaritan allowed his agenda to be interrupted by another person's tragedy. We must interrupt our business as usual to respond to the tragedies and not grow numb to the pain.

Martin Luther King Jr. adds one more powerful dimension to this story that is directly relevant to our gun conversation. He invites us to remember that we are all called to be the good Samaritan and lift our neighbor out of the ditch. But after you lift so many people out of the ditch, you start to think: maybe we need to reimagine the road to Jericho so that people don't keep ending up in the ditch to begin with. Here are King's words: "We are called to play the Good Samaritan on life's roadside. . . . One day we must come to see that the whole Jericho Road must be transformed so that men and women will not be constantly beaten and robbed. . . . True compassion is more than flinging a coin to a beggar. It comes to see that an edifice which produces beggars needs restructuring."[7]

Fearless Love

From the earliest days of the gun, fear has been one of our biggest motivations. Even the gun capitalists know that. Here is one contributor to *Shooting Industry* magazine, writing about how to use fear to drive gun sales: "Customers come to you every day out of fear. Fear of what they read in the newspaper. Fear of what they watch on the 11 o'clock news. . . . Your job, in no uncertain terms, is to sell them confidence in the form of steel and lead. An impulse of fear has sent that customer to your shop, so you want a quality product in stock to satisfy the customer's needs and complete the impulse purchase."[8] Wally Arida, the publisher of *Gun Games* magazine, put it like this: "We scare them to buy one gun. Now let's get these people shooting their guns and educate them to buy more guns. We should tell them, 'Now you have your defense gun, now you need to buy a gun to shoot this sport and another one to shoot this other sport.'"[9]

Violence often begins with fear. But never forget: love casteth out fear. Much of our theology is fundamentally rooted in fear. It's about escaping suffering, either in this life or in the next. Fear of hell. Fear of dying. Fear of scarcity. Fear of not making a difference in the world. So we have fire-and-brimstone preachers of old (and yes, there are a few left today), and we have the prosperity preachers of today talking about how God wants you to be rich, to find your destiny, to "name and claim" your blessings from God. As you take away the layers, you find very little that resembles Jesus and the

THINGS MORE LIKELY TO KILL YOU THAN A TERRORIST

Have you ever thought about whether your fears are justified? Or whether the media has accurately portrayed what—and who—is really dangerous?

A study done by the Cato Institute showed that while many people in the US fear being killed by a refugee terrorist, only three deaths in the past forty years have been attributed to terrorists who were refugees. That's a chance of one in 3.6 billion that a refugee will kill you. More likely you will be killed by stairs, police, roller coasters, hot water, a bathtub, swing sets, state execution, texting, cows, TVs, or a vending machine falling on you.

Of all Americans killed by terrorists, nearly twice as many were killed by home-grown terrorists than by Islamic terrorists—and most of those terrorists were white.

Even outside the US, for every one American killed by an act of terror anywhere in the world in a year, more than 1,049 US citizens died from guns.

teachings of the early church. They were fearless. They mocked death with their courage and their enemy-love.

When I (Shane) was in Afghanistan, I learned the difference between fear and being scared. I went with a group of incredible peacemakers from around the world. Several of them have been nominated for the Nobel Peace Prize, and one—Mairead Maguire—actually won it for her work in Northern Ireland. We were meeting with some women who had escaped unimaginable circumstances under the Taliban. Mairead was sharing her riveting, heroic life story, and one of the women asked, "Were you ever scared?" Mairead paused and responded tearfully: "Of course we were scared. But being scared is different from fear. Being scared is perfectly normal. Fear is when we let being scared stop us from what love requires of us."

We live in a scary world. Evil is real. Violence is everywhere and has many forms—hate crimes, bullying, sexual assault. But the promise of Scripture is that "perfect love drives out fear" (1 John 4:18). *Fear doesn't stand a chance against love.*

Jesus came to set us free from fear, from possessions, even from ourselves. He said things like, If you want to find your life, lose it (Matt. 10:39). If you want to be free, look at the lilies and the sparrows (Matt. 6:26–30). If you want to enter the kingdom of God, come in like a child (Mark 10:15)—vulnerable, free from fear, not worried about tomorrow, entirely dependent on God. We adults get so obsessed with our lives, our possessions, our need to make a difference, that we lose sight of why we are here. We are here to worship God with our whole lives.

St. Francis, one of history's great peacemakers, is attributed with saying that the more stuff we have, the more clubs we need to protect it. Our possessions begin to possess us. And so do our guns. To live without fear is to live like Jesus—like a child, like the lilies and the sparrows.

That doesn't mean everything is going to turn out perfect. Look how things ended up for Jesus: he got killed. Peter got killed. Most of the disciples and many of the early Christians got killed. But their lives were seeds. The movement of God's love spread through their deaths just as it spread through their lives.

Consider Martin Luther King Jr. He was fearless. He knew there was a force stronger than fear in the world. He knew that love would wear evil down.

> We can stand up before our most violent opponent and say: . . . Do to us what you will and we will still love you. . . . Throw us in jail. . . . Threaten our children and bomb our homes, and as difficult as it is, we will still love you. But be assured that we will ride you down by our capacity to suffer. One day we will win our freedom, but we will not only win freedom for ourselves, we will so appeal to your heart and your conscience that we will win you in the process. And our victory will be a double victory.[10]

Grace has the power to dull even the sharpest sword. There is something in the world that is more powerful than fear: love. Nothing in the world—nothing—is more powerful than love.

seventeen

COMMONSENSE CHANGE

> We don't need gun control; we need bullet control. If the bullets cost $5,000 you are going to think twice before you shoot someone. And there will be a lot less stray bullets and innocent bystanders.
>
> —Chris Rock

AFTER THE SANDY HOOK SHOOTING, President Barack Obama made a passionate plea for simple, "commonsense" gun legislation. At the time, 90 percent of Americans backed him up. But the 10 percent held the 90 percent hostage. It is perhaps the biggest, most surprising victory of the NRA in its history.

We have not found the balance between an individual's right to have a gun and the public's right to life, liberty, and the pursuit of happiness—both of which are American treasures.

We cannot honestly, accurately continue to call gun deaths and mass shootings "accidents." The dictionary offers this definition of the word *accident*: "an unforeseen or unplanned event or circumstance," or "an unexpected happening causing loss or injury which is not due to any fault or misconduct."[1]

By definition, it is difficult to say that thirty-eight thousand gun deaths per year are "accidents." After all, it is entirely predictable, easily foreseeable, and very much expected, just as much as it is tragic, heart-wrenching, and horrific.

What we so often call an accident may more accurately be called willful negligence, which, it is worth noting, is a crime. The truth is, we cannot prevent all violence, from guns or from anything else. We can't stop all suicides. But we can save *some* lives if we want to—perhaps many lives.

Here are a few things we might consider: Might it be time to say that automatic and high-capacity semiautomatic guns do not belong on our streets? Semiautomatic guns make up a large portion of guns available for purchase. Should we limit a gun, and the clips that hold the bullets, to, say, six bullets? When would anyone really need to fire off one hundred rounds in one minute? Some guns are designed to kill as many people as possible in as little time as possible. Maybe it's time to put them in museums. Or better yet, turn them into farm tools.

Maybe we can also explore new technology, like smart guns. We've sent people to the moon—we can use our brilliant minds and skilled engineers to improve gun technology in order to save lives. Smart guns have a trigger that recognizes the fingerprint of the designated owner, and without the fingerprint verification, the gun will not shoot. This would eliminate as much as 80 percent of gun crimes, which is the number of those crimes done with lost or stolen guns.[2] This feature would also prevent accidental shootings by kids and by guns that are left out irresponsibly, like my (Shane's) friends in elementary school when one killed the other while playing cops and robbers with his dad's gun.

One idea that has worked in other countries is keeping guns locked until they are needed for hunting or sport. Guns could be used on a monitored system, similar to an alarm system for your home. Or they could be held in a regulated storage facility and signed out as needed. This might also make the home a safer place, since so many deaths happen by firearm suicide and accident. It could be instrumental in curbing the massive rates of suicide by gun, since we saw that studies show many suicides by gun are impulsive, done within a matter of minutes. When there is even a small degree of separation from the gun, it can be what saves someone from taking their life.

A good question is, What makes sense as a prerequisite for owning a gun? Should there be training, safety classes, a license, something similar to what you need to drive a car? Maybe a periodic renewal process and even consequences that come if you develop a criminal record or disability, also similar to a car?

Hopefully many of us can agree that research is a good thing. Whether it is for cancer or opioids or guns, research helps us understand what we are up against and what has been effective in saving lives over time. The restrictions placed on the Centers for Disease Control and Prevention have prohibited it from studying gun violence and need to be removed and the funding restored. It is absurd that we do not have recent data because the gun lobby has forced the data to be destroyed, since what it shows could be bad for the firearms industry. Imagine if automobile makers halted all research on car safety. We'd be outraged. And very unsafe.

We need to do better. **We've been better at protecting guns than people, and it is time to change that.** We are certainly not suggesting that people should not have the right to own a gun for hunting or sport or even for protection. We are suggesting that the rights of a mass murderer, a violent boyfriend, a disgruntled employee, a violent extremist, or a serial killer should not infringe on the rights of everyone else. We will never get rid of all violence. It goes all the way back to Cain and Abel. But we can join much of the industrialized world in making sure that gun violence is rare and we can work hard to make it rarer and rarer—as opposed to it being a normal, everyday reality that claims the lives of over one hundred of God's children each day in our country.

We can save lives. We should be embarrassed to lead the industrialized world in gun deaths. We cannot prevent all deaths, but we can certainly prevent some.

Under a Fig Tree

Laurie Works, a survivor of the New Life Church shooting in 2007 (see chap. 9), helps those who have been through the trauma of gun violence, and she teaches what it looks like to "sit under a vine and fig tree in fear of no other" (see Mic. 4:4). It doesn't mean that we are never afraid, but it means that we heed the call of the angels to "fear not." It means that we acknowledge when we are in a state of fear and confront the fear. It's an active stance of participating in life as it happens. It's the practice of giving and not taking. Whether it's under a fig tree or on our porch, when we see a stranger or a neighbor approaching, we don't retreat and lock our door until they pass. We say hello and offer them a beer or lemonade. We ask how they are doing. Would they like a snack for the rest of their trip? Do they need a cup of sugar? Laurie asks us to be present with each other.

Laurie is a yoga instructor. Not just any yoga, but resilience yoga. If we are in an age of cyborgs, Laurie teaches us how to be less of a cyborg. She teaches us to focus on the triggers inside of us instead of the triggers that can be an extension of us. Sitting under a vine and fig tree is a way for us to be more human.

It sounds weird, but cyborg anthropology is a real thing. It's the study of how humans interact with technology. A cyborg is an organism to which components have been added for the purpose of adapting to new environments.

Cyborg anthropologist Amber Case gave a TED talk about what this means. In traditional anthropology, "somebody goes to another country [and] says, 'How fascinating these people are, how interesting their tools are, how curious their culture is.'" Case goes on to say that "tool use, in the beginning, for thousands and thousands of years, . . . has been a physical modification of self. It has helped us to extend our physical selves, go faster, hit things harder, and there has been a limit on that." This limit is continually stretched with each progress of invention. Case talks about how now, with the advent of smartphones and computers, "what we're looking at is not an extension of the physical self, but an extension of the mental self."[3]

When we think about tools as an extension of the self, and see ourselves as a society of cyborgs, we begin to realize the truth in what philosopher Bruno Latour has said. Evan Selinger explains:

> French philosopher Bruno Latour goes [so] far as to depict the experience of possessing a gun as one that produces a different subject [i.e., a cyborg]: "You are different with a gun in your hand; the gun is different with you holding it. You are another subject because you hold the gun; the gun is another object because it has entered into a relationship with you." While the idea that a gun-human combination can produce a new subject may seem extreme, it is actually an experience that people (with appropriate background assumptions) typically attest to, when responding to strong architectural configurations. When walking around such prestigious colleges as Harvard and the University of Chicago, it is easy to feel that one has suddenly become smarter. Likewise, museums and sites of religious worship can induce more than a momentary inclination towards reflection; they can allow one to view artistic and spiritual matters as a contemplative being.[4]

Depending on what we connect our body to or surround ourselves with, we are then capable of different outcomes. Case extends this into anthropology and how our tools also shape our culture and society. It's why foreign cultures are baffled at the amount of firearms that are present in America. Guns are now part and parcel of American culture. They are part of the genetic makeup of our society. Technology changes us. Think about how different human interactions are now that we have cell phones and airplanes. Owning a gun can also change the way humans interact, even how they process their rage or pain. Technology can determine what we think is possible, and it sets the limits of our imaginations for better or worse.

Despite all this, despite all our inherited sins, God became incarnate. God put skin on and came to us in Jesus. God did not come as a robot, or even as a powerful king. God came as a vulnerable child, as a refugee fleeing persecution. God came as one of us.

We ourselves can't be afraid of being incarnate, of being present, in another's life. We can't be afraid of our neighbors or of what they may require of us. We can't be afraid of being the shoulder to cry on. We can't shy away from hearing someone vent about their day. We can't be afraid to be confronted about our own behavior, either. We need to be able to confront one another without the expectation of violence.

This is how we change the dynamic of the gun debate. We sit and listen to each other. We hear the stories and the background about why we are gun owners and why we are not. We talk about how the handgun moved from unloaded in a safe to loaded and under the pillow. We listen to the circles of mothers who sit across from us and ask, "Then what do I do if you say I shouldn't own a gun? How do I defend my family as a single mom?"

We need to ask these mothers what we can do to help them. Sometimes we'll need to put our body in harm's way for their sake. It means we need to talk to peers. We need to be accountable for our influence in a community. The "least of these" are asking for help to protect their family, and currently our society points them to a gun—even though it's more likely that someone in their house will be harmed by that gun than any intruder will be.

In the fall of 2018 RAWtools partnered with the Pikes Peak Restorative Justice Committee and invited Kay Pranis to teach a three-day workshop on circle training. It's a process in which people gather to listen to each other. It can be linked to conflict mediation and restorative-justice practices where harm is repaired, but it's also a listening tool to prevent harm from happening, because it provides a space for people to hear each other out.

At the same time, RAWtools also launched a RAWpower workshop that trains groups in active bystander intervention, nonviolent confrontation skills, and other practical means of de-escalation. How transformative would it be for churches and community organizations to be known for resolving conflict in their neighborhoods? Christians have a long way to go to fix their reputation of being a major gun-owning group and of being judgmental toward other people. Some of these circle processes may need to start with lament and repentance. It's also important to recognize that the roots of mediation run deep in the Native American tradition. We have a lot to learn from the people who came before us, especially people we actively removed from their homes and land.

Many people have stopped imagining what it might look like to keep a community safe without guns. Guns corrupt the idea from the beginning. As long as they are a possible means of safety, we cannot fully imagine the alternative. With or without guns, we will encounter trauma. There is no way to avoid it. There are no walls high enough or guns fast and powerful and smart enough to keep it from happening. When trauma happens, we turn to the tools at our disposal to heal from it. But we can also grow from it.

We simply aren't using our imaginations! We must go back to the forge. We must offer our self, our families, and our communities to be transformed by the idea of not letting fear dictate our life. Oh, and bring your guns to be transformed too. You'll discover how far the ripple effects of gun violence go. You'll become a storyteller instead of a debater.

Memorial to the Lost

On August 5, 2012, a mass shooting took place at the gurdwara (Sikh temple) in Oak Creek, Wisconsin, where the shooter fatally shot six people and wounded four others. The shooter took his own life. The shooter was an American white supremacist and Army veteran. All of the dead were members of the Sikh faith. These are the names of the victims lost that day:

Paramjit Kaur, 41

Satwant Singh Kaleka, 65

Prakash Singh, 39

Sita Singh, 41

Ranjit Singh, 49

Suveg Singh, 84

Listen to the stories of what each of you is afraid of. We've found that the root of all our fears is exploitation—powerlessness. We're afraid that someone else will take advantage of our situation. More than that, we see it happen every day, mostly in forms that don't involve gun violence. We see it happen in domestic violence. We see it happen in race relations. We see it happen in corporate greed. We see it happen in power vacuums. We see it happen in the marginalization of the LGBTQ community.

The complicated part of gun violence is that it intersects with so many other issues. You can't talk about gun violence without talking about the issues behind each occurrence. Maybe that's what is so hard. We don't want to talk about those things. We don't want to talk about how people in marginalized communities are committing suicide. We don't want to talk about why gangs are formed. And we don't want to do the work of healthy community development. We don't need fancy homeowners associations; we need a radical commitment to love of neighbor *and* enemy.

Politics of Love

Policies affect people, and so one part of loving our neighbor is thinking about and advocating for policies that help them flourish.

To be fully transparent, I (Shane) have a lot of distaste for partisan politics and have some major reservations about putting too much power or hope in politicians. I don't naturally think of looking to the government to solve our problems—the government seems to be perpetuating many of them.

We need to think through what an authentic political imagination looks like for Christians, who are citizens of heaven (Phil. 3:20) and who are in the world but not of the world. We can't legislate love. Laws, as important as they are, cannot change the evil of a human heart.

The Catholic activist Ammon Hennacy once said, "The good people don't need [laws], and the bad people don't obey them."[5] So in the end, I don't look to the government as my messianic hope. I already have a Savior. But I do think we can expect the government to limit harm. I often think of voting as damage control.

Politics has its root in the Greek word *polis*, which means "city." This is why we have cities to this day that end in "polis," like Indianapolis and Minneapolis. *Metropolis* means "mother city." *Cosmopolitan* is "world city." And the Greek term *politēs* means "citizen"—politics has to do with how people relate and live together in society. So when we think about politics, it's helpful to think about people.

We need to take the word back from the folks who have hijacked it. No one has much love for "politics," but we do care about people. And all of us, especially those of us trying to follow Jesus, are deeply concerned about the *politēs*. Loving our neighbors requires thinking about how we live together well, how we organize our shared life, how we protect our most vulnerable citizens, and how we protect life and the common good of all.

We have come to care about policies because they affect people, whom we love. Policies don't solve everything. You can't legislate love or force compassion. But policies can free people up or hold people down. They can lock people out or open doors of opportunity. Politics is not just about empty rhetoric, stale debates, and broken promises. It may be all those things too. But politics is also about real, concrete, real-time policies that affect our everyday lives.

Policies affect how we get food and water, how we care for the young and the old people in our midst. Policies shape how we live, where we live, how we educate our kids, and how we take care of the sick among us—making sure we don't have lead in our water or all get Ebola and die.

So let's think of politics with fresh imagination and a little more openness. Politics is about human survival and flourishing.

We have no doubt that all of you reading this are a diverse bunch—especially when it comes to politics. Some of you think health care is the government's job, and others, not so much. Some of you probably think pot should be legal, and others might think tobacco shouldn't be. You have lots of different parties and camps, labels and categories.

We want to invite you to find common ground—by starting from the same place.

Our fundamental starting point, with guns and everything else, is this: What policies help us live well together? What's best for the most? What's good for the common good? What policies are vital for humans to thrive? We are not just thinking individualistically but as a "polis," as a people—less about "I" and "me" and more about "we" and "us." There is something that unites us that is deeper and more profound than all the stuff that divides us. Something unites us across party lines and blows all the labels and categories out of the water: our shared humanity.

We can all probably think of areas where we wish there was more regulation, and other areas where we wish there was less. How far is too far when it comes to the control we give the government? We may believe in the freedom of speech, but should we have to allow Nazis to protest on our college campuses? When does one person's freedom begin to encroach on another person's freedom? Even if you believe pornography should be legal to view in the privacy of your home, that doesn't necessarily mean you want to see a naked body on a billboard, and it doesn't mean you should be able to sell naked photos of young kids, does it?

Too many rules can stifle human flourishing, and too few rules can stifle human flourishing. Where do we need more regulation, and where do we need less? What if Wall Street had no rules? What if oil companies could dump chemicals anywhere they want? Overregulation versus underregulation is a never-ending tension in society.

Tension is a good thing. It's sort of like the trellis of a garden. If you don't have some structure for your tomatoes, they flop over and rot on the ground. If you have too much structure, it stifles their growth; you won't get many good tomatoes until you have a good structure for them to flourish on.

COMMONSENSE CHANGES

Consider these possible reforms that many gun owners and gun-violence victims agree would save lives.

- Limit the amount of handguns one person can acquire to one per month. If someone is buying more than twelve handguns in a year, they may not be making the world safer.
- Require licensing, registration, and waiting periods to allow comprehensive background checks and cooling-off periods. Before you can drive a car, you spend some time learning safety, preparing to drive, and practicing, and then you pass a test to get a license. Might this also be a good idea for owning a gun?
- Close the gun-show loophole by not making exceptions for gun-show purchases. Gun shows, too, would have to require background checks for all buyers. Crazy idea?
- Ban semiautomatic assault weapons, armor-piercing ammunition, and high-capacity cartridges. Basically, do not allow war weapons on the streets—any more than we allow grenades on the streets.
- Since most gun deaths are occurring at the hands of eighteen- to twenty-year-olds, raise the legal handgun ownership age to twenty-one. Why do we trust our youth with handguns or military service before we trust them with alcohol or the ability to rent a car?
- Advocate for new technologies and new resources that would allow government and nongovernment agencies to trace guns used in crimes and thereby protect lives.
- Eliminate the Tiahrt Amendment that requires the Justice Department to destroy records of gun buyers.
- Repeal laws that don't allow law enforcement to destroy confiscated weapons when owners have lost their right to bear arms.
- Add your own suggestion:

There are always tensions in the complex political ecosystem.

But is our current status quo working? Or could we be doing more to save even a portion of the thirty-eight thousand lives lost each year to guns? What could we do better? And what is stopping us?

We're always making adaptations in other areas of society to try to save lives—guns are one of the extraordinary exceptions. After one guy tried to set off a bomb in his shoes, we all have to take off our shoes in the airport so they can be scanned. James Atwood points out the radical steps taken when there was a threat of *E. coli*. When five people were hospitalized in the Southwest with *E. coli* found in spinach, the government immediately shut down the entire spinach industry, putting it under surveillance 24/7 and quarantining suspected farms.[6]

And yet when more than thirty-eight thousand Americans die by gunfire each year, Congress reacts to protect guns, along with their institutions, factories, distribution systems, and private sellers, which only guarantees that there will be more human sacrifices in the days to come. It's like protecting the companies that gave us *E. coli*.

We appreciate the multifaceted approach to ending gun violence. We've kept vigil. We've prayed. We've taught classes on nonviolence and conflict mediation. We've marched in the streets, made phone calls, met with gun dealers—all that important stuff.

But there comes a time when we start to think that maybe there are some things the government can do as well. For instance, the one-handgun-a-month law, which would limit the amount of handguns that one person can buy to twelve a year. It makes a lot of sense to almost everyone we've talked to, even our NRA-card-carrying family members. No one is talking about taking away hunting rifles or the pistol under the bed. It would just put a sensible limit on the number of handguns a person can buy. If you are buying more than a dozen a year, you may not be making the world a safer place—not good for the common good. And yet bills like this one get blocked over and over by a small minority of gun advocates. Should we really have that Barrett .50-caliber gun that can shoot a plane out of the sky? Does anyone need to be able to shoot one hundred bullets in one minute? Should we have bullets that are designed to penetrate a bulletproof vest of a police officer? Why does a law-abiding citizen need a silencer on their gun? These are good questions. And we can't let the few gun extremists convince us that, if we ask any of these good questions, our ultimate goal is to take away hunting rifles.

Often cities, like Philadelphia, see the carnage on their streets and set some limits, such as banning assault rifles. Cities come to the conclusion that such weapons don't belong on their streets any more than grenades do. But over and over, these laws are reversed at a state or federal level, putting more and more people at risk.

We are not talking about banning all guns. We're not talking about taking away hunting rifles or even handguns. The question we ask is this: Can we create better policies that better protect our "polities"—our people, our shared life together? How can we organize our shared common life so that we all can flourish, so that one person's freedom is not another person's bondage? What stands in the way?

Just because something is legal doesn't make it right. Slavery was legal, but that didn't make it right. Societies evolve. Laws change. There are things that are not legal now that used to be one hundred years ago. And there are things that are legal now that were illegal one hundred years ago. Some things, like the death penalty, are legal in some places and illegal in others. Places prone to drought and fire regulate fireworks.

Such regulations are not meant to be mindless, unnecessary, bureaucratic barriers. They are meant to keep people safe. To help people flourish. They exist for the common good. Limits are put on individual freedoms—like how fast you can drive or how much you can drink before driving—to create some order and organization to our common life. Few people actually want to do away with the Second Amendment and the right to have guns. Most just want it to be regulated.

Corporate Accountability

As citizens, we must be a moral conscience for those who profit from the madness of gun sales today. Perhaps one of our best strategies can be to organize and leverage consumer power against these companies and stir their conscience. It's beginning to happen even now. Walmart has voluntarily signed on to a code of conduct to try to reduce gun violence. Dick's Sporting Goods voluntarily stopped selling assault weapons and destroyed its inventory. We need to applaud these decisions and keep encouraging other gun profiteers to take steps in the right direction.

It has been incredible to watch the public outcry against the NRA create such a groundswell that some of the largest corporations in the world have severed ties: United, Enterprise, Alamo, National, Hertz, Avis, Symantec, MetLife, Wyndham, and Delta. Some of them now face lawsuits as a result.

We need courage. And imagination. Perhaps we can even incentivize good decisions like creating safer guns and new technology such as fingerprint readers for guns. We've sent people to the moon, after all, and have drones that can operate like bumblebees—we've got this!

PARKLAND TEENS INSPIRE GUN OWNER TO TURN IN AR-15

Mic ✓
@mic

Because of the Parkland teens, Chris Shields just decided to give up his AR-15. Now, the 18-year member of the military and owner of 10 guns, is calling on fellow gun owners to give theirs up too.

2:49 PM - Feb 24, 2018

♡ 55K ○ 24.9K people are talking about this

We also need to call out the lies, as the students of Marjory Stoneman Douglas High School in Florida are doing, who are famous now for the saying "We call B.S." when they hear the gun industry cover up truth to make money. The very idea that we need guns to protect us from all the guns sure sounds like a marketing pitch from people who are out to sell as many guns as possible, no matter what the hidden costs to life are.

The industry that creates one of the most dangerous products you can buy enjoys total immunity when it comes to any responsibility for harm done. Toy weapons have more regulations than real weapons. If you shoot your friend's eye out with a Nerf gun, you can sue Nerf. But not so with a Winchester rifle or an AR-15. It's time for the weapons industry to take the same responsibility as every other industry. Guns should not be exempt from safety requirements and wise regulations. Likewise, gun shops that sell guns irresponsibly should be accountable for the lives that are lost. If a liquor store turns a blind eye to a minor buying alcohol or sells booze to someone they know is already drunk, they can be held responsible.

Guns should not be exempt from safety requirements, responsible regulations, and sensible restrictions. Think about cars. We've learned some lessons in how to keep people safe from this technology, which can be deadly. We've added seat belts. We require driver's licenses. You need to register your car and, at least in some states, have it checked for emissions periodically. You need to pass a test before you drive one. There is a limit to the alcohol you can consume before operating one. There are speed limits. And on and on. As society evolves, so do our laws—for instance, some states now make it illegal to text and drive, a new law responding to new technology.

Certainly, irresponsible people still break the rules. But you don't get rid of traffic laws because some people refuse to stop at red lights. Someone can still acquire a car, legally or illegally, and deliberately use it as a weapon, driving into a crowd like we've seen far too often, from Charlottesville to London to Manhattan. We will never stop all violence and murder. People can use a gun to kill, and they can use a van—or a hammer or, apparently, a spoon. At a conference, I (Shane) mentioned how guns exponentially increase the capacity of a person who wants to destroy life, saying, "After all, it's hard to kill someone with a spoon." Later I got a flood of emails with links to murders or attempted murders by spoon (mostly in prisons), though I have yet to find a mass murder by spoon. Our goal is to save as many lives as possible. If we knew, just hypothetically, that people were ten times more likely to die from a car in the United States than in Canada or Japan or Belgium, we're pretty sure we'd work around the clock to solve the problem.

The noteworthy difference between automobiles and guns is that guns are designed to kill. Cars *can* kill but are not *made* to kill. It is all the more reason that the gun industry does not deserve the unprecedented immunity it currently enjoys and exploits.

That "freedom" is killing us.

Eighteen

REIMAGINING THE WORLD

> What if this darkness is not the darkness of the tomb, but the darkness of the womb?
>
> —Valarie Kaur

THERE IS SOMETHING POWERFUL, transcendent, and mystical about seeing a gun transformed into something else. When you take the hammer and begin beating, you can hear the sharp thump of metal on metal, rattle and echo. You can feel the impact up your arm and through your body. There's something sacramental about the process, like how some Christians believe God is present in the Communion table as we eat the bread and drink the wine. There is something holy about seeing an instrument of death transformed into an instrument of life—when swords become plows, when guns become garden tools.

Chopping an assault rifle

With every gun we transform at RAW-tools, it feels as if the world becomes a little safer, as if the heaviness of death lingering over us like a cloud lifts a little. We've beaten guns into plows all over the country. We've done it on the altars of churches during worship. We've done it live on stages at convention centers. We've done it in the streets, in garages, in parking lots, and in backyards. We were forging peace.

We did a cross-country trip and turned 9mm pistols into plows in honor of Trayvon Martin. A tool from those guns was auctioned off for thousands of dollars, which we proudly gave to the Trayvon Martin Foundation.

There is one event, though, that we'll never forget. We teamed up with Terri Roberts, the mother of Charlie Roberts, who was responsible for the Nickel Mines shooting nine years ago. When she picked up a hammer and beat on the barrel of a gun, it wasn't just about the gun. Terri (who passed away in 2017) was a living witness that God is transforming hearts, not just metal, as she developed a relationship with the Amish families that baffled the mind and healed the soul.

Terri Roberts, mother of the Nickel Mines shooter, transforming a gun

Rosanna, a young girl who survived the shooting, is in a wheelchair and eats with a feeding tube. Every other Thursday, Terri visited Rosanna and helped bathe her, read with her, and sang with her. Spending time together helped heal the wounds of the tragedy. Every time Terri visited, she was confronted with the damage her son caused. But she was also reminded that violence does not have to get the last word. And each year in October,

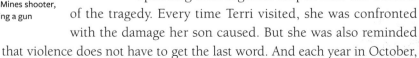

WE HAVE A DREAM

We have a dream. A dream for every city and rural town in America to have a designated drop spot where people can bring their guns to be donated and repurposed. Each of those locations will have tools and people trained to disable guns. The guns will be disabled and made inoperative as they arrive. Then, scattered throughout the country will be mobile blacksmithing trailers that can collect the gun parts to transform them into tools. We could hire citizens returning from incarceration and thereby create jobs. Then we can bring those tools back to the communities to be instruments of life. Let's do it.

around the time of the shooting, she had tea with the Amish mothers as a way of remembering the season and redeeming it.[1]

As we worked with Terri on transforming the gun, she reminded us that we need God to transform both our hearts and our nation. As we beat on the barrel of that gun, it felt like we were participating in the redemptive work of God in healing hearts and healing streets—beating guns into plows, turning hatred into love.

Growing Hope

It is our prayer that God will heal our heart problem and that some of our politicians will have the courage to help heal our gun problem. The varying perspectives have too long demonized the "other" perspective to the point of no longer being able to dialogue. Many of us have family all across the spectrum. Let's tell our stories and move forward together. The prerequisite for a solution to end gun violence is that it does not involve more violence and death.

So we ask you to follow the wounded healers to a table. Maybe that table is the top of the anvil, or maybe that table is at your neighbor's home or at a local park. Go to the table and tell your story. Celebrate your story.

We'd celebrate a community that no longer trains for war but that plots for peace, a community that doesn't let fear dictate how neighbors interact with one another and whether they welcome a stranger. These celebrations can be built with tools that have been transformed from a past we are ready to leave behind. We can recognize the past through the ritual transformation of swords into plowshares.

We've seen activists and police officers take the hammer together. We've had folks shot by guns and folks who have shot people with guns beat on the same anvil.

We've seen standing side by side at the forge Republicans and Democrats, war vets and pacifists, old people and young kids, homeless folks and survivors of genocides, politicians and anarchists, conservatives and liberals, Christians and atheists, Jews and Muslims, war hawks and peaceniks—the forge brings us all together. We have hope for a world free from fear and violence. We stand together around the warmth of the forge and dream of a new world.

We've seen veterans transform the guns they brought back from war.

We've had guns donated that people had intended to use to kill themselves. We've transformed assault rifles and handguns.

We may not all agree on politics, or even on the gun control debate, but something feels right about taking the hammer together and transform-

ing an AR-15 into garden tools. It unites former adversaries and creates common ground where there's previously been misunderstanding. It creates a space to pray, to breathe, to heal. The fire of the forge softens every heart.

As we embarked on this adventure of transforming weapons, we started getting stories and images sent to us from around the world of others doing the same thing.

The fire of the forge
is a refining fire

Memorial to the Lost

On October 2, 2006, a man entered a one-room Amish schoolhouse in Lancaster County, Pennsylvania, with a 9mm semi-automatic handgun. By the end of the shooting, five young girls had been killed and several others injured.

The response from the Amish community at Nickel Mines was one of anguish but also forgiveness. They fascinated the world as they comforted the family of the shooter and attended his funeral to mourn the loss of his life as well as their own children. They also shared the donations given to them with the shooter's family, to help support the children of the shooter. In the end the families found a way forward together that stunned the world. We detail this story further in this chapter, and we have had the privilege of finishing a gun transformation with Terri Roberts, the mother of the shooter.

The schoolhouse was demolished and a new school building was constructed with the name New Hope School. Here are the names of the lives lost that day:

Naomi Rose Ebersol, 7

Marian Stoltzfus Fisher, 13

Lena Zook Miller, 8

Mary Liz Miller, 7

Anna Mae Stoltzfus, 12

Sami Rasouli

Peace Day in Najaf, Iraq

One guy made a guitar out of handguns. Someone else made a bicycle.

Another fellow in Mozambique made a saxophone out of a semiautomatic.

Our friends in Iraq poured guns into the street and ran over them with a steamroller, crushing them into oblivion. And they let kids drive.

In the holy city where Jesus was born, the "little town of Bethlehem," violence is still real. Tear-gas canisters are regularly fired at Palestinians there. Some creative minds came together and began gathering the canisters and making Christmas ornaments out of them, creating jobs for Palestinian families and making something beautiful out of something terrible.

People are hearing the ring of the anvil. It echoes both to those lost to gun violence in the past and to those fed from community gardens in the future. We must not let guns beat us any longer. They do not need to be a part of the weave of the fabric of our society.

Christmas ornament made from a tear-gas canister, https://peaceparcels.com

There is a way to beat guns. And it addresses the triggers in our hearts as well as the triggers in our streets. We need everyone at the table. Those who believe we don't have a gun problem need to be at the table teaching us how to deal with our heart problem. Those who believe we do have a gun problem need to be at the table offering creative ways to move our society away from nearly unfettered access to guns and toward responsible gun ownership. We must not allow ourselves to be cold and removed from the softening of the forge. We must lean into each other, without fear of the other.

Forging a New World

The paradox we find ourselves in is that we use the same resources to make tools for either kingdom—the kingdom of this world and God's kingdom. We use wood and metal to make guns and to make plows. In fact, in my (Mike's) local library the reference section has gunsmithing literally book-ended with woodworking and blacksmithing. There aren't any books near there on plowshares—yet.

This captures an important part of the power of going from swords to plows. We're not doing this because the world is devoid of the threat of violent conflict and it is now safe to lay down our weapons. We're doing it because transformation occurs when you turn swords into plows in spite of the threat of violence. This transformation is a witness to a way of life that says, "I am not only committing to never taking life from a person; I am also committing to keeping the tools that do so out of my life and habits."

This is when I hear, "Hammers and cars kill people too—why not make them into plowshares while you're at it?" This is a more deflective than constructive argument. I know that somewhere in history there has been someone killed with a garden tool, and I've been told that RAWtools' garden tools would make good blunt-force killing objects. All of this misses what changing swords to plows is about. The more we surround ourselves with plows, the more we will find ourselves creating life. The more we produce with plows, the more we see others as recipients of that (sometimes actual) produce. The more we surround ourselves with guns, the more we will see people, animals, and things as targets. *Our imaginations work with the tools we have.* We expand on the possibility of our tools by reinventing them. Sometimes we use things in ways they were not designed for. The empire of violence can take almost any device and weaponize it. The kingdom of God needs to be better at taking any device and transforming it. This is the hard work ahead. To make something new often leaves little that resembles the past, but it also opens new possibilities for the future.

Violence is all around us. But so are the seeds of a new world.

Some will say, "All we can do is pray." That's a lie.

We can pray, and we must pray. Gun violence is spiritual.

But we can do more than pray. We can organize. We can dialogue. We can boycott and keep vigil. We can write letters and make phone calls and go to jail for nonviolent civil disobedience. Gun violence is social and political and economic; it is also a moral issue.

We need courage. We need to turn up the volume for love and life. After a string of mass shootings with AR-15s (and similar guns), we teamed up in Philadelphia for an event called "Demand the Ban," focusing on assault weapons, those military-style guns that are designed to kill as many people as possible as quickly as possible, and that are often the weapon of choice for mass shooters.

Shane Claiborne

Marching at Demand the Ban

We took an AR-15 and turned it into a plow. Then hundreds of us marched together, carrying the plow and wearing T-shirts with the names of hundreds of people killed by assault rifles. We delivered the plow as a gift to Senator Pat Toomey. And we were determined not to leave until he agreed to champion the current bill before Congress that would ban assault weapons. He hasn't agreed yet, but we are hopeful. We sat in the rain, singing and praying. And thirty-three of us were arrested (the charges were later dropped). As the police led us into a bus where we were held, many of them thanked us for what we were doing

And they shall
beat their swords into
beautiful
things . . .

Shane arrested at Demand the Ban

and the spirit in which we did it. After all, AR-15s kill police officers too. We're still hoping Senator Toomey and other politicians will have courage, but we will not wait on them. We cannot wait.

When we ask God why thirty-eight thousand lives are lost each year, God may throw the question back to us: Why do we allow it?

When we ask God to move a mountain, sometimes God hands us a shovel. Or an anvil. One of the greatest mysteries of our faith is that, for some strange reason, God does not want to change the world without us.

When we make changes in society, we need rituals to help us transition. Sometimes we repeat them to build habits.

Turning swords to plows is a ritual. It's a ritual of celebration and a ritual of lament, a ritual of commitment and a ritual of letting go. It's a ritual of wounded healing so that there are no more wounds.

And it's a party. The anvil rings and rejoices with the roar of the forge as we all lean into each other. There is dancing too. And music is played on instruments made from weapons of war. Slides on handguns are made into tuning forks.

We are different with a plow in our hands than we are with a gun in our hands. We move from a life of individualism into a life of community, away from a life where we can dictate what we do, no matter the season, into a life that is centered on seasons: harvest, planting, resting, plowing. Seasonal life brings seasonal celebrations, a life where we no longer enter seasons of mass shootings but instead enter seasons of great harvests.

Mike at the anvil

Shane Claiborne

So we come back to the blacksmith shop. The place where every tool can trace its origin to. It's a place where we are given the opportunity to create anew. It's a place with an opportunity for a fresh start. We can use steel to make plows, and we can use guns as source material. And when the guns run out, nation will not lift up sword against nation, because there will be no swords left to lift. Turning swords to plows brings us away from the immediate, instant, and fatal consequences of empire and toward the patient, seasonal, and creative consequences of Jesus's kingdom.

The Bible doesn't end with us returning to the garden of Eden. It ends with the vision of the new Jerusalem—a city that has been healed and restored, with a river of life and a tree of life and a gate that is left open to all. How beautiful it is that the Bible begins in a garden and ends in a city! The new Jerusalem is a city brought back to life, a city where the gates are left open and kids can play without fear.

If that is the end of the story, it should influence the way we live now: we live into the future the prophets foretold and we inaugurate the new world. Let's keep the forge ready and the fire hot as we wait for the next person to disarm. There are about three hundred million guns in the US. That'll take a while. But imagine the tools, art, and musical instruments we can make with all that metal.

The prophets spoke of beating guns into plows. And we are committed to building the world the prophets dreamed of. The prophets leave us with a final glimpse of that world: Zechariah says "the city streets will be filled with boys and girls playing" (Zech. 8:5). And Zephaniah adds, "No one will make them afraid" (Zeph. 3:13). Don't forget: according to the prophets, the vision of a renewed world ends with the wolf and the lamb living together, and the lion and the calf lying down together, and nation not rising up against nation, and kids playing without fear, and people no longer learning violence. But it begins with us. It is not the kings and presidents and politicians who lead the way to peace. It is the people who rise up, refuse to kill, and begin beating their weapons into garden tools. **We are the people we are waiting for.**

May we be the midwives of a better world—through our prayers, by our lives, and with our hammers.

ACKNOWLEDGMENTS

These little sections in which authors give shout-outs to everyone who helped them with the book often get skipped over by readers, like the credits at the end of a movie. But we want you to know that we literally could not have done this book without the love and support and gifted talents of these friends.

This book would be incomplete without thanking them.

First, we are grateful beyond words for Shane's wife, Katie Jo, and Mike's wife, Hannah (who came up with the name for RAWtools). And Mike's two boys who have lovingly welcomed him home after traveling. We are thankful for our families, some of whom are gun owners who have patiently read this book with an open mind, and especially for Mike's dad, Fred, who helped found and shape RAWtools from the very beginning. We'd like to thank Angela Scheff, Rebekah Devine, and Adam Bacher, as well as Eric Salo, Jeremy Wells, Jim Kinney, and our whole team at Brazos Press. Without them this book would not be nearly as beautiful or as poignant or as precise as what you have here (our first draft had over seven hundred fact checks!). We are grateful for the countless artists and photographers, especially Pedro Reyes, Paul Villinski, and Esther Augsburger (who have made so many marvelous things from guns), who have opened the imaginations of many people.

Acknowledgments

There are so many who have contributed to this book—with their stories and lives, their expertise and imagination: Sharletta Evans, Laurie Works, Benjamin Corey, Michael McBride, Lucy McBath, Sami Rasouli, Fr. Michael Pfleger, Bryan Miller, and Rob Schenck. We've built on the great scholarship of folks like James Atwood, Pamela Haag, Vox, Everytown for Gun Safety, and many others to whom we are indebted. And we're thrilled and honored about the film *Beating Guns* produced by our pal Rex Harsin, released alongside this book.

Finally, to the everyday peacemakers who are committed to beating guns into plows and reimagining the world, you inspire us: folks like Christian Peacemaker Teams, Preemptive Love Coalition, Mennonite Central Committee, Beth-El Mennonite Church, About Face, Veterans for Peace, Campaign Nonviolence, PICO's Live Free Campaign, Moms Demand Action, the Movement for Black Lives, the students from Parkland, Pax Christi, Fellowship of Reconciliation, Global Immersion Project, Heeding God's Call, CeaseFire, the Plowshares movement, and so many others.

NOTES

Introduction

1. We are indebted to James Atwood for his tireless scholarship and work on gun violence, particularly his books *America and Its Guns: A Theological Exposé* (Eugene, OR: Cascade, 2012) and *Gundamentalism* (Eugene, OR: Cascade, 2017). We have built on some of his ideas and his scholarship here and are grateful for his friendship and support. Few folks have done a better job at shaping the conversation around God and guns than Atwood. We highly recommend reading his work.

Chapter 1: Turning Weapons into Farm Tools (and Other Lovely Things)

1. Centers for Disease Control and Prevention, "Fatal Injury Reports, National, Regional and State, 1981–2016," WISQARS (Web-based Injury Statistics Query and Reporting System), updated February 19, 2017, https://webappa.cdc.gov/sasweb/ncipc/mortrate.html.

2. Mekialaya White, "Colorado Springs Group Holds Silent Walk, Sending Loud Message about Gun Violence," KRDO (News Channel 13), updated July 15, 2016, http://www.krdo.com/news/local-news/colorado-springs-group-holds-silent-walk-sending-loud-message-about-gun-violence/35507160.

3. Dale Frederickson, "Fragile Trigger" (poem), in *Keeping Pulse* (n.p.: Samizdat Creative, 2016), available at https://youtu.be/loH5w5Uroho.

4. Rachel Yehuda et al., "Holocaust Exposure Induced Intergenerational Effects on FKBP5 Methylation," *Biological Psychiatry* 80, no. 5 (September 2016): 372–80, https://doi.org/10.1016/j.biopsych.2015.08.005.

Chapter 2: The Mess We Find Ourselves In

1. Eli Rosenberg, "A Teen Missed the Bus to School. When He Knocked on a Door for Directions, a Man Shot at Him," *Washington Post*, April 13, 2018, https://www.washingtonpost.com/news/post-nation/wp/2018/04/13/a-teen-missed-the-bus-to-school-when-he-knocked-on-a-door-for-directions-a-man-shot-at-him.

2. Nicole Flatow, "Father Shoots and Kills 14-Year-Old Daughter, Saying He Mistook Her for Burglar," ThinkProgress, December 24, 2013, https://thinkprogress.org/father-shoots-and-kills-14-year-old-daughter-saying-he-mistook-her-for-burglar-a4bf5e6d3290.

3. This statistic is from E. G. Krug, K. E. Powell, and L. L. Dahlberg, "Firearm-Related Deaths in the United States and 35 Other High- and Upper-Middle-Income Countries," *International Journal of Epidemiology* 27, no. 2 (April 1998): 214–21, cited in James Atwood, *America and Its Guns: A Theological Exposé* (Eugene, OR: Cascade, 2012), 160.

4. Libby Nelson and Javier Zarracina, "A Shocking Statistic about Gun Deaths in the US," Vox, December 4, 2015, https://www.vox.com/policy-and-politics/2015/12/4/9851102/gun-deaths-us-children. Vox used information from Erin Grinshteyn and David Hemenway, "Homicide, Suicide, and Unintentional Firearm Fatality: Comparing the United States with Other High-Income Countries, 2003," *Journal of Trauma* 70, no. 1 (January 2011): 238–43, https://doi.org/10.1097/TA.0b013e3181dbaddf.

5. Centers for Disease Control and Prevention, "Fatal Injury Reports, National, Regional and State,

1981–2016," WISQARS (Web-based Injury Statistics Query and Reporting System), updated February 19, 2017, https://webappa.cdc.gov/sasweb /ncipc/mortrate.html.

6. More American citizens were killed with guns in the eighteen-year period between 1979 and 1997 (651,697) than all the US servicemen and women killed in all the foreign wars since 1775 (650,858). Atwood, *America and Its Guns*, 52.

7. Arwa Mahdawi, "Sacha Baron Cohen's Scheme to Arm Toddlers Isn't Far from Reality," *Guardian* (US edition), July 16, 2018, https://www .theguardian.com/us-news/2018/jul/16/sacha-bar on-cohen-guns-children-toddlers-who-is-america -reality.

8. Ryan Sit, "More Children Have Been Killed by Guns since Sandy Hook Than U.S. Soldiers in Combat since 9/11," *Newsweek*, March 16, 2018, https://www.newsweek.com/gun-violence-children -killed-sandy-hook-military-soldiers-war-terror-9 11-848602.

9. Gregg Zoroya, "Suicide Surpassed War as the Military's Leading Cause of Death," *USA Today*, October 31, 2014, https://www.usatoday.com/story /nation/2014/10/31/suicide-deaths-us-military -war-study/18261185; Leo Shane III and Patricia Kime, "New VA Study Finds 20 Veterans Commit Suicide Each Day," *Military Times*, July 7, 2016, https://www.militarytimes.com/veterans/2016 /07/07/new-va-study-finds-20-veterans-commit-sui cide-each-day.

10. Lindsey Donovan, "Disgraceful Gun Bill Endangers Veterans: Army Vet," *USA Today*, March 29, 2017, https://www.usatoday.com/story/opinion/20 17/03/29/gun-bill-endangers-mentally-ill-veterans -suicide-army-vet-column/99740790.

11. German Lopez, "America's Gun Problem, Explained," Vox, May 18, 2018, https://www.vox .com/2015/10/3/9444417/gun-violence-united-sta tes-america. One source says thirty-one gun deaths per million: Kevin Quealy and Margot Sanger-Katz, "Comparing Gun Deaths by Country: The U.S. Is in a Different World," *New York Times*, June 13, 2016, https://www.nytimes.com/2016/06/14/upshot/com pare-these-gun-death-rates-the-us-is-in-a-different -world.html. Another source says 38.5 gun deaths per million: Nurith Aizenman, "Gun Violence: How the U.S. Compares with Other Countries," *Goats*

and Soda (NPR), October 6, 2017, https://www.npr .org/sections/goatsandsoda/2017/10/06/5558618 98/gun-violence-how-the-u-s-compares-to-other -countries.

12. Lopez, "America's Gun Problem, Explained."

13. Alan I. Leshner, Bruce M. Altevogt, Arlene F. Lee, Margaret A. McCoy, and Patrick W. Kelley, eds., *Priorities for Research to Reduce the Threat of Firearm-Related Violence* (Washington, DC: National Academies Press, 2013), http://nap.edu/18319.

14. National Institute of Justice, "Gun Violence," updated March 13, 2018, https://www.nij.gov /topics/crime/gun-violence/pages/welcome.aspx.

15. "Handguns for 18-Year-Olds?," editorial, *New York Times*, November 25, 2010, https://www .nytimes.com/2010/11/26/opinion/26fri1.html.

16. Lopez, "America's Gun Problem, Explained."

17. Leanna Garfield, "There Are 50,000 More Gun Shops Than McDonald's in the US," *Business Insider*, October 6, 2017, http://www.businessins ider.com/gun-dealers-stores-mcdonalds-las-vegas -shooting-2017-10.

18. Christopher Ingraham, "40 Million More Guns Than People," *Washington Post*, October 5, 2015, https://www.washingtonpost.com/news/wonk /wp/2015/10/05/guns-in-the-united-states-one-for -every-man-woman-and-child-and-then-some.

19. Gun sales for 2016 were over 4 million more than in 2015. Leonard Greene, "Record 27 Million Guns Sold across the U.S. in 2016, 4 Million More Than the Previous Year," *New York Daily News*, January 4, 2017, http://www.nydailynews.com/ne ws/national/record-27-million-guns-sold-u-s-2016 -article-1.2934554.

There were 11 million guns manufactured in 2016. Damian Paletta, "U.S. Gun Manufacturers Have Produced 150 Million Guns since 1986," *Denver Post*, February 23, 2018, https://www.denver post.com/2018/02/23/how-many-guns-are-there.

There were 9.36 million guns produced in 2015: "Number of Firearms Manufactured in the U.S. from 1986 to 2015," Statista, accessed June 6, 2018, https://www.statista.com/statistics/215395 /number-of-total-firearms-manufactured-in-the-us.

20. Harry Enten, "There's a Gun for Every American. But Less Than a Third Own Guns," CNN, February 15, 2018, https://www.cnn.com

/2018/02/15/politics/guns-dont-know-how-many
-america/index.html.

21. Rick Jervis, "3% of Americans Own Half the Country's 265 Million Guns," *USA Today*, updated September 22, 2016, https://www.usatoday.com /story/news/2016/09/22/study-guns-owners-viole nce/90858752.

22. Enten, "There's a Gun for Every American."

23. Dara Lind, "Who Owns Guns in America? White Men, Mostly," Vox, December 4, 2015, https://www.vox.com/2015/12/4/9849524/gun -race-statistics.

24. Martin Luther King Jr., "Beyond Vietnam" (sermon, New York, April 4, 1967), https://king institute.stanford.edu/king-papers/documents /beyond-vietnam.

25. This is from one of the most thorough studies of crime guns available: US Department of the Treasury, Bureau of Alcohol, Tobacco, and Firearms, "Commerce in Firearms in the United States," February 2000, http://www.joebrower.com/RKBA/RKBA _FILES/GOV_DOCS/BATF_report_020400.pdf. Also cited at Christopher Ingraham, "New Evidence Confirms What Gun Rights Advocates Have Said for a Long Time about Crime," *Washington Post*, July 27, 2016, https://www.washingtonpost.com/ne ws/wonk/wp/2016/07/27/new-evidence-confirms -what-gun-rights-advocates-have-been-saying-for -a-long-time-about-crime; Mayors against Illegal Guns, "Inside Straw Purchasing: How Criminals Get Guns Illegally," Everytown for Gun Safety, April 15, 2008, https://everytownresearch.org/reports/in side-straw-purchasing-criminals-get-guns-illegally; and Atwood, *America and Its Guns*, 170.

26. "The Truth about Gun Dealers in America," Brady Campaign and Brady Center, accessed July 23, 2018, http://www.bradycampaign.org/sites/default /files/TheTruthAboutGunDealersInAmerica.pdf.

Chapter 3: Gun History 101

1. We are grateful for the brilliant work of Pamela Haag, whose book *The Gunning of America: Business and the Making of American Gun Culture* (New York: Basic Books, 2016) was instrumental in this section on gun history and is one of the most thorough histories on guns in America. Her bibliography is seventy-three pages long.

2. Haag, *Gunning of America*, 189.
3. Haag, *Gunning of America*, 189.
4. Haag, *Gunning of America*, 354.
5. Ramon F. Adams, *Six-Guns and Saddle Leather: A Bibliography of Books and Pamphlets on Western Outlaws and Gunmen* (New York: Dover, 1969), cited in Haag, *Gunning of America*, 354.
6. Haag, *Gunning of America*, 355.
7. Haag, *Gunning of America*, 357.
8. Stegner, *The American West as Living Space* (Ann Arbor: University of Michigan Press, 1987), 69.
9. Cartwright, "The Cowboy Subculture," in *Guns in America: A Reader*, ed. Jan E. Dizard, Robert Muth, and Stephen P. Andrews (New York: New York University Press, 1999), 86–87, cited in Haag, *Gunning of America*, 201.
10. Thomas McDade, *The Annals of Murder: A Bibliography of Books and Pamphlets on American Murders from Colonial Times to 1900* (Norman: University of Oklahoma Press, 1961).
11. "Fist, feet, sticks and bricks still outnumbered guns and knives combined." Roger Lane, *Murder in America: A History* (Columbus: Ohio State University Press, 1997), 129, cited in Haag, *Gunning of America*, 418n1.
12. Haag, *Gunning of America*, 355.
13. Haag, *Gunning of America*, 13.
14. Haag, *Gunning of America*, 109.
15. Haag, *Gunning of America*, 53.
16. Haag, *Gunning of America*, 34.
17. Haag, *Gunning of America*, 30.
18. Haag, *Gunning of America*, 63.
19. Haag, *Gunning of America*, 29.
20. Henry Barnard, *Armsmear: The Home, the Arm, and the Armory of Samuel Colt* (New York, 1866), 198, https://books.google.com/books?id=BEE BAAAAQAAJ.
21. "How I Invented Maxim Gun—Hiram Maxim, Outbreak of World War Moves Veteran American to Describe for the Times His Epoch-Making Invention," *New York Times*, November 1, 1914, cited in Haag, *Gunning of America*, 36.
22. Haag, *Gunning of America*, 104.
23. Haag, *Gunning of America*, 113.
24. Haag, *Gunning of America*, xvii.
25. Winchester Repeating Arms Company Archives Collection (WRAC), D. H. Veader and

A. W. Earle, typescript, "The Story of the WRAC. This Includes Its Predecessors, the Volcanic Repeating Firearms Company and the New Haven Arms Company," 27, quoted in Haag, *Gunning of America*, 122.

26. Haag, *Gunning of America*, 40.

27. Haag, *Gunning of America*, 119.

28. House of Representatives Report #46, "Sales of Ordnance Stores," April 15, 1872 (Washington, DC: US Government Printing Office, 1872), 181, 29, 144, 155, 156, quoted in Haag, *Gunning of America*, 120.

29. Haag, *Gunning of America*, 40.

30. Haag, *Gunning of America*, 42.

31. Haag, *Gunning of America*, 43.

32. Scott Kraft, "End War Now, Mandela Tells Blacks," *Los Angeles Times*, February 26, 1990, http://articles.latimes.com/1990-02-26/news/mn-1165_1_south-africa.

33. Haag, *Gunning of America*, 110.

34. Haag, *Gunning of America*, 110.

35. Haag, *Gunning of America*, 75.

36. Haag, *Gunning of America*, 76.

37. Haag, *Gunning of America*, 56.

38. Haag, *Gunning of America*, 250–51.

39. WRAC, series 1, box 6, folder 7, July 7, 1917; series 6, box 13, folder 20, from T. G. Bennett to "The Trade," 1918, 6; series 6, box 13, folder 20, from Win Bennett "To the Trade," 22, cited in Haag, *Gunning of America*, xv, 324.

40. Haag, *Gunning of America*, 7.

41. Haag, *Gunning of America*, 87.

42. Quoted in Wiley Sword, *The Historic Henry Rifle: Oliver Winchester's Famous Civil War Repeater* (Woonsocket, RI: Andrew Mowbray, 2006), 64, cited in Haag, *Gunning of America*, 88.

43. A phrase used by Homer Sprague, brother-in-law of Sarah Winchester. Homer Sprague, *History of the Thirteenth Infantry Regiment of Connecticut Volunteers during the Great Rebellion* (Hartford, CT: Case, Lockwood, 1867), 114, quoted in Haag, *Gunning of America*, 87.

44. Haag, *Gunning of America*, 72.

45. M. L. Brown, *Firearms in Colonial America: The Impact on History and Technology, 1492–1792* (Washington, DC: Smithsonian Institution, 1980), 347, cited in Haag, *Gunning of America*, 10.

46. Haag, *Gunning of America*, 18.

47. William Hallahan, *Misfire: The History of How America's Small Arms Have Failed Our Country* (New York: Scribner's, 1994), 48–50, 62–77, cited in Haag, *Gunning of America*, 23.

Chapter 4: The Gun Empire

1. Marco Brunner, "The NRA Wasn't Always about the Promiscuous Toting of Guns and Arming of Teachers," *Timeline*, March 13, 2018, https://timeline.com/old-nra-endorsed-gun-control-6584fda35d7f; Michael S. Rosenwald, "The NRA Once Believed in Gun Control and Had a Leader Who Pushed for It," *Washington Post*, February 22, 2018, https://www.washingtonpost.com/news/retropolis/wp/2017/10/05/the-forgotten-nra-leader-who-despised-the-promiscuous-toting-of-guns.

2. Gil Troy, "The Teen Killer Who Radicalized the NRA," *Daily Beast*, October 8, 2017, https://www.thedailybeast.com/the-teen-killer-who-radicalized-the-nra.

3. "Letter of Resignation Sent by Bush to Rifle Association," *New York Times*, May 11, 1995, https://www.nytimes.com/1995/05/11/us/letter-of-resignation-sent-by-bush-to-rifle-association.html.

4. "1989 Reagan Condemns Assault Weapons," C-SPAN, February 6, 1989, https://www.c-span.org/video/?c4462648/1989-reagan-condemns-assault-weapons.

5. Steven Rosenfeld, "7 Uncovered Quotes That Reveal Just How Crazy the NRA's Become," *Salon*, January 23, 2013, https://www.salon.com/2013/01/23/7_uncovered_quotes_that_reveal_just_how_crazy_the_nras_become.

6. John M. Bruce and Clyde Wilcox, eds., *The Changing Politics of Gun Control* (Lanham, MD: Rowman & Littlefield, 1998), 158–59.

7. This particular bill was ruled unconstitutional, but that has not stopped the NRA from suing municipalities if they deem their local laws a violation of the Second Amendment, often taking them to federal court.

8. "NRA Ad," YouTube, June 29, 2017, https://youtu.be/PrnIVVWtAag.

9. Jacob Sullum, "What Does the NRA Think about the Shooting of Philando Castile?," *Newsweek*, July 19, 2017, https://www.newsweek.com

/what-does-nra-think-about-shooting-philando
-castile-639224.

10. Kim Parker, "Among Gun Owners, NRA Members Have a Unique Set of Views and Experiences," Pew Research Center, July 5, 2017, http://www.pewresearch.org/fact-tank/2017/07/05/among-gun-owners-nra-members-have-a-unique-set-of-views-and-experiences.

11. King, "The Casualties of the War in Vietnam" (speech, The Nation Institute, Los Angeles, February 25, 1967), http://www.aavw.org/special_features/speeches_speech_king02.html.

12. Jim Zumbo, "Assault Rifles for Hunters?," *Outdoor Life*, February 16, 2007, available at http://razoreye.net/mirror/zumbo/zumbo_assault_rifles.html.

13. Blaine Harden, "'Terrorist' Remark Puts Outdoorsman's Career in Jeopardy," *Washington Post*, February 24, 2007, http://www.washingtonpost.com/wp-dyn/content/article/2007/02/23/AR2007022301709.html.

14. "NRA Publications Suspends Ties to Jim Zumbo," NRA Institute for Legislative Action, February 22, 2007, https://www.nraila.org/articles/20070222/nra-publications-suspends-ties-to-jim-z.

15. Tom Kertscher, "Do 90% of Americans Support Background Checks for All Gun Sales?," Politifact, October 3, 2017, https://www.politifact.com/wisconsin/statements/2017/oct/03/chris-abele/do-90-americans-support-background-checks-all-gun-/.

16. Kim Parker et al., "America's Complex Relationship with Guns," Pew Research Center, June 22, 2017, http://www.pewsocialtrends.org/2017/06/22/americas-complex-relationship-with-guns; Mayors against Illegal Guns, "2012 Frank Luntz National Poll of Gun Owners and NRA Members," Everytown for Gun Safety, October 20, 2012, https://everytownresearch.org/2012-polling-on-support-for-background-checks; Colleen L. Barry et al., "After Newtown—Public Opinion on Gun Policy and Mental Illness," *New England Journal of Medicine* 368 (March 21, 2013): 1077–81, http://doi.org/10.1056/NEJMp1300512.

17. Christal Hayes, "NRA Says It Faces Financial Crisis, Claims It Might Be 'Unable to Exist' in Future: Lawsuit," *USA Today*, August 4, 2018, https://www.usatoday.com/story/news/politics/2018/08/03/nra-faces-financial-crisis-claims-might-una ble-exist/902918002.

Chapter 5: Do Black Guns Matter?

1. Alexandra Filindra, "How Racial Prejudice Helps Drive Opposition to Gun Control," *Washington Post*, June 21, 2016, https://www.washingtonpost.com/news/monkey-cage/wp/2016/06/21/heres-the-surprising-reason-some-white-americans-oppose-gun-regulation.

2. Dave Gilson, "The NRA's Board Members Are—Shockingly—Mostly White Guys," Mother Jones, March 1, 2018, https://www.motherjones.com/politics/2018/03/nra-board-members-tom-selleck.

3. "The Origins of the Second Amendment," YouTube, February 28, 2018, https://youtu.be/NSFsU2NzJv0.

4. Carroll Colby, *Firearms by Winchester* (New York: Coward-McCann, 1957), 4, cited in Pamela Haag, *The Gunning of America: Business and the Making of American Gun Culture* (New York: Basic Books, 2016), 105.

5. Haag, *Gunning of America*, 184.

6. Haag, *Gunning of America*, 196.

7. Ida B. Wells, *Crusade for Justice: The Autobiography of Ida B. Wells* (Chicago: University of Chicago Press, 1970), 62, quoted in Nicholas Johnson, *Negroes and the Gun: The Black Tradition of Arms* (Amherst, MA: Prometheus, 2014), 105.

8. Nicholas Johnson, "Negroes and the Gun: A Winchester 'in Every Black Home,'" *Washington Post*, January 29, 2014, https://www.washingtonpost.com/news/volokh-conspiracy/wp/2014/01/29/negroes-and-the-gun-a-winchester-in-every-black-home.

9. DuBois, *The Autobiography of W. E. B. Dubois: A Soliloquy on Viewing My Life from the Last Decade of Its First Century* (New York: International Publishers, 1968), 286, quoted in Johnson, *Negroes and the Gun*.

10. Gunnar Myrdal, *An American Dilemma*, vol. 2, *The Negro Problem and Modern Democracy*, 7th ed. (New York: Harper & Row, 2009), 560, cited in Haag, *Gunning of America*, 198.

11. Thad Morgan, "The NRA Supported Gun Control When the Black Panthers Had the Weapons,"

History, March 22, 2018, https://www.history.com/news/black-panthers-gun-control-nra-support-mulford-act.

12. Haag, *Gunning of America*, 195.

13. H. C. Brearly, *Homicide in the United States* (Chapel Hill: University of North Carolina Press, 1932), cited in Haag, *Gunning of America*, 198.

14. Niall McCarthy, "Homicides in Chicago Eclipse U.S. Death Toll in Afghanistan and Iraq," *Forbes*, September 8, 2016, https://www.forbes.com/sites/niallmccarthy/2016/09/08/homicides-in-chicago-eclipse-u-s-death-toll-in-afghanistan-and-iraq-infographic.

15. Molly Pahn, Anita Knopov, and Michael Siegel, "Gun Violence in the US Kills More Black People and Urban Dwellers," *The Conversation*, November 8, 2017, https://theconversation.com/gun-violence-in-the-us-kills-more-black-people-and-urban-dwellers-86825.

16. Katherine A. Fowler et al., "Childhood Firearm Injuries in the United States," *Pediatrics* 140, no. 1 (June 2017), http://doi.org/10.1542/peds.2016-3486; Centers for Disease Control and Prevention, "Fatal Injury Reports, Leading Causes of Death, United States," WISQARS (Web-based Injury Statistics Query and Reporting System), data from 2016, children and teenagers aged one to nineteen, black defined as non-Hispanic, number of deaths by known intent (homicide, suicide, unintentional deaths), ages zero to one calculated separately by the CDC because leading causes of death for newborns and infants are specific to the age group. See also Melonie Heron, "Deaths: Leading Causes for 2015," *National Vital Statistics Reports* 66, no. 5 (November 27, 2017), https://www.cdc.gov/nchs/data/nvsr/nvsr66/nvsr66_05.pdf; Everytown for Gun Safety, "Gun Violence in America," accessed September 10, 2018, https://everytownresearch.org/gun-violence-america.

17. King, *The Autobiography of Martin Luther King, Jr.*, ed. Clayborne Carson (New York: Warner, 1998), 82.

18. King, *Autobiography of Martin Luther King, Jr.*, 331.

19. Ben Popken, "Trump's Victory Has Fearful Minorities Buying Up Guns," NBC News, November 23, 2016, updated November 27, 2016, https://www.nbcnews.com/business/consumer/trump-s-victory-has-fearful-minorities-buying-guns-n686881.

20. Teryn Payne, "Gun Sales among Blacks See Increase," *Ebony*, November 29, 2016, http://www.ebony.com/news-views/gun-sales-blacks-increase.

21. Herman Wong, "Calling for Civility, Ted Nugent Explains Why He Once Told Obama to 'Suck on My Machine Gun,'" *Washington Post*, June 18, 2017, https://www.washingtonpost.com/news/the-fix/wp/2017/06/17/ted-nugent-once-said-obama-should-suck-on-my-machine-gun-now-he-wants-to-tone-down-the-hateful-rhetoric.

22. Stephen Rex Brown, "Ted Nugent Posts Racist Image on Facebook—One Month after Anti-Semitic Controversy," *New York Daily News*, March 31, 2016, http://www.nydailynews.com/news/national/nra-board-member-ted-nugent-posts-racist-image-facebook-article-1.2584368.

23. Jeff Cooper, "Cooper's Corner," *Guns & Ammo*, April 1991, 104, quoted in "NRA Family Values," Violence Policy Center, 1998, http://www.vpc.org/studies/nrafamst.htm.

24. Alexandra Filindra, "How Racial Prejudice Helps Drive Opposition to Gun Control," *Washington Post*, June 21, 2016, https://www.washingtonpost.com/news/monkey-cage/wp/2016/06/21/heres-the-surprising-reason-some-white-americans-oppose-gun-regulation.

25. Barbara Goldberg and Gina Cherelus, "Corporate Partners Cut Cord with NRA as Gun Control Debate Rages," Reuters, February 23, 2018, https://www.reuters.com/article/us-usa-guns-boycott/corporate-america-under-pressure-to-cut-ties-with-nra-idUSKCN1G71OX.

26. "Armed in America: Faith & Guns Townhall," PBS, May 10, 2016, https://www.pbs.org/video/armed-america-faith-guns-armed-america-faith-guns-townhall.

Consider This: Gallery of the Absurd

1. Erik Schelzig, "Sponsor of Law Allowing Guns in Bars Arrested on DUI, Gun Charges," Associated Press, October 12, 2011, cited in James Atwood, *America and Its Guns: A Theological Exposé* (Eugene, OR: Cascade, 2012), 106.

2. "Tennessee Man Accidentally Shoots Self, Wife during Church Gun-Violence Chat," Reuters,

November 17, 2017, https://www.reuters.com/art
icle/us-tennessee-shooting/tennessee-man-acciden
tally-shoots-self-wife-during-church-gun-violence
-chat-idUSKBN1DH247.

3. Corky Siemaszko, "Sicilian Wedding Photographer Accidentally Shot, Killed by Couple after He Had Them Pose with Guns," *New York Daily News*, July 27, 2010, www.nydailynews.com/news/world/sicili
an-wedding-photographer-accidentally-shot-killed
-couple-pose-guns-article-1.466571.

4. Dan Zimmerman, "Irresponsible Gun Owner of the Day: Dylan Gremore," Truth about Guns, January 27, 2012, http://www.thetruthaboutguns
.com/2012/01/daniel-zimmerman/irresponsible
-gun-owner-of-the-day-dylan-gremore.

5. Dees-Thomases, *Looking for a Few Good Moms* (Emmaus, PA: Rodale, 2004), 17.

6. Barrett Firearms Manufacturing Inc., brochure advertising Model 82A1 .50-caliber sniper rifle, cited in Atwood, *America and Its Guns*, 79.

7. Turner Hutchens, "Aiming for Success," *Daily News Journal*, Murfreesboro, Tennessee, December 24, 2006.

8. "Statement by the President Announcing the Use of the A-Bomb at Hiroshima," Harry S. Truman Presidential Library & Museum, August 6, 1945, https://www.trumanlibrary.org/publicpapers/index
.php?pid=100; "Radio Report to the American People on the Potsdam Conference," Harry S. Truman Presidential Library & Museum, August 9, 1945, https://www.trumanlibrary.org/publicpape
rs/?pid=104.

9. "The Truth about Gun Dealers in America," Brady Campaign and Brady Center, accessed July 23, 2018, http://www.bradycampaign.org/sites/defa
ult/files/TheTruthAboutGunDealersInAmerica.pdf.

10. "Fatal Force," *Washington Post*, accessed July 24, 2018, https://www.washingtonpost.com/graph
ics/national/police-shootings-2017.

11. Brian Freskos, "Up to 600,000 Guns Are Stolen Every Year in the US—That's One Every Minute," *Guardian* (US edition), September 21, 2016, https://www.theguardian.com/us-news/2016/sep
/21/gun-theft-us-firearm-survey.

12. Chelsea Parsons and Eugenio Weigend Vargas, "Stolen Guns in America," Center for American Progress, July 25, 2017, https://www.americanprog

ress.org/issues/guns-crime/reports/2017/07/25/436
533/stolen-guns-america.

13. Testimony of Eileen R. Larance, Director of Homeland Security and Justice, before the Senate Committee on Homeland Security and Governmental Affairs, May 5, 2010, U.S. Government Accountability Office, cited in Atwood, *America and Its Guns*, 163.

14. Eduardo Munoz, "Couples Lug AR-15 Assault Rifles to Pennsylvania Church Blessing," Reuters, February 28, 2018, https://www.reuters
.com/article/us-usa-guns-church/couples-lug-ar-15
-assault-rifles-to-pennsylvania-church-blessing-id
USKCN1GC2V3.

15. Ruben Gallego and Dan Gross, "Crack Down on 'Bad Apple' Gun Dealers," CNN, August 13, 2015, https://www.cnn.com/2015/08/13/opin
ions/gallego-gross-gun-dealers/index.html.

16. David Williams, "Americans Can Legally Download 3-D Printed Guns Starting Next Month," CNN, updated July 20, 2018, https://www.cnn.com
/2018/07/19/us/3d-printed-gun-settlement-trnd.

Chapter 6: Mythbusting

1. Michael Luo, "NRA Stymies Firearms Research, Scientists Say," *New York Times*, January 25, 2011, https://www.nytimes.com/2011/01/26/us/26
guns.html.

2. Studies have repeatedly shown this to be true: Scott H. Decker, "Americans Mostly Kill the Ones We Know," Zócalo Public Square, August 6, 2016, http://www.zocalopublicsquare.org/2016/08
/06/americans-mostly-kill-ones-know/ideas/nexus.

3. Evan Defilippis and Devin Hughes, "Gun-Rights Advocates Claim Owning a Gun Makes a Woman Safer. The Research Says They're Wrong," The Trace, May 2, 2016, https://www.thetrace.org
/2016/05/gun-ownership-makes-women-safer-de
bunked.

4. Christopher Ingraham, "For Every Gun Used in Self-Defense, Six More Are Used to Commit a Crime," *Washington Post*, June 14, 2016, https://
www.washingtonpost.com/news/wonk/wp/2016
/06/14/for-every-gun-used-in-self-defense-six-mo
re-are-used-to-commit-a-crime.

5. Arthur Kellerman, "Guns for Safety? Dream On, Scalia," *Washington Post*, June 29, 2008, http://

www.washingtonpost.com/wp-dyn/content/article/2008/06/27/AR2008062702864.html.

6. David Hemenway and Sara J. Solnick, "The Epidemiology of Self-Defense Gun Use: Evidence from the National Crime Victimization Surveys 2007–2011," *Preventative Medicine* 79 (October 2015): 22–27, https://doi.org/10.1016/j.ypmed.2015.03.029, cited in Harvard Injury Control Research Center, "Gun Threats and Self-Defense Gun Use," Harvard School of Public Health, accessed September 11, 2018, https://www.hsph.harvard.edu/hicrc/firearms-research/gun-threats-and-self-defense-gun-use-2.

7. David Hemenway, "Does Owning a Gun Make You Safer?," *Los Angeles Times*, August 4, 2015, http://www.latimes.com/opinion/op-ed/la-oe-0804-hemenway-defensive-gun-home-20150730-story.html.

8. Hemenway and Solnick, "Epidemiology of Self-Defense Gun Use."

9. Everytown for Gun Safety, "Gun Violence in America," accessed September 10, 2018, https://everytownresearch.org/gun-violence-america.

10. Arthur Kellermann et al., "Injuries and Deaths Due to Firearms in the Home," *Journal of Trauma, Injury, Infection, and Critical Care* 45, no. 2 (August 1998): 263–67.

11. Emiko Petrosky et al., "Racial and Ethnic Differences in Homicides of Adult Women and the Role of Intimate Partner Violence—United States, 2003–2014," *Morbity and Mortality Weekly Report* 66 (2017): 741–46, http://dx.doi.org/10.15585/mmwr.mm6628a1.

12. Jacquelyn Campbell et al., "Risk Factors for Femicide in Abusive Relationships: Results from a Multisite Case Control Study," *American Journal of Public Health* 93, no.7 (2003): 1089–97.

13. Gary Kleck and Marc Gertz, "Armed Resistance to Crime: The Prevalence and Nature of Self-Defense with a Gun," *Journal of Criminal Law and Criminology* 86, no. 1 (Fall 1995): 150–87, https://scholarlycommons.law.northwestern.edu/jclc/vol86/iss1/8.

14. Flyer from Realco Guns of District Heights, Maryland, cited in James Atwood, *America and Its Guns: A Theological Exposé* (Eugene, OR: Cascade, 2012), 100.

15. Hemenway and Solnick, "Epidemiology of Self-Defense Gun Use."

16. "Q and A: Guns, Crime, and Self-Defense," *Orange County Register*, September 19, 1993, cited in Atwood, *America and Its Guns*, 101.

17. "Number of Justifiable Homicides by Law Enforcement Officers and Private Citizens in the United States from 2007 to 2015," accessed September 11, 2018, https://www.statista.com/statistics/251894/number-of-justifiable-homicides-in-the-us. See also Samantha Raphelson, "How Often Do People Use Guns In Self-Defense?," *Here & Now* (NPR), April 13, 2018, https://www.npr.org/2018/04/13/602143823/how-often-do-people-use-guns-in-self-defense; and Michael Planty and Jennifer L. Truman, "Firearm Violence, 1993–2011," Bureau of Justice Statistics, May 2013, https://www.bjs.gov/content/pub/pdf/fv9311.pdf.

18. Centers for Disease Control and Prevention, "Fatal Injury Reports, National, Regional and State, 1981–2016," WISQARS (Web-based Injury Statistics Query and Reporting System), updated February 19, 2017, https://webappa.cdc.gov/sasweb/ncipc/mortrate.html.

19. "Armed Bystander's Reaction in Ariz. Shootings Illustrates Complexity of Gun Debate," *Denver Post*, published January 15, 2011, updated May 4, 2016, https://www.denverpost.com/2011/01/15/armed-bystanders-reaction-in-ariz-shootings-illustrates-complexity-of-gun-debate.

20. Christopher Ingraham, "For Every Gun Used in Self-Defense, Six More Are Used to Commit a Crime," *Washington Post*, June 14, 2016, https://www.washingtonpost.com/news/wonk/wp/2016/06/14/for-every-gun-used-in-self-defense-six-more-are-used-to-commit-a-crime.

21. Glenn Kessler, "The NRA's Fuzzy, Decades-Old Claim of '20,000' Gun Laws," *Washington Post*, February 5, 2013, https://www.washingtonpost.com/blogs/fact-checker/post/the-nras-fuzzy-decades-old-claim-of-20000-gun-laws/2013/02/04/4a7892c0-6f23-11e2-ac36-3d8d9dcaa2e2_blog.html.

22. Cited in Glenn Kessler, "The NRA's Fuzzy, Decades-Old Claim of '20,000' Gun Laws," *Washington Post*, February 5, 2013, https://www.washingtonpost.com/blogs/fact-checker/post/the-nras-fuzzy-decades-old-claim-of-20000-gun-laws/2013

/02/04/4a7892c0-6f23-11e2-ac36-3d8d9dcaa2e
2_blog.html.

23. "1989 Reagan Condemns Assault Weapons,"
C-SPAN, February 6, 1989, https://www.c-span
.org/video/?c4462648/1989-reagan-condemns-as
sault-weapons. A ban on assault weapons existed
from 1994 to 2004, a law endorsed by three ex-
presidents: Ronald Reagan, Gerald Ford, and Jimmy
Carter. However, the ban was allowed to expire
in 2004.

24. Mayors against Illegal Guns, "2012 Frank
Luntz National Poll of Gun Owners and NRA Members," Everytown for Gun Safety, October 20, 2012,
https://everytownresearch.org/2012-polling-on
-support-for-background-checks.

25. Studies such as these: Kim Parker et al.,
"America's Complex Relationship with Guns," Pew
Research Center, June 22, 2017, http://www.pewso
cialtrends.org/2017/06/22/americas-complex-relati
onship-with-guns; Public Policy Polling, "National
Survey Results," Center for American Progress, November 11–12, 2015, https://cdn.americanprogress
.org/wp-content/uploads/2015/11/17054452/PPP
-GunOwnersPollResults-11.17.15.pdf.

26. Benton Strong, "Release: Gun Owners
Overwhelmingly Support Background Checks, See
NRA as Out of Touch, New Poll Finds," Center for
American Progress, November 17, 2015, https://
www.americanprogress.org/press/release/2015
/11/17/125618/release-gun-owners-overwhelmin
gly-support-background-checks-see-nra-as-out-of
-touch-new-poll-finds/d.

Chapter 7: Kids and Guns

1. Portions of the segment can be seen at "Who
Is America? (2018) | First Look | Sacha Baron Cohen
SHOWTIME Series," YouTube, July 15, 2018,
https://youtu.be/QkXeMoBPSDk.

2. Adam Harris, "A World Where School Shootings Feel Inevitable," Atlantic, May 18, 2018, https://
www.theatlantic.com/education/archive/2018
/05/a-world-where-school-shootings-feel-inevitable
/560735.

3. Libby Nelson and Javier Zarracina, "A Shocking Statistic about Gun Deaths in the US," Vox, December 4, 2015, https://www.vox.com/policy-and
-politics/2015/12/4/9851102/gun-deaths-us-chil

dren. Vox used information from Erin Grinshteyn
and David Hemenway, "Homicide, Suicide, and Unintentional Firearm Fatality: Comparing the United
States with Other High-Income Countries, 2003,"
Journal of Trauma 70, no. 1 (January 2011): 238–43,
https://doi.org/10.1097/TA.0b013e3181dbaddf.

4. Everytown for Gun Safety, "The Impact of
Gun Violence on American Children and Teenagers," August 15, 2018, https://everytownresearch
.org/impact-gun-violence-american-children-teens,
citing Centers for Disease Control and Prevention,
"Fatal Injury Reports, National, Regional and State,
1981–2016," WISQARS (Web-based Injury Statistics Query and Reporting System), updated February
19, 2017, https://webappa.cdc.gov/sasweb/ncipc
/mortrate.html.

5. Judy Schaechter, "Guns in the Home,"
Healthy Children, updated June 5, 2018, https://
www.healthychildren.org/English/safety-prevent
ion/at-home/Pages/Handguns-in-the-Home.aspx.

6. Child Trends Data Bank, Centers for Disease Control and Prevention, Statistics on Guns in
Schools 2008, 1–2, cited in James Atwood, America
and Its Guns: A Theological Exposé (Eugene, OR: Cascade, 2012), 117.

7. As of December 2016, there were approximately 14,146 McDonald's and 25,400 grocery
stores in the US—and yet there were 64,417 firearm
dealers. Leanna Garfield, "There Are 50,000 More
Gun Shops Than McDonald's in the US," Business
Insider, October 6, 2017, http://www.businessin
sider.com/gun-dealers-stores-mcdonalds-las-vegas
-shooting-2017-10.

8. Mandela, Long Walk to Freedom (New York:
Little, Brown, 2008), 622.

9. Quentin Fottrell, "Walmart and Dick's Sporting Goods Surge in Public's Esteem after Breaking
Ties with NRA," MarketWatch, March 6, 2018,
https://www.marketwatch.com/story/americans-a
ppear-divided-over-companies-breaking-ties-with
-nra-2018-03-01.

10. Ryan Dunn, "Toledo Mother Grieves 3-Year-
Old's Shooting Death," The Blade, October 31, 2016,
http://www.toledoblade.com/Police-Fire/2016
/10/31/Toledo-mother-grieves-3-year-old-s-shoot
ing-death.html.

11. Ryan Foley, Larry Fenn, and Nick Penzen-
stadler, "Chronicle of Agony: Gun Accidents Kill at

Least 1 Kid Every Other Day," *USA Today*, October 14, 2016, https://www.usatoday.com/story/news /2016/10/14/ap-usa-today-gun-accidents-children /91906700.

12. Melissa Healy, "Guns Kill Nearly 1,300 Children in the U.S. Each Year and Send Thousands More to Hospital," *Los Angeles Times*, June 19, 2017, http://www.latimes.com/science/sciencenow/la-sci -sn-gun-deaths-children-20170619-story.html.

13. Ryan Bort, "Kids and Guns: Shootings Now Third Leading Cause of Death for U.S. Children," *Newsweek*, June 19, 2017, http://www.newsweek .com/guns-kids-third-leading-cause-death-627209.

Chapter 8: Another Dark Secret

1. National Institute of Mental Health, "Suicide," last updated May 2018, https://www.nimh .nih.gov/health/statistics/suicide.shtml.

2. National Institute of Mental Health, "Suicide."

3. This data reflects the five-year average (2012 to 2016) of gun deaths by intent. Centers for Disease Control and Prevention, "Fatal Injury Reports, National, Regional and State, 1981–2016," WISQARS (Web-based Injury Statistics Query and Reporting System), updated February 19, 2017, https://weba ppa.cdc.gov/sasweb/ncipc/mortrate.html.

4. Matthew Miller, Deborah Azrael, and David Hemenway, "The Epidemiology of Case Fatality Rates for Suicide in the Northeast," *Annals of Emergency Medicine* 43, no. 6 (2004): 723–30, https://doi .org/10.1016/j.annemergmed.2004.01.018.

5. National Institute of Mental Health, "Suicide."

6. Everytown for Gun Safety, "Firearm Suicide in the United States," 2017, https://everytownrese arch.org/wp-content/uploads/2017/09/Suicide-in -USA-FACT-SHEET-091917A.pdf.

7. David Owens, Judith Horrocks, and Allan House, "Fatal and Non-Fatal Repetition of Self-Harm: Systematic Review," *British Journal of Psychiatry* 181, no. 3 (September 2002): 193–99, cited by Everytown for Gun Safety, "Firearm Suicide."

8. German Lopez, "What Many People Get Wrong about Suicide," Vox, September 17, 2015, https://www.vox.com/2015/7/30/9068255/suicide -impulsive-gun-control.

9. Corey Adwar, "The Role of Impulsiveness Is One of the Saddest Things about Suicide," *Business Insider*, August 13, 2014, http://www.businessinsider .com/many-suicides-are-based-on-an-impulsive -decision-2014-8.

10. Everytown for Gun Safety, "Firearm Suicide."

11. Greg Allen, "Florida Bill Could Muzzle Doctors on Gun Safety," NPR, May 7, 2011, https://www .npr.org/2011/05/07/136063523/florida-bill-could -muzzle-doctors-on-gun-safety.

12. Zack Beauchamp, "Australia Confiscated 650,000 Guns: Murders and Suicides Plummeted," Vox, May 18, 2018, https://www.vox.com/2015/8/27 /9212725/australia-buyback.

13. Andrew Leigh and Christine Neill, "Do Gun Buybacks Save Lives? Evidence from Panel Data," *American Law and Economics Review* 12, no. 2 (Fall 2010): 509–57.

14. "Suicide Prevention in the Israeli Military," Suicide Prevention Resource Center, January 26, 2017, https://www.sprc.org/news/suicide-prevention -israeli-military.

15. US Department of Veterans Affairs, "VA National Suicide Data Report, 2005–2015," June 2018, https://www.mentalhealth.va.gov/docs/data -sheets/OMHSP_National_Suicide_Data_Report _2005-2015_06-14-18_508-compliant.pdf.

16. Everytown for Gun Safety, "Firearm Suicide."

Chapter 9: Dudes and Their Guns

1. David Mikkelson, "Hunting for Bambi," Snopes, October 26, 2008, https://www.snopes.com /fact-check/hunting-for-bambi.

2. Laura Kiesel, "Don't Blame Mental Illness for Mass Shootings; Blame Men," *Politico*, January 17, 2018, https://www.politico.com/magazine/story /2018/01/17/gun-violence-masculinity-216321; Frank T. McAndrew, "If You Give a Man a Gun: The Evolutionary Psychology of Mass Shootings," *The Conversation*, December 4, 2015, https://thecon versation.com/if-you-give-a-man-a-gun-the-evoluti onary-psychology-of-mass-shootings-51782.

3. Lauren F. Winner, "Unexpected Metaphors for God," lecture at TheoEd Talks (First Presbyterian

Church of Atlanta, February 25, 2018), available at https://vimeo.com/258838358.

4. Shane Claiborne and Chris Haw, *Jesus for President: Politics for Ordinary Radicals* (Grand Rapids: Zondervan, 2008); Shane Claiborne and Ben Cohen, *Jesus, Bombs, and Ice Cream: Building a More Peaceful World* (Grand Rapids: Zondervan, 2013), DVD and study guide.

5. Jiaquan Xu, Sherry L. Murphy, Kenneth D. Kochanek, and Brigham A. Bastian, "Deaths: Final Data for 2013," *National Vital Statistics Reports* 64, no. 2 (February 16, 2016), https://www.cdc.gov /nchs/data/nvsr/nvsr64/nvsr64_02.pdf; Arthur L. Kellermann et al., "Gun Ownership as a Risk Factor for Homicide in the Home," *New England Journal of Medicine* 329, no. 15 (1993); Peter Cummings et al., "The Association Between the Purchase of a Handgun and Homicide or Suicide," *Journal of Public Health* 87, no. 6 (1997): 974–78; Shannan Catalano et al., "Selected Findings: Female Victims of Violence," US Department of Justice, Bureau of Justice Statistics, September 2009, http://www.bjs .gov/content/pub/pdf/fvv.pdf; Jacquelyn Campbell et al., "Risk Factors for Femicide in Abusive Relationships: Results from a Multisite Case Control Study," *American Journal of Public Health* 93, no.7 (2003): 1089–97, cited in Pamela Haag, *The Gunning of America: Business and the Making of American Gun Culture* (New York: Basic Books, 2016), 367.

6. Everytown for Gun Safety, "Guns and Violence against Women," 2014, https://everytownre search.org/documents/2015/04/guns-and-violence -against-women.pdf.

7. Scottish Trades Union Congress, Stop Violence against Women Conference, cited in James Atwood, *America and Its Guns: A Theological Exposé* (Eugene, OR: Cascade, 2012), 109.

8. Amina Khan, "Domestic Violence Homicide Rate Drops with Stricter Gun Law, Study Finds," *Los Angeles Times*, September 19, 2017, http://www .latimes.com/science/sciencenow/la-sci-sn-gun-vio lence-women-20170919-story.html.

9. Natalie Wilkins et al., "Connecting the Dots: An Overview of the Links among Multiple Forms of Violence," National Center for Injury Prevention and Control (Centers for Disease Control and Prevention) and Prevention Institute, July 2014, https:// www.preventioninstitute.org/sites/default/files /publications/Connecting the Dots Links Among M ultiple Forms of Violence2.pdf.

10. Evan Defilippis, "Having a Gun in the House Doesn't Make a Woman Safer," *Atlantic*, February 23, 2014, https://www.theatlantic.com/na tional/archive/2014/02/having-a-gun-in-the-house -doesnt-make-a-woman-safer/284022.

11. Winchester Repeating Arms Company Archives Collection (WRAC), series 1, box 6, folder 7, July 7, 1917; series 6, box 13, folder 20, from T. G. Bennett to "The Trade," 1918, 6; series 6, box 13, folder 20, from Win Bennett "To the Trade," 22, cited in Haag, *Gunning of America*, xv, 324.

12. Haag, *Gunning of America*, 333, 467n36, cites several examples of the many "real boy" advertisements released by Winchester in this time period.

13. WRAC, series 1, box 6, folder 9, Sales Bulletin, June 29, 1917; series 6, box 13, folder 20, from T. G. Bennett to "The Trade," 1918, 12, cited in Haag, *Gunning of America*, 326.

14. Unless noted otherwise, facts in this section are from Haag, *Gunning of America*, 143–297.

15. Haag, *Gunning of America*, 294.

16. Laurie has recited this poem at several public events. It is used here with her permission.

17. Laurie Works, "Becoming a Wounded Healer," TEDxJacksonHole, published September 26, 2017, 10:18, https://youtu.be/J784v__FVjE.

18. Kevin Simpson, "Denver Woman Feels the Power of Restorative Justice after Son Murdered," *Denver Post*, July 9, 2012, updated October 13, 2016, https://www.denverpost.com/2012/07/09/den ver-woman-feels-the-power-of-restorative-justice -after-son-murdered.

19. You can support Laurie Works at www .laurieworks.com and find her on Instagram at @healingembodied. And support the women in your community who are leading the way toward less violent neighborhoods.

Chapter 10: The Second Amendment and the Sermon on the Mount

1. David Anderson, "The Lynchburg Revival with Shane Claiborne," YouTube, June 5, 2018, https://youtu.be/a1TaITKluL8.

2. James Madison, *Federalist*, no. 63, March 1, 1788, in Alexander Hamilton, James Madison, and John Jay, *The Federalist*, ed. Jacob E. Cooke (Middletown, CT: Wesleyan University Press, 1961), http://press-pubs.uchicago.edu/founders/documents/v1ch4s27.html.

3. "New SPLC Report: 'Patriot' Groups, Militias Surge in Number in Past Year," Southern Poverty Law Center, March 2, 2010, https://www.splcenter.org/news/2010/03/02/new-splc-report-patriot-groups-militias-surge-number-past-year.

4. District of Columbia et al. v. Heller, 554 U.S. 570 (2008), https://www.supremecourt.gov/opinions/07pdf/07-290.pdf.

5. Ida B. Wells, *Crusade for Justice: The Autobiography of Ida B. Wells* (Chicago: University of Chicago Press, 1970), 62, quoted in Nicholas Johnson, *Negroes and the Gun: The Black Tradition of Arms* (Amherst, MA: Prometheus, 2014), 105.

6. Brian Naylor, "Retired Supreme Court Justice Stevens Calls for Repeal of Second Amendment," NPR, March 27, 2018, https://www.npr.org/2018/03/27/597259426/retired-supreme-court-justice-stevens-calls-for-repeal-of-second-amendment.

7. This is Michael Moore's suggested rewrite of the amendment. "My Proposal to Repeal the Second Amendment and Replace It with This," Facebook, October 4, 2017, https://www.facebook.com/mmflint/posts/10154778028796857.

8. We are thankful for the work of Walter Wink, who coined the phrase the "third way" of Jesus and who works in detail on these texts from the Sermon on the Mount. See Wink, *The Powers That Be* (New York: Doubleday, 1998). Shane (with Chris Haw) builds on Wink's ideas in *Jesus for President: Politics for Ordinary Radicals* (Grand Rapids: Zondervan, 2008).

9. We highly recommend our friend Walter Brueggemann's book *The Prophetic Imagination*, 2nd ed. (Minneapolis: Fortress, 2001).

Consider This: Laying It All Out There

1. This *Guinness Book of World Records* was using data from *Small Arms Survey 2007: Guns and the City* (Cambridge: Cambridge University Press, 2007), http://www.smallarmssurvey.org/publications/by-type/yearbook/small-arms-survey-2007.html.

2. German Lopez, "America's Unique Gun Violence Problem, Explained in 17 Maps and Charts," Vox, updated June 29, 2018, https://www.vox.com/policy-and-politics/2017/10/2/16399418/us-gun-violence-statistics-maps-charts.

3. Lopez, "America's Unique Gun Violence Problem."

4. A mass shooting is defined as when four or more people are shot. Here is a map of recent mass shootings: http://www.gunviolencearchive.org/charts-and-maps.

5. Lopez, "America's Unique Gun Violence Problem."

6. Kim Parker et al., "America's Complex Relationship with Guns," Pew Research Center, June 22, 2017, http://www.pewsocialtrends.org/2017/06/22/americas-complex-relationship-with-guns.

7. Richard Florida, "The Geography of Gun Deaths," *Atlantic*, January 13, 2011, https://www.theatlantic.com/national/archive/2011/01/the-geography-of-gun-deaths/69354.

8. Lopez, "America's Unique Gun Violence Problem."

9. David Owens, Judith Horrocks, and Allan House, "Fatal and Non-Fatal Repetition of Self-Harm: Systematic Review," *British Journal of Psychiatry* 181, no. 3 (September 2002): 193–99, cited by Everytown for Gun Safety, "Firearm Suicide in the United States," 2017, https://everytownresearch.org/wp-content/uploads/2017/09/Suicide-in-USA-FACT-SHEET-091917A.pdf. See also Lopez, "America's Unique Gun Violence Problem."

10. Here are a few websites that track police-involved shootings: https://www.fatalencounters.org; https://www.washingtonpost.com/graphics/2018/national/police-shootings-2018; https://mappingpoliceviolence.org.

11. David I. Swedler et al., "Firearm Prevalence and Homicides of Law Enforcement Officers in the United States," *American Journal of Public Health* 105, no. 10 (October 2015): 2042–48, https://doi.org/10.2105/AJPH.2015.302749.

12. Swedler et al., "Firearm Prevalence and Homicides."

13. WRAC, Winchester letter book, from Winchester to Charles Bradford, Indiana, October 18, 1862, cited in Pamela Haag, *The Gunning of America:*

Business and the Making of American Gun Culture (New York: Basic Books, 2016), 59.

14. US Department of Justice, Bureau of Alcohol, Tobacco, Firearms, and Explosives, "Firearms Commerce in the United States," 2017, https://www.atf.gov/resource-center/docs/undefined/firearms-commerce-united-states-annual-statistical-update-2017/download.

Chapter 11: In Guns We Trust

1. Richard Lacayo, "Under Fire," *Time*, June 24, 2001, http://content.time.com/time/magazine/article/0,9171,153695,00.html.

2. *Turf, Field and Farm*, March 19, 1875, advertisements in this volume; Colt Collection (Connecticut State Library), box 66, folder 3, advertisement, "The Pioneers of Civilization, Colt's Repeating Firearms," cited in Pamela Haag, *The Gunning of America: Business and the Making of American Gun Culture* (New York: Basic Books, 2016), 168.

3. Closing remarks, NRA annual meeting, Charlotte, North Carolina, 2000, available at "Charlton Heston; From My Cold Dead Hands. Long Version," YouTube, April 26, 2008, https://youtu.be/5ju4Gla2odw.

4. Check out a more detailed account of this in Shane Claiborne and Chris Haw, *Jesus for President: Politics for Ordinary Radicals* (Grand Rapids: Zondervan, 2008), 65–137.

5. Tertullian, *On Idolatry* 19.

6. Tertullian, *Apology* 50.

7. A great compilation of quotes from early Christians is Eberhard Arnold, ed., *The Early Christians in Their Own Words* (Farmington, PA: Plough, 2007), https://www.holybooks.com/wp-content/uploads/The-Early-Christians-in-their-own-Words.pdf.

8. Andy Crouch, *Playing God: Redeeming the Gift of Power* (Downers Grove, IL: IVP Books, 2013), 56.

9. Garry Wills, "Our Moloch," *New York Review of Books*, December 15, 2012, https://www.nybooks.com/daily/2012/12/15/our-moloch.

10. Peter G. Peterson Foundation, "U.S. Defense Spending Compared to Other Countries," May 7, 2018, https://www.pgpf.org/chart-archive/0053_defense-comparison. See also Shane Claiborne and Ben Cohen, *Jesus, Bombs, and Ice Cream:*

Building a More Peaceful World (Grand Rapids: Zondervan, 2013), DVD and study guide, which details the military economy; and "Ben Cohen's Dessert—Another World is Possible Vol 1 with Shane Claiborne," YouTube, August 31, 2010, https://youtu.be/YVPGb21oaq8.

11. "A Moral Agenda Based on Fundamental Rights," Poor People's Campaign, accessed July 26, 2018, https://www.poorpeoplescampaign.org/demands.

12. Nick Turse, "Does the Pentagon Really Have 1,180 Foreign Bases?," *Huffington Post*, originally published January 10, 2011, updated December 6, 2017, https://www.huffingtonpost.com/nick-turse/does-the-pentagon-really-_b_806817.html.

13. Our pal Rob Bell did a great podcast series on this. Rob Bell, "Politics and Guns—Part 4—The United States of America," *The Robcast* (podcast), https://robbell.podbean.com/e/episode-57-politics-and-guns-part-4-the-united-states-of-america.

14. Wilson Andrews et al., "Taking Apart the Federal Budget," *Washington Post*, accessed September 20, 2018, http://www.washingtonpost.com/wp-srv/special/politics/budget-2010; Tanza Loudenback, "Middle-Class Americans Made More Money Last Year Than Ever Before," *Business Insider*, September 12, 2017, https://www.businessinsider.com/us-census-median-income-2017-9.

15. US Government Accountability Office, "Public Relations Spending: Reported Data on Related Federal Activities," September 30, 2016, https://www.budget.senate.gov/imo/media/doc/GAO%20PR%20Agency%20Spending.pdf; Derek Thompson, "War and Peace in 30 Seconds: How Much Does the Military Spend on Ads?," *Atlantic*, January 30, 2012, https://www.theatlantic.com/business/archive/2012/01/war-and-peace-in-30-seconds-how-much-does-the-military-spend-on-ads/252222.

16. Bill Theobald, "Pentagon Paid Sports Teams Millions for Patriotic Events," *USA Today*, November 4, 2015, https://www.usatoday.com/story/news/2015/11/04/millions-paid-pro-teams-patriotic-events-sens-flake-mccain-say/75141688.

17. Noah Shachtman, "27,000 Work in Pentagon PR and Recruiting," *Wired*, February 5, 2009, https://www.wired.com/2009/02/27000-work-in-p.

18. Hans M. Kristensen and Robert S. Norris, "Status of World Nuclear Forces," Federation of American Scientists, updated June 2018, https://fas .org/issues/nuclear-weapons/status-world-nuclear -forces.

19. This incredible video gives a sense of the scale: "The Terrifying True Scale of Nuclear Weapons," YouTube, October 7, 2016, https://youtu.be /fs1CIrwg5zU.

20. "Nuclear Weapons—the Facts," New Internationalist, June 2, 2008, https://newint.org/features /2008/06/01/nuclear-weapons-facts.

21. Skye Gould and Jeremy Bender, "Here's How the US Military Spends Its Billions," *Business Insider*, August 29, 2015, https://www.businessin sider.com/how-the-us-military-spends-its-billions -2015-8.

22. Philip J. Cook and Jens Ludwig, *Gun Violence: The Real Costs* (Oxford: Oxford University Press, 2000), 11.

23. Hugh Waters et al., *The Economic Dimensions of Interpersonal Violence* (Geneva: Department of Injuries and Violence Prevention, World Health Organization, 2004), 24–25, http://apps.who.int/iris /bitstream/handle/10665/42944/9241591609.pdf.

24. C. S. Lewis, *The Problem of Pain*, in *The Complete C. S. Lewis Signature Classics* (Grand Rapids: Zondervan, 2007), 626 (emphasis original).

25. Alexa Liautaud, "White House Acknowledges the U.S. Is at War in Seven Countries," VICE News, March 15, 2018, https://news.vice.com/en _us/article/a3ywd5/white-house-acknowledges-the -us-is-at-war-in-seven-countries.

26. F. Brinley Bruton, "U.S. Bombed Iraq, Syria, Pakistan, Afghanistan, Libya, Yemen, Somalia in 2016," NBC News, January 9, 2017, https://www .nbcnews.com/news/world/u-s-bombed-iraq-syria -pakistan-afghanistan-libya-yemen-somalia-n704 636.

27. Martin Luther King Jr., "Beyond Vietnam" (sermon, New York, April 4, 1967), https://king institute.stanford.edu/king-papers/documents /beyond-vietnam.

28. Dwight D. Eisenhower, "The Chance for Peace" (address delivered before the American Society of Newspaper Editors, April 16, 1953), http:// www.presidency.ucsb.edu/ws/?pid=9819.

Chapter 12: Exorcising Demons

1. Carma Hassan and Steve Almasy, "During Sermon on Violence, N.C. Pastor Confronts Man with Rifle," CNN, January 4, 2016, https://www .cnn.com/2016/01/02/us/north-carolina-pastor -man-with-gun/index.html; "Pastor Says Armed Man in N.C. Church Disarmed with Prayer," CBS News, January 3, 2016, https://www.cbsnews.com/news /pastor-says-armed-man-north-carolina-church -disarmed-with-prayer.

2. John Dear, "Expelling the Demons of War," *National Catholic Reporter*, March 29, 2011, https:// www.ncronline.org/blogs/road-peace/expelling -demons-war.

3. The pig was also the mascot of Rome's Tenth Fretensis Legion stationed in Antioch (Warren Carter, *Matthew and Empire: Initial Explorations* [Harrisburg, PA: Trinity Press, 2001], 71). It's interesting to note the places where Jesus drove demons out of people: often in the temple and in the militarized zones. The words "come out" that usually accompany an exorcism are the same words with which Jesus exorcised the temple, calling the money changers to "come out" because they had made a market of God's temple and marginalized visiting gentiles. We're thankful for John Dominic Crossan, Ched Meyers, and the numerous scholars whose work on this text has given us new eyes to see. For an in-depth study of Mark's Gospel, we suggest Ched Myers, *Binding the Strong Man: A Political Reading of Mark's Story of Jesus*, rev. ed. (Maryknoll, NY: Orbis, 2008).

4. Someone caught this encounter on video, and it's powerful to watch: "Pro-gun Advocates Sing 'God Bless America' Over Top 'the Lord's Prayer,'" YouTube, March 8, 2010, https://youtu.be/9YTajZ fqTYI.

Chapter 13: Christians with Guns

1. Chuck Shepherd, "Bible-Quoting Contest: Loser Shoots, Kills Winner," *Montgomery Advertiser*, Associated Press, July 18, 1996, cited in James Atwood, *America and Its Guns: A Theological Exposé* (Eugene, OR: Cascade, 2012), 8.

2. "Argument over Bible, Forgiveness Leads to Man Being Shot Twice in Head, Say Police," WLTX, Oc-

tober 30, 2017, https://www.wltx.com/article/news
/crime/argument-over-bible-forgiveness-leads-to
-man-being-shot-twice-in-head-say-police/101-48
7309612.

3. Madeleine Albright, *The Mighty and the Almighty: Reflections on America, God, and World Affairs* (New York: HarperCollins, 2006), 25, cited
in Atwood, *America and Its Guns*, 59.

4. Ed Mazza, "Gun Maker Creates 'Crusader'
Assault Rifle with Bible Verse on It," *HuffPost*, September 3, 2015, https://www.huffingtonpost.com
/entry/crusader-assault-rifle_us_55e7ff20e4b0b7a
9633bcb11; https://www.spikestactical.com/prod
ucts/complete-rifle-crusader.

5. Sarah Eekhoff Zylstra, "Praise the Lord and
Pass the Ammunition, Quantified," *Christianity
Today*, July 24, 2017, https://www.christianitytoday
.com/news/2017/july/praise-lord-pass-ammunition
-who-loves-god-guns-pew.html, citing Kim Parker
et al., "America's Complex Relationship with Guns,"
Pew Research Center, June 22, 2017, http://www
.pewsocialtrends.org/2017/06/22/americas-compl
ex-relationship-with-guns.

6. Sarah Pulliam Bailey, "Jerry Falwell Jr.: 'If
More Good People Had Concealed-Carry Permits,
Then We Could End Those' Islamist Terrorists,"
Washington Post, December 5, 2015, https://www
.washingtonpost.com/news/acts-of-faith/wp/2015
/12/05/liberty-university-president-if-more-good
-people-had-concealed-guns-we-could-end-those
-muslims.

7. For a thorough survey of early Christian
views on violence, we recommend Ron Sider's
edited volume, *The Early Church on Killing: A Comprehensive Sourcebook on War, Abortion, and Capital
Punishment* (Grand Rapids: Baker Academic, 2012).

8. T. Rees Shapiro, "Gun-Friendly Liberty
University to Open On-Campus Shooting Range,"
Washington Post, December 15, 2016, https://www
.washingtonpost.com/news/grade-point/wp/2016
/12/15/gun-friendly-liberty-university-to-open-on
-campus-shooting-range.

9. William Barclay, *The Gospel of Luke* (Louisville: Westminster John Knox, 2001), 92.

Chapter 14: Unlearning Violence

1. Norman Herr, "Television & Health," Sourcebook for Teaching Science, accessed August 21,
2018, https://www.csun.edu/science/health/docs
/tv&health.html.

2. Cited in James Atwood, *America and Its
Guns: A Theological Exposé* (Eugene, OR: Cascade,
2012), 33.

3. Alan Dawson, "The 51 Best-Selling Pay-Per-
View Fight Nights in History," *Business Insider*, August 25, 2017, http://www.businessinsider.com/the
-50-best-selling-pay-per-view-events-boxing-ufc
-wrestling-tv-history-2017-8.

4. Robert Johnson, "Call of Duty: Modern Warfare 2 Destroys Records in First Day Sales Rampage,
Pulls in $310M," *New York Daily News*, November 12,
2009, http://www.nydailynews.com/news/money
/call-of-duty-modern-warfare-2-destroys-records-day
-sales-rampage-article-1.417049.

5. Sasha Emmons, "Is Media Violence Damaging
to Kids?," CNN, February 21, 2013, https://www
.cnn.com/2013/02/21/living/parenting-kids-violen
ce-media/index.html.

6. Angelo Dargenio, "10 Call of Duty Facts That
Will Blow Your Mind!," Arcade Sushi, June 1, 2014,
http://arcadesushi.com/call-of-duty-facts-that-will
-blow-your-mind; Brian Fung, "Humankind Has
Now Spent More Time Playing Call of Duty Than
It Has Existed on Earth," *Washington Post*, August
13, 2013, https://www.washingtonpost.com/news
/the-switch/wp/2013/08/13/humankind-has-now
-spent-more-time-playing-call-of-duty-than-it-has
-existed-on-earth.

7. Jeremy Diamond, "Trump: I Could 'Shoot
Somebody and I Wouldn't Lose Voters,'" CNN,
January 24, 2016, https://www.cnn.com/2016
/01/23/politics/donald-trump-shoot-somebody-sup
port/index.html.

8. Benjamin Carlson, "Yes, Language Does
Shape Culture," *Atlantic*, July 26, 2010, https://www
.theatlantic.com/national/archive/2010/07/yes-lang
uage-does-shape-culture/340451; Lera Boroditsky,
"How Language Shapes the Way We Think," TED-
Women 2017, November 2017, 14:13, https://www
.ted.com/talks/lera_boroditsky_how_language_sha
pes_the_way_we_think.

9. Craig A. Anderson and Brad J. Bushman, "Effects of Violent Video Games on Aggressive Behavior, Aggressive Cognition, Aggressive Affect, Physiological Arousal, and Prosocial Behavior: A Meta-Analytic Review of the Scientific Literature," *Psychological Science* 12, no. 5 (September 2001): 353–59, https://doi.org/10.1111/1467-9280.00366.

10. Atwood, *America and Its Guns*, 36.

11. Sami Yenigun, "A Real-World Connection between Video Games and Guns," *All Tech Considered* (NPR), April 29, 2013, http://www.npr.org/sections/alltechconsidered/2013/04/29/179853504/a-real-world-connection-between-video-games-and-guns.

12. The NFL and sports reference found in Atwood, *America and Its Guns*, 206. Perhaps the New Orleans Saints can petition other teams for a new name!

13. Ronald J. Sider, ed., *The Early Church on Killing: A Comprehensive Sourcebook on War, Abortion, and Capital Punishment* (Grand Rapids: Baker Academic, 2012).

Chapter 15: The Third Way of Jesus

1. Daniel Berrigan, *No Bars to Manhood* (Garden City, NY: Doubleday, 1970), 49.

2. Jim Forest, *At Play in the Lions' Den: A Biography and Memoir of Daniel Berrigan* (Maryknoll, NY: Orbis, 2017).

3. Vivian Giang, "What It Takes to Change Your Brain's Patterns after Age 25," *Fast Company*, April 28, 2015, https://www.fastcompany.com/3045424/what-it-takes-to-change-your-brains-patterns-after-age-25.

4. Daniel J. Siegel, *The Developing Mind: How Relationships and the Brain Interact to Shape Who We Are*, 2nd ed. (New York: Guilford, 2012), 24. Donald Hebb, author and psychologist, developed a theory that is often paraphrased as "Neurons that fire together wire together."

5. Michael N. Nagler documents this in his book *Is There No Other Way? The Search for a Nonviolent Future* (Berkeley, CA: Berkeley Hills, 2001).

6. Walter Wink, *The Powers That Be* (New York: Doubleday, 1998), 111.

7. Wink, *Powers That Be*, 111.

8. Wink, *Powers That Be*, 111.

9. Robert Ellsberg, ed., *Dorothy Day: Selected Writings* (Maryknoll, NY: Orbis, 1992), 339.

10. Pope Francis, "Words of Holy Father Francis" (Vigil of Prayer for Peace, Saint Peter's Square, September 7, 2013), http://w2.vatican.va/content/francesco/en/homilies/2013/documents/papa-francesco_20130907_veglia-pace.html.

11. Tertullian, *Apology* 50.

12. Martin Luther King Jr., *Strength to Love* (Minneapolis: Fortress, 2010), 47.

13. Ronald J. Sider, "God's People Reconciling" (speech, Mennonite World Conference, Strasbourg, France, summer 1984), https://www.cpt.org/resources/writings/sider.

Chapter 16: Love Casteth Out Fear (and Fear Casteth Out Love)

1. S. L. A. Marshall, *Men against Fire: The Problem of Battle Command* (1947; repr., Norman: University of Oklahoma Press, 2000). See also Dave Grossman, *On Killing: The Psychological Cost of Learning to Kill in War and Society*, rev. ed. (New York: Back Bay Books, 2009); Grossman, "S. L. A. Marshall Revisited . . . ?," *Canadian Military Journal* 9, no. 4 (2008), http://www.journal.forces.gc.ca/vo9/no4/18-grossman-eng.asp.

2. Richard C. Dieter, "Battle Scars: Military Veterans and the Death Penalty," Death Penalty Information Center, 2015, https://deathpenaltyinfo.org/files/pdf/BattleScars.pdf; "Suicide among Veterans and Other Americans 2001–2014," U.S. Department of Veteran Affairs, Office of Suicide Prevention, August 3, 2016, https://www.mentalhealth.va.gov/docs/2016suicidedatareport.pdf.

3. Michael Martin, "Radical Red Letters: A Story from a Gun Donor," *Voices of RAWtools* (blog), April 25, 2018, http://www.patheos.com/blogs/voicesofrawtools/2018/04/radical-red-letters-a-story-from-a-gun-donor.

4. Shane has written in depth about this in *Executing Grace: How the Death Penalty Killed Jesus and Why It's Killing Us* (San Francisco: HarperOne, 2016).

5. Sarah McCammon, "The Warfare May Be Remote but the Trauma Is Real," *All Things Considered* (NPR), April 24, 2017, https://www.npr.org/2017/04/24/525413427/for-drone-pilots-warfare-may

-be-remote-but-the-trauma-is-real. See also Medea Benjamin, *Drone Warfare: Killing by Remote Control* (New York: OR Books, 2012).

6. Katherine Weber, "Rick Warren: Why God Encourages Christians to 'Fear Not' 365 Times in the Bible," *Christian Post*, April 30, 2016, https://www.christianpost.com/news/rick-warren-why-god-encourages-christians-to-fear-not-365-times-in-the-bible-163029.

7. Martin Luther King Jr., "Beyond Vietnam" (sermon, New York, April 4, 1967), https://kinginstitute.stanford.edu/king-papers/documents/beyond-vietnam.

8. Massad Ayoob, "Trend Crimes and the Gun Dealer," *Shooting Industry*, March 1993, 18, cited in James Atwood, *America and Its Guns: A Theological Exposé* (Eugene, OR: Cascade, 2012), 90.

9. Quoted by Tom Diaz, *Making a Killing: The Business of Guns in America* (New York: New Press, 1999), 164, cited in Atwood, *America and Its Guns*, 90.

10. Martin Luther King Jr., "The American Dream" (sermon, Ebenezer Baptist Church, Atlanta, GA, July 4, 1965), https://kinginstitute.stanford.edu/king-papers/documents/american-dream-sermon-delivered-ebenezer-baptist-church.

Chapter 17: Commonsense Change

1. *Merriam-Webster Collegiate Dictionary*, s.v. "accident (n.)," accessed July 27, 2018, http://unabridged.merriam-webster.com/collegiate/accident.

2. Anthony Fabio et al., "Gaps Continue in Firearm Surveillance: Evidence from a Large U.S. City Bureau of Police," *Social Medicine* 10, no. 1 (July 2016): 13–21; Christopher Ingraham, "New Evidence Confirms What Gun Rights Advocates Have Said for a Long Time about Crime," *Washington Post*, July 27, 2016, https://www.washingtonpost.com/news/wonk/wp/2016/07/27/new-evidence-confirms-what-gun-rights-advocates-have-been-saying-for-a-long-time-about-crime.

3. Amber Case, "We Are All Cyborgs Now," TEDWomen 2010, filmed December 2010, 7:46, https://www.ted.com/talks/amber_case_we_are_all_cyborgs_now.

4. Evan Selinger, "The Philosophy of the Technology of the Gun," *Atlantic*, July 23, 2012, https://www.theatlantic.com/technology/archive/2012/07/the-philosophy-of-the-technology-of-the-gun/260220.

5. Quoted in Rosalie Riegle Troester, ed., *Voices from the Catholic Worker* (Philadelphia: Temple University Press, 1993), 114.

6. James Atwood, *America and Its Guns: A Theological Exposé* (Eugene, OR: Cascade, 2012), 132.

Chapter 18: Reimagining the World

1. Terri writes about that journey in her book *Forgiven: The Amish School Shooting, a Mother's Love, and a Story of Remarkable Grace* (Minneapolis: Bethany House, 2015).

NOTES TO SIDEBARS

Mel Bernstein (chapter 2)

The information on Mel Bernstein in this section is drawn from an ABC interview: Michael Koenigs, "What the 'Most Armed Man in America' Has to Say about Mass Shootings," *ABC News*, November 9, 2017, http://abcnews.go.com/US/armed-man-america-mass-shootings/story?id=50704521.

Greg St. Martin, "Study: 70M More Firearms Added to US Gun Stock over Past 20 Years," *News at Northeastern*, September 26, 2016, https://news.northeastern.edu/2016/09/26/study-70m-more-firearms-added-to-us-gun-stock-over-past-20-years.

Oversupply and Overdemand (chapter 2)

US Department of Justice, Bureau of Alcohol, Tobacco, Firearms, and Explosives, "Firearms Commerce in the United States," 2017, https://www.atf.gov/resource-center/docs/undefined/firearms-commerce-united-states-annual-statistical-update-2017/download.

Gun Facts (chapter 2)

German Lopez, "America's Gun Problem, Explained," Vox, May 18, 2018, https://www.vox.com/2015/10/3/9444417/gun-violence-united-states-america.

Aaron Smith, "Black Friday Was Huge for Gun Sales," CNN, November 27, 2017, http://money.cnn.com/2017/11/27/news/companies/black-friday-gun-sales.

Michael Luo, Mike McIntire, and Griff Palmer, "Seeking Gun or Selling One, Web Is a Land of Few Rules," *New York Times*, April 17, 2013, https://www.nytimes.com/2013/04/17/us/seeking-gun-or-selling-one-web-is-a-land-of-few-rules.html.

Leanna Garfield, "There Are 50,000 More Gun Shops Than McDonald's in the US," *Business Insider*, October 6, 2017, http://www.businessinsider.com/gun-dealers-stores-mcdonalds-las-vegas-shooting-2017-10.

Wikipedia, s.v. "Estimated Number of Civilian Guns Per Capita by Country," last modified July 23, 2018, https://en.wikipedia.org/wiki/Estimated_number_of_guns_per_capita_by_country.

Centers for Disease Control and Prevention, "Fatal Injury Reports, National, Regional and State, 1981–2016," WISQARS (Web-based Injury Statistics Query and Reporting System), updated February 19, 2017, https://webappa.cdc.gov/sasweb/ncipc/mortrate.html.

Alan I. Leshner et al., eds., *Priorities for Research to Reduce the Threat of Firearm-Related Violence* (Washington, DC: National Academies Press, 2013), http://nap.edu/18319.

National Institute of Justice, "Gun Violence," updated March 13, 2018, https://www.nij.gov/topics/crime/gun-violence/pages/welcome.aspx.

"Handguns for 18-Year-Olds?," editorial, *New York Times*, November 25, 2010, https://www.nytimes.com/2010/11/26/opinion/26fri1.html.

Erin Grinshteyn and David Hemenway, "Homicide, Suicide, and Unintentional Firearm Fatality: Comparing the United States with Other High-Income Countries, 2003," *Journal of Trauma* 70, no. 1 (January 2011): 238–43, https://doi.org/10 .1097/TA.0b013e3181dbaddf.

Everytown for Gun Safety, "Gun Violence in America," accessed September 10, 2018, https:// everytownresearch.org/gun-violence-america.

Libby Nelson and Javier Zarracina, "A Shocking Statistic about Gun Deaths in the US," Vox, December 4, 2015, https://www.vox.com/policy-and-poli tics/2015/12/4/9851102/gun-deaths-us-children.

Harry Enten, "There's a Gun for Every American. But Less Than a Third Own Guns," CNN, February 15, 2018, https://www.cnn.com/2018/02/15/politics /guns-dont-know-how-many-america/index.html.

Rick Jervis, "3% of Americans Own Half the Country's 265 Million Guns," *USA Today*, updated September 22, 2016, https://www.usatoday.com/story /news/2016/09/22/study-guns-owners-violence/90 858752.

Dara Lind, "Who Owns Guns in America? White Men, Mostly," Vox, December 4, 2015, https://www .vox.com/2015/12/4/9849524/gun-race-statistics.

Elspeth Reeve, "Some Uncomfortable Numbers about Guns in America," *Atlantic*, December 17, 2012, https://www.theatlantic.com/politics/archive /2012/12/guns-in-america-statistics/320409.

"Nearly Half of Guns in U.S. Owned by 3 Percent of Population, Study Finds," *All Things Considered* (NPR), September 20, 2016, https://www.npr .org/2016/09/20/494765559/nearly-half-of-guns -in-u-s-owned-by-3-percent-of-population-study -finds. See also Tibi Puiu, "Just 3% of Americans Own 50% of the Country's Guns," *ZME Science*, updated October 5, 2017, https://www.zmescience .com/medicine/just-3-americans-50-countrys-guns; Youyou Zhou, "Three Percent of the Population Own Half of the Civilian Guns in the US," *Quartz*, October 6, 2017, https://qz.com/1095899/gun-ow nership-in-america-in-three-charts.

As of 2014, Japan has an even lower gun-death rate. There were only six gun deaths in 2014 (that's total, not per capita). Harry Low, "How Japan Has Almost Eradicated Gun Crime," *BBC World Service*, January 6, 2017, http://www.bbc.com/news/maga zine-38365729. Japan is one of four countries that have nearly eliminated gun violence. Chris Weller, "These Four Countries Have Nearly Eliminated Gun Deaths—Here's What the US Can Learn," *Independent*, February 18, 2018, https://www.independent

.co.uk/news/world/americas/gun-deaths-eliminated -america-learn-japan-australia-uk-norway-florida -shooting-latest-news-a8216301.html.

Gun Timeline (chapter 3)

This sidebar is adapted from "Gun Timeline," PBS, accessed August 21, 2018, http://www.pbs.org/opb /historydetectives/technique/gun-timeline.

Developing a Domestic Gun Market after the Civil War (chapter 3)

Pamela Haag, *The Gunning of America: Business and the Making of American Gun Culture* (New York: Basic Books, 2016), 54; "The Remington Works, Ilion, NY," *Scientific American*, April 13, 1872, 240, cited in Haag, *Gunning of America*, 110; WRAC, Winchester letter book, from Winchester to Charles Bradford, Indiana, October 18, 1862, cited in Haag, *Gunning of America*, 59; Haag, *Gunning of America*, 113.

The Teen Killer Who Radicalized the NRA (chapter 4)

Gil Troy, "The Teen Killer Who Radicalized the NRA," *Daily Beast*, October 8, 2017, https://www .thedailybeast.com/the-teen-killer-who-radicalized -the-nra.

A Gun in the Home (chapter 7)

American Academy of Pediatrics, Committee on Injury and Poison Prevention, "Firearm-Related Injuries Affecting the Pediatric Population," *Pediatrics* 105, no. 4 (April 2000), 888–95.

"It's a Fact That God Loves You" (chapter 8)

Benjamin L. Corey, "Why I'll Always Be a God Believer (about the Day I Was Going to Die)," *The Official Blog of Benjamin L. Corey*, January 17, 2014, http://www.patheos.com/blogs/formerlyfundie/why -ill-always-be-a-god-believer-about-the-day-i-was -going-to-die.

Beating Plows into Swords (chapter 11)

Kyle Mizokami, "Here Is Every Aircraft Carrier in the World," *Popular Mechanics*, January 25, 2016, https://www.popularmechanics.com/military/navy-ships/g2412/a-global-roundup-of-aircraft-carriers.

Gathering around the Forge (chapter 12)

"Neighborhood Economics: Walter Brueggemann," QC Family Tree, keynote address at Neighborhood Economics Conference, Louisville, Kentucky, November 12–13, 2014, http://qcfamilytree.org/neighborhood-economics-walter-brueggemann.

The Language of Violence (chapter 14)

From James Atwood, *America and Its Guns: A Theological Exposé* (Eugene, OR: Cascade, 2012), 45.

Early Christians on Violence (chapter 14)

Justin Martyr, *Dialogue with Trypho* 11.3, 11.4, in Eberhard Arnold, ed., *The Early Christians in Their Own Words* (Farmington, PA: Plough, 2007), 81; Tertullian, *Against Marcion* 3.21, in *The Ante-Nicene Fathers: Translations of the Writings of the Fathers down to A.D. 325* (hereafter *ANF*), edited by Alexander Roberts and James Donaldson, 10 vols. (New York: Christian Literature, 1885–1887; repr., Peabody, MA: Hendrickson, 1994), 3:339–40; Arnobius, *Against the Pagans* 1.6 (*ANF* 6:415); Athenagoras, *A Plea for the Christians* 35 (*ANF* 2:147); Tertullian, *Apology* 37 (*ANF* 3:45); Tertullian, *On the Spectacles* 2 (*ANF* 3:80); Minucius Felix, *The Octavius of Minucius Felix* 30 (*ANF* 4:192); Origen, *Against Celsus* 3.7 (*ANF* 4:467); Cyprian, *On the Good of Patience* 16 (*ANF* 5:488); Cyprian, *To Donatus* 6 (*ANF* 5:277).

A Fear-Filled People (chapter 16)

Jonathan Merritt, "Moving beyond a Fear-Based Faith," Religion News Service, January 19, 2018, https://religionnews.com/2018/01/19/moving-beyond-a-fear-based-faith.

Things More Likely to Kill You Than a Terrorist (chapter 16)

Alex Nowrasteh, "Terrorism and Immigration: A Risk Analysis," Cato Institute, *Policy Analysis* 798 (September 13, 2016), 13, https://object.cato.org/sites/cato.org/files/pubs/pdf/pa798_1_1.pdf.

Kyra Russell, "13 Things More Likely to Kill You Than a Refugee Terrorist," Odyssey, February 13, 2017, https://www.theodysseyonline.com/13-things-more-likely-kill-than-refugee-terrorist.